CW00524327

Collected Plays
Volume One

Volume One offers four major plays from roughly the first half of
Girish Karnad's career.

Tughlaq, an acknowledged classic of the contemporary stage, uses the troubled
reign of a fourteenth-century sultan of Delhi to presciently dramatize the
crisis of secular nationhood in post-independence India.

Hayavadana combines a twelfth-century folktale about 'transposed heads'
with indigenous performance traditions to offer a path-breaking model for
a quintessentially 'Indian' theatre in postcolonial times.

Nāga-Mandala draws on the folktale about a woman with a snake lover to
explore gender relations within marriage. The play was presented by the
Guthrie Theatre in Minneapolis as part of its thirtieth anniversary season.

Bali: The Sacrifice connects individual human sexuality to the historical
debate on violence in Indian culture, and received its premiere at the
Haymarket Theatre, Leicester.

Collected Plays
Volume One

Tughlaq
Hayavadana
Bali: The Sacrifice
Nāga-Mandala (*Play with a Cobra*)

GIRISH KARNAD

With an Introduction by
Aparna Bhargava Dharwadker

OXFORD
UNIVERSITY PRESS

OXFORD

UNIVERSITY PRESS

Oxford University Press is a department of the University of Oxford.
It furthers the University's objective of excellence in research, scholarship,
and education by publishing worldwide. Oxford is a registered trademark of
Oxford University Press in the UK and in certain other countries

Published in India by
Oxford University Press
YMCA Library Building, 1 Jai Singh Road, New Delhi 110 001, India

ISBN-13: 978-0-19-567310-4
ISBN-10: 0-19-567310-7

Typeset in Minion in 10.5/14
by Excellent Laser Typesetters, Pitampura, Delhi 110034
Printed in India by G.H. Prints Pvt Ltd, New Delhi 110020

CONTENTS

INTRODUCTION

I

Girish Karnad (b. 1938) belongs to the formative generation of Indian playwrights who came to maturity in the two decades following independence, and collectively reshaped Indian theatre as a major national institution in the later twentieth century. The work of these playwrights has a historical connection with the modern theatre forms that emerged under the influence of Western models in metropolises such as Calcutta and Bombay during the colonial period. Their modernity, however, is shaped by the unprecedented experience of political autonomy and new nationhood, and entails a rejection rather than continuation of colonial theatre practices. In modern Indian theatre, the years leading up to and following independence in 1947 marked a period of disjunction during which both the commercialism of the Parsi stage (dominant until the 1930s) and the radical populism of the Indian People's Theatre Association (dominant during the 1940s) became unsatisfactory models for the future development of urban drama. This sense of disconnection from the immediate past led the more ambitious post-independence playwrights to rethink the issues of dramatic form and presentational style, to forge radical connections with an older past as well as the postcolonial present in India, and to put the resources of world theatre (especially modern Euro-American theatre) to novel use. Along with such contemporaries as Dharamvir Bharati, Mohan Rakesh, Vijay Tendulkar, Badal Sircar, Utpal Dutt, Habib Tanvir, G. P. Deshpande, and Mahesh Elkunchwar, Karnad is a playwright whose work reveals a determined and self-conscious effort towards a new Indian drama.

The members of Karnad's theatrical generation therefore share a number of important qualities that separate them as a group from their precursors. In varying degrees, these authors approach playwriting as a serious literary activity and drama as a complex verbal art, potentially connected to, but also independent of, theatrical practice: the play-as-meaningful-text is thus detached equally from the genres of commercialized entertainment and topical political performance. At the same time, they constitute the first group of modern playwrights in India who belong simultaneously to the economies of print and performance. All of them have had notable success on the stage, while their work has also circulated in print and become available for analysis, commentary, and interpretation outside the boundaries of performance. Each playwright is committed to an indigenous language (rather than English) as his medium of original composition, and hence to the literary and performative traditions of the region where that language is dominant. But each has also participated actively in the process of interlingual translation that gives his plays national (and often international) visibility, and establishes them as contemporary classics. In yet another perspective, Karnad and his contemporaries have rendered the role of 'dramatic author' largely synonymous with that of 'theorist' and 'critic'. By advancing theoretical and polemical arguments about form, language, style, purpose, and influence in a range of rhetorical genres, they have offered the first fully developed, often antithetical theories of dramatic representation and reception in the modern period in India, and formulated competing conceptions of the role of theatre in cultural and national life.

With drama as his chosen literary form and Kannada as his principal language of original composition, Karnad certainly exemplifies the transformative practices of his generation, but he has also carved out a distinctive niche for himself with respect to subject matter, dramatic style, and authorial identity. The majority of his plays employ the narratives of myth, history, and folklore to evoke an ancient or premodern world that resonates in contemporary contexts because of his uncanny ability to remake the past in the image of the present. Karnad's engagement with myth (especially certain episodes in the Mahabharata) begins with *Yayati* in 1961, continues in *Hittina Hunja* (The Dough Rooster, 1980; rewritten in English as *Bali: The Sacrifice*, 2002), and culminates in *Agni Mattu Malé* (The Fire and the Rain) in 1994. The line of history plays moves from *Tughlaq* (1964) to *Talé-Daṇḍa* (Death by Decapitation, 1990) and *The Dreams of Tipu Sultan* (1997). Folktales from different periods and sources provide the basis of *Hayavadana* (Horse-Head, 1971), *Nāga-Mandala* (Play with a Cobra, 1988), and *Flowers: A Monologue* (2004). *Anjumallige* (literally, 'Frightened Jasmine,' 1977) is the only early play by Karnad with a contemporary setting—Britain during the early 1960s—and his most recent work, *Broken Images* (2004) is the only one to be set in present-day India. During the 1961–77 period, therefore, each successive play by Karnad marks a departure in a major new direction and the invention of a new form appropriate to his content—ancient myth in *Yayati*, fourteenth-century north Indian history in *Tughlaq*, a twelfth-century folktale interlineated with Thomas Mann's retelling of it in *Hayavadana*, and early-postcolonial Britain in *Anjumallige*. In the later plays this quadrangulated pattern repeats itself in a different order, creating a cycle of myth-folklore-history in *Hittina Hunja*, *Nāga-Mandala*, and *Talé-Daṇḍa* (1980–90), and a second cycle of myth-history-myth- contemporary life-folklore in *Agni Mattu Malé, Tipu Sultan, Bali, Broken Images,* and *Flowers* (1994–2004).

The dominant presence of the ancient and medieval past in Karnad's drama is a result of both personal and cultural compulsions. He has argued from the beginning that the deep-rooted narratives of myth, oral history, and legend constitute a vital connection between an author and his or her audience, and theatre is a particularly powerful medium for the communication of such culturally resonant fictions. Karnad belongs perhaps to the last generation of *urban* Indian writers who encountered the 'great' and 'little' traditions of myth, poetry, history, legend, and folklore at first hand in their earliest childhood, and internalized them deeply enough to have their adult authorial selves shaped by them. Such a vibrant culture of orality is no longer available to the Western playwright, and Karnad is fully aware that it is being rapidly eroded in India by the processes of urbanization, Westernized education, and economic development. Orality and print, however, are also carefully balanced in his oeuvre. All his major plays, from *Yayati* to *Agni Mattu Malé* and *Bali*, originate in remembered stories but depend extensively on printed sources for their textual complexity and weight. Karnad comes uncannily close, therefore, to the kind of modern writer T. S. Eliot imagined in 'Tradition and the Individual Talent', one of the founding critical texts of twentieth-century modernism:

[Tradition] involves, in the first place, the historical sense, which we may call nearly indispensable to anyone who would continue to be a poet beyond his twenty-fifth year; and the historical sense involves a perception, not only of the pastness of the past, but of its presence;... This historical sense, which is a sense of the timeless as well as of the temporal and of the timeless and the temporal together, is what makes a writer traditional. And it is at the same time what makes the writer acutely conscious of his place in time, of his own contemporaneity.

Karnad's ability to contend with 'the timeless and the temporal together' is clearest in his juxtaposition of myth and history, in the simultaneous embrace of the ahistorical and the historical. The plays based on myth and folklore evoke a chronologically indeterminate (but unambiguously premodern) realm of kings and queens, goddesses and concubines, horses and elephants, bullock carts and country fairs. They create character-types rather than individuals, but give them memorable voices, along with a local habitation and a name. The history plays draw extensively on printed sources, combine real-life individuals with fictional characters, and recreate particular places at particular moments in time. More than any of his contemporaries, Karnad therefore possesses a dramatic imagination that ranges widely in time and space, and allows him to 'speak through' a remarkably diverse cast of characters.

Karnad also persistently describes playwriting as the vocation that best expresses his self-perceptions and abilities, and the identity of playwright as his chosen literary identity, despite a multifaceted engagement with the media of film, television, and video, and a larger-than-life presence in the public realm. As an actor, director, screenplay-writer, high-profile administrator, and public figure Karnad has been—to use an Americanism—a 'celebrity' for more than three decades. No other contemporary author in India is more likely to be recognized on cinema and television screens or the pages of a magazine than within the covers of a printed book or on the stage, and certainly no other Indian playwright has been more visible in the national print and broadcast media. In addition, Karnad has held administrative positions in key cultural institutions, serving as Director of the Film and Television Institute of India in Pune (1974–5), Chair of the Sangeet Natak Akademi in New Delhi (1988–93), and Director of the Nehru Centre in London (2000–3). Yet, as the double honour of the Jnanpith Award and the Kalidasa Samman (India's two most prestigious literary prizes) confirmed in 1999, Karnad makes very serious claims on our literary attention, and values the recognition of his work as a playwright above all other distinctions. He thus appears to have maintained a unique separation and balance between his contributions to 'high', 'popular', and 'official' culture—between the responsibilities of authorship and the demands of the marketplace as well as the public sphere.

Furthermore, Karnad is atypical among contemporary playwrights in being the principal translator of his own plays, and an important commentator on the nature and contexts of his drama. With the exception of *Yayati*, he has rendered all his major plays from Kannada into English, and reversed the process with three recent plays—*The Dreams of Tipu Sultan* (1997), *Broken Images* (2004), and *Flowers* (2004)—which he wrote originally in English and then translated into Kannada. The acts of translation in both directions indicate Karnad's equal facility in the two languages (unique in an Indian-language playwright), and his interest in a wider audience, whether a play was written originally in Kannada or English. But they also indicate his desire to retain control over his plays, and occasionally to act as critic and censor of his own work. For instance, Karnad came to regard *Yayati* as part of his juvenilia, and although the play had successful productions in Kannada and Hindi, he did not translate it into English. A Hindi translation by B. R. Narayan was published in 1979, but the English translation by Priya Adarkar has not yet appeared in print. Similarly, *Anjumallige* and *Hittina Hunja* did not appear in English translations after the Kannada editions were published in 1977 and 1980, again because of the author's ambivalence towards those versions.

In a related practice, for more than three decades Karnad has used the forms of the newspaper or journal interview, the essay, and the author's introduction to comment extensively on his own new plays, the broader trajectory of his work, and the direction of both modern and contemporary Indian theatre. Because of the frequency with which he is interviewed in newspapers and magazines, Karnad's journalistic appearances are too numerous to mention, but two interviews recorded at very different phases in his career—the first with Rajinder Paul for *Enact* in 1971, and the second with me for *New Theatre Quarterly* in 1993 (published in 1995)—showcase his ability to move between the particular and the general in theatre practice, and to address important cultural and political issues while commenting on his own work. In an essay titled 'Theatre in India' which first appeared in *Daedalus* (1989), and then in revised form as the Author's Introduction to *Three Plays* (Oxford University Press, 1994; cited hereafter as *TP*), Karnad offers an elegant commentary on the challenges confronting his generation in Indian theatre, and the impulses and questions that led to the writing of major plays such as *Tughlaq* and *Hayavadana*. Karnad's readers have come to expect this ongoing self-reflection on his part, so much so that the present volumes mark the first occasion when he has not introduced a new collection of his plays in English.

The publication of the two-volume *Collected Plays* thus offers Karnad's readers and critics an opportunity for the kind of discerning assessment of his drama that he has favoured and practiced for several decades. The playwright's controlling hand continues to be in evidence here. *Yayati* (1961) does not appear in the collection for the reasons mentioned earlier. Karnad has also excluded *Anjumallige*, the play set in 1960s London, and included *Hittina Hunja* only in the reworked English version of 2002 that he titled *Bali*. On the other hand, the author has included two very recent one-act plays which constitute a double bill and were written originally in English—*Broken Images* and *Flowers* (both 2004). The remainder of this Introduction is devoted to a sequential discussion of the plays first written between 1961 and 1988. The Introduction to volume two considers the plays from 1990–2004 in chronological sequence, and also takes up several issues of general significance to Karnad's career as a playwright: the relationship of various theatrical languages and the translator's role in a multilingual field; the relation of his plays to his work in the other media and his visibility as a public figure; and the most important stage interpretations and performance venues for his drama.

II

Yayati (1961) does not appear in the present collection, but it is the appropriate point of departure for a discussion of Karnad's work because it launched his career as a playwright, and established an approach to mythic narrative that has shaped many of the mature later plays. The play was written over a few weeks in 1960 as Karnad was preparing to leave India for a three-year stint as a Rhodes Scholar at Oxford, and found himself caught up in his family's anxieties about the potential implications of his departure. The conflict centered on 'the terrible choice...implicit in the very act of going away', and was framed in idealistic terms: 'Should I...return home for the sake of my family, my people and my country,...or should I rise above such parochial considerations and go where the world drew me?' (*TP* 2). According to Karnad, his youthful ambition was to be a poet, and he had trained himself to write in English, the lingua franca of urban life in contemporary India. Hence he was surprised to find himself writing a play in Kannada about Yayati, the Chandravamshi king in the Mahabharata who exchanged his decrepitude with the youth of his youngest son, Puru, in order to stave off the curse of premature old age.

The play, however, proved to be much more than a fictional displacement of the conflict between family expectations and personal aspirations. 'When you follow the trail of the past,' the Sutradhar comments at the beginning of *Yayati*, 'you're like a lost wayfarer, groping in a huge cavern filled with the ruins of an old and unfamiliar mode of life. You grope...and yet you must listen to the call of the past, give it the ears of the present.' The result is 'a story of our ancestors, but we see our own image there' (1). As Karnad noted with the advantage of hindsight, the myth of Yayati 'enabled me to articulate for myself a set of values that I had been unable to arrive at rationally. Whether to return home finally seemed the most minor of issues; the myth had nailed me to my past' (*TP* 3). Yet he also acknowledged that modern Indian theatre offered him no appropriate theatrical form for his mythical content, and consequently his chosen form was an eclectic synthesis of the Greek tragic playwrights, Jean Anouilh, Jean-Paul Sartre, and Eugene O' Neill. Karnad's tireless formal experiments in the later plays stem in part from this early paradox—that while the past 'had come to my aid with a ready-made narrative within which I could contain and explore my insecurities, there had been no dramatic structure in my own tradition to which I could relate myself' (*TP* 3). In practical terms, the immediate attention *Yayati* attracted among readers when it appeared in Kannada under the imprint of G. B. Joshi's Manohar Granth Mala in 1961 convinced Karnad that he had a future as a playwright in India, and prompted his return home at the end of the Rhodes scholarship period. The play itself resolved, as a literary work, the existential crisis that had generated and shaped it.

Yayati is a wordy, didactic, dialectical play in the style of Anouilh, but it prefigures Karnad's later work in the modernist thoroughness with which it reshapes mythical material, redistributes thematic emphases, and invents new characters to complicate the dramatic potential of a story. In the *Adiparvan*, the first major book of the Mahabharata, Yayati is a 'mighty' and 'invincible' descendent of the Kurus who has already achieved greatness as a king when he is cursed with premature old age for cohabiting with Sharmishtha, the Asura princess who is the rival and slave of his wife, sage Shukracharya's daughter Devayani. The epic does not question or criticize Yayati's motives when he demands that one of his sons assume the curse because he himself is 'not yet sated of youth' (191). On the contrary, Yayati curses his four older sons for refusing the challenge because 'the strict do not deem him a son who is contrary to his father,' and blesses his youngest son for accepting it. After a thousand years, Yayati assumes his old age again and gives the kingdom to Puru, because 'like a true son, Puru did my pleasure' (194). The myth validates the father's authority and the son's obedience, reinforcing the counter-oedipal logic of filial relations in Hindu mythology.

Karnad restructures the story as an ironic drama of discontent, futility, and death. Yayati is a self-centered epicurean who invites the curse because he cannot overcome his desire for Sharmishtha, although Devayani has warned him about the destructive consequences of his choice. Puru is a philosophical but self-hating 'outsider' who feels unsettled by the questionable legitimacy of his birth, and oppressed by the weight of dynastic tradition. When the curse is pronounced, Puru accepts it because he thinks the sacrifice of his youth would counteract his feelings of unworthiness, and enable him to fulfil his destiny as a Chandravamsha prince. However, in deviation from the Mahabharata story, Karnad's Puru has just returned home with a new bride, Chitralekha, who tries to accept his sacrifice but commits suicide in revulsion against her blighted future. Too late, Yayati tries to atone for his actions by restoring Puru's youth and withdrawing into the forest, but Sharmishtha points out to him the inescapable foundations of his future: 'a corpse, a lunatic, a fallen woman' (Act IV). Like the effete figures in Eliot's poem who 'had the experience but missed the meaning', Puru ends the play on a note of stark bewilderment, unable to comprehend the point of what he has endured.

Karnad's portrait of an overbearing patriarch and a weak-willed son is a displaced expression of his resentment against the element of 'emotional blackmail' in family relations, and this method of indirect reference to the present characterizes all his myth and history plays. But the most memorable feature of *Yayati*—and a striking accomplishment for a twenty-two year-old author—is its quartet of sentient, articulate, embittered women, all of whom are subject in varying degrees to the whims of men, but succeed in subverting the male world through an assertion of their own rights and privileges. Devayani the Brahman queen and Sharmishtha the slave-princess are caught in a fierce rivalry that allegorizes the hierarchical divisions of caste while also visiting upon both women the destructive effects of Yayati's amoral desire. Such a triangulation, between two men and one woman or one man and two women, reappears so consistently in Karnad's myth and folk-based plays as to constitute a basic plot device as well as a central thematic. In *Yayati*, the fictional Chitralekha adds another dimension to gender conflicts because, unlike Puru, she rejects the king's authority over her, and sees no reason why 'my life existence [should be] immolated at the altar of some empty bubble in the future' (Act IV). Before killing herself, she also reminds Yayati that incestuous adultery between them would be the logical implication of his assumption of Puru's youth. As the play's most complex female character, Sharmishtha is quite unlike her counterpart in the Mahabharata: she endures rather than seeks Yayati's attentions, knows that she is doomed by his pursuit of her, and confronts him with the immorality of his quest for a surrogate victim. In dialogue that is transparently contemporary, she also tries to dissuade Puru from assuming the curse because 'sacrificing oneself needlessly is a form of perversity. Pride in being self-denying all the time can become a fatal habit' (Act III). The performance history of *Yayati* reinforces the women's centrality: in Satyadev Dubey's celebrated production for the Indian National Theatre in 1967, for instance, Sunila Pradhan played Devayani, Tarla Mehta played Sharmishtha, Sulabha Deshpande was Swarnalata, and Rekha Sabnis was Chitralekha, with Amrish Puri as Yayati and Dubey himself as Puru.

This chorus of unusual female voices, mixed in with the flawed male utterances, humanizes the myth and gives it ethical and dialectical weight. *Yayati* establishes at the outset of Karnad's career that myth is not merely a narrative to be bent to present purposes, but a structure of meanings worth exploring in itself because it offers opportunities for philosophical reflection without the constraints of realism or the necessity of a contemporary setting. *Bali* and *Agni Mattu Malé*, the two later myth plays, exhibit the same qualities at a higher level of skill and maturity. Like the characters of a Greek tragedy, Karnad's mythic figures have human depth even when they are caught in a predetermined course of action, and he does not hesitate to alter both character and event to create effective drama.

III

Karnad's next play, *Tughlaq* (1964), marked a radical change of direction after *Yayati*, and inaugurated a second genre that has since been central to his dramaturgy. While still at Oxford, he felt challenged by the verdict of noted Kannada critic Kirtinath Kurtkoti that modern Kannada drama had no first-rate historical plays, and began a process of self-education in pre-modern Indian history to search for a possible dramatic subject. The 'marvellous' discovery of the fourteenth-century sultan Muhammad bin Tughlaq in an elementary-level textbook motivated Karnad to take on the full range of historiographic materials available at Oxford, which in turn led to a series of revelations about the uncanny persistence of the past in India. In the 1971 interview with Rajinder Paul, Karnad recalled that Tughlaq struck him as 'the most idealistic, the most intelligent king ever to come [to] the throne of Delhi, including the Mughals', who nevertheless ended as 'one of the greatest failures' because of contradictions within his personality and the self-defeating nature of his politics. The twenty-year period of Tughlaq's decline as a ruler also offered a 'striking parallel' to the first two decades of Indian independence under Jawaharlal Nehru's idealistic but troubled leadership, and Nehru appeared remarkably like Tughlaq in his propensity for failure despite an extraordinary intellect. Yet the play was not meant either as an 'obvious comment on Nehru' or an 'exact parallel' of the present: rather, it addressed the emerging ambivalence of power relations in the political and public spheres which were based, for the first time in Indian history, on the principles of mass representation and enfranchisement. 'In a sense,'

Karnad observes, 'the play reflected the slow disillusionment
my generation felt with the new politics of independent India:
the gradual erosion of the ethical norms that had guided the
movement for independence, and the coming to terms with
cynicism and realpolitik' ('In Search' 98).

This connection with a specific phase in post-independence
politics was material to the play's genesis and early reception,
but *Tughlaq* has emerged as a modern masterpiece because of
its seemingly endless capacity to make history resonate with
contemporary meaning, and to encapsulate political experience
as it evolves under the conditions of modernity and postcolonialism.
The power and cultural vitality of the play stem principally from
the multifold engagement with history and politics that lies
behind and beyond the words. *Tughlaq* is the first major post-
independence play to engage with the sultanate period (twelfth
to early-sixteenth century), which brought the 'golden age' of
classical Hinduism to a decisive end, and introduced Islam as a
dominant political and cultural force on the subcontinent. The
sultanate represents an important phase of Islamic imperialism
in India, but in the national imaginary it has been marginalized
by the later periods of Mughal and British imperialisms. Karnad's
play reinscribes the narrative of Tughlaq in the collective memory
of contemporary audiences, refining legend and oral tradition
through a detailed historical reenactment. In another perspective,
Tughlaq is a play *about* history: about how it is written, transmitted,
and accepted as a valid image of the past, and about how a
'historical play' relates to history itself. Even a superficial familiarity
with Karnad's written sources confirms that our seemingly
'objective' views of Tughlaq come either from medieval Muslim
historians like Zia-ud-din Barani, who regarded him as a dangerous
heretic, or from orientalist British historians like James Mill and
Vincent Smith, who regarded him as a type of the brilliant but
unprincipled 'Oriental despot' that British rule had eliminated
in India. Karnad revives the paradoxical Tughlaq of history and

occasionally constructs his dialogue verbatim out of various historical documents, especially Barani's contemporaneous account of Tughlaq's reign, the *Tarikh-i Firoz Shahi* (1357). He also follows the chronology of Tughlaq's reign closely, mixes historical characters (such as Barani, Najib, Sheikh Imam-ud-din, and the stepmother) with fictional inventions (such as Aazam and Aziz), and thus creates a complex ideological and intertextual connection between history, historiography, and his own fiction. The effect of such interlineation, morever, is not to perpetuate but to problematize the received history of Tughlaq: the play urges contemporary Indian audiences to scrutinize the premodern and colonial institutions that have created their understanding of the past, and to question institutionalized history as a source of knowledge.

In a move that is characteristic of the historical parallel as a genre (and acknowledged by Karnad), *Tughlaq* also invokes significant elements in modern Indian political and cultural experience by presenting an ostensibly self-sufficient historical narrative that viewers and readers can apply to their own situation. For the audience of the 1960s, Karnad's play certainly expressed the disenchantment and cynicism that attended the end of the Nehru era in Indian politics. A decade later, the play appeared to be an uncannily accurate portrayal of the brilliant but authoritarian and opportunistic political style of Nehru's daughter and successor, Indira Gandhi. Now (yet another thirty years later) *Tughlaq* seems concerned less with specific figures than with two general issues that have assumed increasing importance in the Indian political and public spheres. At one level, the play acts out the polarity between politics as the selfless extension of individual spirituality (Mahatma Gandhi) and vision (Jawaharlal Nehru), and politics as the self-serving, sometimes demonic expression of individual fantasies of power (evidenced in Indira Gandhi, Sanjay Gandhi, and, more recently, in Sikh, Muslim, and Hindu fundamentalist leaders). These two models of political action in turn imply radically different relations between leaders and citizens, but by embodying both impulses within Tughlaq, Karnad also suggests an ironic identity between them.

At another level, *Tughlaq* offers an ironic, clearly prophetic commentary on the ideology of secularism and the forces that subvert that ideology. The 'idea of India' as an assimilative, tolerant, multiform political entity was central to the nationalist thinking that emerged under the leadership of Gandhi, Nehru, Abul Kalam Azad, and others during the 1920s and 1930s. The demand for a separate Pakistan undercut this idea tragically and led to the trauma of partition in 1947. Since then, the emergence of ethnoreligious nationalisms in various parts of the country, the national frenzy over the Babri Masjid in Ayodhya, the unabated terrorist violence in Kashmir (which became embroiled in the global 'war on terrorism' after 11 September 2001), and the escalation of militant Hindu nationalism to a point which brought on India's first organized 'pogrom' against the minority Muslim population in the state of Gujarat in February 2002—these are only some of the events that have reduced the idea of secularism to 'an unattainable utopia'. Enmeshed in this experience, *Tughlaq* now invokes not merely the loss of political innocence in the 1960s but the gradual attrition of the larger political and cultural processes that created the imagined community of India as an independent nation in the mid-twentieth century. The religious issues in the play pose a question important to all 'traditional' or 'diverse' societies experimenting with democratic structures: whether religion can be, or indeed can be prevented from becoming, the primary basis of nationhood.

Predictably, the resonance of *Tughlaq* as a complex text has been reinforced over four decades by its status as a stage classic. The actors who have created the title role include such major performers as Om Shivpuri (Urdu, 1966 and 1972), Arun Sarnaik (Marathi, 1971), and Manohar Singh (Urdu, 1972, 1974, and 1982), as well as more occasional players like Kabir Bedi (English,

1970) and Ashok Mandanna (English, 2003). Shivpuri directed himself in the role, but the other productions also involve celebrated actor-director partnerships—between Sarnaik and Arvind Deshpande, Singh and Ebrahim Alkazi, and Bedi and Alyque Padamsee. Manohar Singh, in particular, established a reputation as 'the actor born to play Tughlaq': the image of him 'looming large over the ramparts of Alkazi's cognisance' to enact a 'Macbethian high drama' at Purana Qila in 1974 has become an indelible memory for the Delhi audiences who watched that production. In a different location, C. R. Simha monopolized the role of Tughlaq in Kannada for three decades, from 1969 to 1999. The resilience of *Tughlaq* as a political vehicle also appears in the interpretive shifts through which successive productions have accommodated the changing politics of the nation since the 1970s. The move from the 'disenchantment' of the Nehruvian decades to a new phase of corruption and violence is evident in the program note to Arun Kuckreja's Delhi production of *Tughlaq* in September 1975, three months after Indira Gandhi had suspended constitutional rights and turned India (temporarily) into a police state:

Our interpretation of the play is one in which the politics of the entire situation are all-important and the violence of the second half of the play evident. It is for this purpose that all the murders merely mentioned in the script are presented on stage. The choice of contemporary-looking costumes, the use of pop music and an abstract setting are all geared to one main purpose—to make the play as modern as possible, so that it has relevance to us today. The play now no longer remains merely the tragic history of a medieval monarch, but grows to larger proportions with Tughlaq himself becoming a symbol of our times. (Jacob, 'Tughlaq')

As a 'symbol of the times,' since the mid-1970s the visionary Tughlaq of the play's first half has also receded, giving prominence to the vengeful tyrant of the second half. In the production directed by Prasanna in 1982, Manohar Singh appeared as a 'loud and mad Sultan, short-tempered and violent, with little to offer

to his subjects. His idealism, scholarship or statesmanship are
hardly in evidence' (Paul, 'Last Month'). Predictably, the communal
issues in the play have become even more controversial, if not
incendiary. Commenting on Arjun Sajnani's 2003 English production
in Bangalore, G. N. Prashanth notes the 'movement from the
Nehruvian "socialist" setting, through the Emergency, to what is
now Savarkar's time', arguing that the play's present context is
'the rise of the Hindu Right' and its 'virulent' twenty-first century
politics. To continue creating viable political meaning for present-
day Indian audiences, directors of *Tughlaq* must now contend
with a public sphere that has come to regard politics as empty
of all morality.

IV

Karnad's third play, *Hayavadana* (1971), marked another major
change of direction, not only in his playwriting but in post-
independence theatre as a whole, because it was the first work to
translate into notable practice the debate over the usefulness of
indigenous performance genres in the development of a new,
quintessentially 'Indian' theatre. Having explored the genres of
mythic-existentialist and historical drama in *Yayati* and *Tughlaq*,
Karnad had experienced the urge to 'begin again': In 1970–2 he
held the prestigious Homi Bhabha Fellowship 'for creative work
in folk theatre', and in 1971 he was a key participant in the
'National Roundtable on the Contemporary Relevance of Traditional
Theatre' organized by the Sangeet Natak Akademi. Given his
predilection for taking on any form if (but only if) it served his
authorial purposes, the endless arguments about the revitalizing
effects of traditional forms prompted him to inquire what
playwrights like him, 'basically city dwellers, [were] to do with
this stream. What did the entire paraphernalia of theatrical
devices, half-curtains, masks, improvisation, music, and mime
mean? I remember that the idea of my play *Hayuvadana* started
crystallizing in my head right in the middle of an argument

with B. V. Karanth...about the meaning of masks in Indian theatre and theatre's relationship to music' (*TP* 12). The story about switched heads in the twelfth-century Sanskrit collection, the *Kathasaritasagara*, interested him initially because of the possibilities it offered for the use of masks on stage. However, refracted through Thomas Mann's philosophical novella *The Transposed Heads*, Karnad's distinctive view of femininity, and a reflexive double frame, the traditional conventions underwent a process of defamiliarization in *Hayavadana* that produced a genuinely original work for the urban Indian stage, and created a unique intellectual and theatrical excitement throughout the decade of the 1970s.

The play's credentials were impeccable and its timing fortuitous. In 1972 *Hayavadana* won both the annual Sangeet Natak Akademi award, and the Kamaladevi Award of the Bharatiya Natya Sangh, for best Indian play. During the same year, in a rare transposition of languages, it received three major productions, not in the original Kannada (which would have been the obvious medium) but in Hindi: under the direction respectively of Satyadev Dubey for Theatre Group in Bombay, of Rajinder Nath for Anamika in Calcutta, and of B. V. Karanth (who had also composed the music) for Dishantar in Delhi. Undertaken simultaneously by three directors with a preference for important new plays, these productions pointed to the intense interest *Hayavadana* had generated within an engaged, experimentally-oriented national theatre community. Karanth's Kannada production, for the Bangalore-based group Benaka, followed in September 1972, while Vijaya Mehta directed the play in Marathi in 1983, incorporating elements of the Tamasha form. Karanth and Mehta also emerged as the play's most ambitious and persistent directors. Karanth revived his Hindi version in 1974 and 1982 and the Kannada version for the Nehru Shatabdi Natya Samaroh in 1989, and undertook a new English version for the National Institute of Dramatic Arts in Australia. In 1984, Mehta also took the play

to the Deutsches Nationaltheater, Weimar, for a German production
with German actors. With this succession of major productions
virtually complete by 1990, *Hayavadana* is still one of Karnad's
most frequently performed plays, having found an enduring
popularity with amateur urban theatre groups, college drama
societies, and even audiences in the Indian diaspora.

In keeping with Karnad's interest in a usable 'structure of
expectations', the outstanding quality of *Hayavadana* as an 'urban
folk' play is that it joins the conventions of Yakshagana folk
performance (stock characters, music, dance, masks, talking dolls,
etc.) with a core narrative that poses philosophical riddles about
the nature of identity and reality. In the *Kathasaritasagara*, the
story of 'The Heads That Got Switched' contains a simple riddle.
A woman travelling with her husband and her brother discovers
the men's decapitated bodies in the temple of Parvati, receives a
boon from the goddess to bring them back to life, but switches
their heads by mistake. The resulting problem of 'true' identity
has an unambiguous solution in this version: 'The one with her
husband's head is her husband because the head rules the limbs
and personal identity depends on the head' (Sattar 219). In the
mythic genealogy of caste, first offered in the Purusha-sukta in
the *Rg-veda* (Book 10, hymn 90) around 1000 BC, Brahmans
emerged from Purusha's head, and the supremacy of that part of
the body is so firmly established in the subsequent Hindu tradition
that it overrides the implications of incest in the twelfth-century
narrative (in some versions of the story, however, the second male
is a friend rather than the woman's brother).

Thomas Mann's philosophical elaboration of this story in *The
Transposed Heads* (1940) is a fully developed parable about
conjugality, proscribed desire, and an 'accidental' disruption of
identity that can be resolved only by death. Sita is married to
Shridaman, who is cerebral, delicate, and sensitive, but she feels
an intense physical attraction for his friend Nanda, who is visceral,
strong, and emotionally crude. In Mann's version, the husband

beheads himself in Parvati's temple out of jealousy and despair; the friend follows suit out of guilt and fear; and the pregnant wife prepares to die in order to avoid ignominy for herself and her child. After the accident of transposition a holy ascetic grants Sita to the new Shridaman by using the same logic that appears in the folktale, but in Mann's text the supremacy of the head is both sustained and challenged far beyond the moment of crisis. The new bodies of the two men change inexorably until they are compatible with the heads once again; but the original bodies also exert their own subversive power, and change the heads indefinably. Sita, to whom the man with the husband-head and friend-body had given 'full enjoyment of the pleasures of sense' for a time, finds herself yearning once again for the man with the friend-head and husband-body, and returns to him in full knowledge of the consequences of her action. Shridaman and Nanda kill each other in the forest, and Sita commits *sati* on their funeral pyre, leaving her precocious four-year old son behind to keep alive the memory of her strange sacrifice. The story of Devadatta, Kapila, and Padmini in Karnad's *Hayavadana* follows elements of characterization and the order of events in Mann's novella closely enough to be considered, in some respects, a 'de-orientalized', contemporary Indian theatrical version of it. The play's real originality lies in the reflexive frames Karnad constructs for the story, and the thematic force of its representation of femininity, desire, and identity *in and for the present*, independent of its sources.

Karnad's first radical move is to multiply the contexts in which the problem of incongruity, as symbolized by the disjunction between head and body, appears. In the human world of Devadatta and Kapila, transposition offers a symbolic but temporary resolution to the problem of mind/body dualism: for a brief period of time, Devadatta-Kapila possesses the ideal mind as well as the ideal body, while the other hybrid being, Kapila-Devadatta, is deficient in both respects. But when each man's body reverts to its original qualities, the problem of dualism returns, and the human condition appears as essentially one of disunity and imperfection culminating in death. Karnad diffuses this human 'tragedy' by placing it alongside two other realms of experience—the divine and the animal. Despite his comical appearance, the elephant-headed, pot-bellied Ganesha is the patron deity of scribes and performers, the remover of obstacles (*vighneshwara*), and the god of all auspicious beginnings—an embodiment of both divinity and perfection. On the other hand, Hayavadana, the horse-headed man who gives the play its title, lacks any vestige of divinity and appears painfully suspended between the animal and *human* worlds. Unlike the god, Hayavadana cannot endure to remain mixed up; unlike the humans, he does not possess a prior self that can reassert itself. But as in the human world, the head determines identity, even if that means the triumph of the animal over the human: Hayavadana achieves wholeness by relinquishing his human characteristics, and turning completely into a horse. This triple perspective on disrupted selves puts into practice Karnad's belief that the various conventions of Indian folk theatre create effects similar to those associated with Brecht's notion of 'complex seeing': 'the chorus, the masks, the seemingly unrelated comic episodes, the mixing of human and nonhuman worlds permit the simultaneous presentation of alternative points of view, of alternative attitudes to the central problem' (*TP* 14).

The second level of complication in *Hayavadana* involves the author's self-conscious manipulation of the structure of folk performance. While the action of folk theatre moves between a frame and the inner play, in *Hayavadana* there are two outer frames, both belonging to the historical present, which intersect unpredictably with each other and with the action of the inner play. The first frame consists of the Bhagavata, the female chorus, and the two male actors who are not merely *characters* in a folk performance but *performers* in a provincial troupe preparing to enact the story of Padmini and her two husbands for a contemporary audience. Just as the action of the inner play is about to begin, the performance is disrupted by the appearance of Hayavadana, the talking horse who wants a solution to his own predicament. The disruption forces the characters of folk drama to revert to their 'real' personae as actors, and the performance of Padmini's story begins only after the Bhagavata has persuaded Hayavadana to leave and seek divine intervention for the solution of his problem. Similarly, the end of Padmini's story is not the end of the play: the two framing narratives continue until Hayavadana, who now reappears as a horse with a human voice, has lost—as he wants to—this last human attribute. The conventional folk structure of a play-within-a-play is therefore yoked in *Hayavadana* to a reflexive rehearsal format, whose function is to subject the defining conventions of folk performance to ironic scrutiny.

Beyond its philosophical reflection on identity and its self-reflexive structure, *Hayavadana* also resonates in present dramatic and cultural contexts because it gives primacy to women in the psychosexual relations of marriage, and creates a space for the expression, even the fulfilment, of amoral female desire within the constraints of patriarchy. In this respect, the genre of 'urban folk' theatre to which both *Hayavadana* and *Nāga-Mandala* belong offers a radical contrast to the representation of women in the 'urban realist' drama of such playwrights as Mohan Rakesh, Vijay Tendulkar, the early Badal Sircar, Mahesh Elkunchwar, Jayawant Dalvi, and Mahesh Dattani. The essential basis of difference here is not the gender of the author, which continues to be exclusively male (Karnad, Chandrashekhar Kambar, Tanvir, K. N. Panikkar, Ratan Thiyam), but the qualitatively different attitudes to gender that emerge *within* the plays when male authors move out of the urban social-realist mode into the anti-modern, anti-realistic, charismatic realm of folk culture. Plays such as *Hayavadana* and *Nāga-Mandala* (as well as Kambar's *Jokumaraswami* and Tanvir's *Charandas Chor*) are important in

the discourse of gender because they embody several principles
largely absent in realist drama.

First, women in these works are objects of desire as well as
desiring subjects, and they want something other than what
society has ordained for them. The very presence of such
desire violates the norms of feminine behaviour and disturbs
established notions of propriety. Second, women succeed in their
quest because of the interchangeability of male partners. The
proscribed object of desire magically replaces the husband in
three of these plays, usually in the *form* of the husband. Since the
men can 'stand in' for each other, there is no unique male self
to which the woman owes fidelity—a notion that questions the
principle of male proprietorship, and hence undermines a basic
premise of patriarchy. Third, while realist drama emphasizes and
often romanticizes the maternal role, folk narratives stress the
feminine but not necessarily the maternal. Or, to put it differently,
fertility and motherhood are important in folk plays, but can be
detached from the constraints of marital fidelity. In all these
plays, the women want or get men they cannot legitimately have;
each one accomplishes her desire, but only provisionally, and like
the queen bee destroys her male partner (lover or husband) in
the process. The ideology of urban folk drama thus manifests
itself most conspicuously in the treatment of femininity, sexuality,
desire, and power: although the challenge to patriarchy is not
absolute, women in folk drama find the means of exercising an
ambivalent freedom within its constraints, unlike their urban
counterparts in such plays as Rakesh's *Adhe Adhure* or Vijay
Tendulkar's *Shantata! Court Chalu Ahe*.

V

Nāga-Mandala (1988), which came seventeen years after
Hayavadana, can be considered a companion play because it
creates variations on many of the same themes. Written in 1987–8
during Karnad's residency as a Fulbright fellow at the University

of Chicago, the play combines another reflexive frame—this time about a fictional playwright who can continue to live only if he keeps awake for one whole night—with two oral tales that Karnad had heard several years earlier from his friend and mentor, A. K. Ramanujan. The first story, about the lamp flames that gather in a village temple to exchange gossip about the households they inhabit, is part of the outer play and gives imaginative expression to the idea of community life. The second story, about the woman who was visited by a king cobra in the form of her husband, is personified in the play as a beautiful young woman in a sari, and it 'tells itself' (as the inner play) to an audience composed of the playwright and the flames. This amalgamation of human, abstract, and magical elements creates a synthesis that is thematically and philosophically simpler than the polysemy of *Hayavadana*; it allows for innovative staging and rich visual effects, but appeals more to the fancy than the imagination.

By making Rani almost a pure embodiment of feminine simplicity, innocence, and powerlessness, Karnad pares his drama of gender relations down to an elemental level. Marriage for Rani means the loss of the secure world of childhood and parental love, and she has to reimagine that world in her fantasies merely to keep herself from psychic collapse. As the ill-tempered, tyrannical, two-dimensional husband, Appanna rapidly reduces her daily life to a featureless existence without companionship or community, except for the clandestine visits by Kurudavva, the old blind village woman. Because the marriage is unconsummated, Rani's latent power as wife and mother also remains unrealized. The snake-lover's magical visits in the form of the husband are thus virtually overdetermined by the familiar folk logic that beauty and innocence must triumph without the overt violation of moral norms. Once the visits have begun, Rani's experience points to two qualities that have 'realistic' resonance in the context of the extended Indian family—the difference between 'day' and 'night' selves, and the liberating effects of sexual fulfilment. Rani is willing to accept that the brutish husband of the day turns into the ardent lover at night because those are the conditions of her sexual initiation and emancipation: as Naga explains, 'the husband decides on the day visits. And the wife decides on the night visits.'

The announcement of Rani's pregnancy begins a third movement in the inner play and marks the return of patriarchal control by the husband as well as the community, but by then she has matured from a girl into a woman, wife, and mother-to-be, and needs a definite resolution to her predicament. The snake ordeal is another magical way for Rani to 'get everything she has ever wanted', but her apotheosis, and the perfect life that follows, are riddled with irony and compromise. In a reversal of Rama's classic rejection of Sita, the wayward husband in the folktale has to accept the chastity of a wife who undoubtedly had a lover, and a child he knows he did not engender. For her part, Rani comes to realize that her two husbands were not the same person, and her new life of contentment is not free of remembrance and regret. Furthermore, as in *Hayavadana*, Rani's story does not end with the inner play. The characters in the frame narrative question the 'happily ever after' convention because it leaves too many questions unanswered, and the playwright creates two alternative endings, one tragic and one happy, to give the story of the snake-lover a conclusion as well. Once again, the use of folk material by an urban playwright serves as an occasion for reflections on the nature of writing and performance, the manipulation of conventions, and a reaffirmation of the centrality of women that is all the more significant because unlike Padmini, Rani moves from a position of total abjection to one of unqualified power.

More than any other full-length play by Karnad, *Nāga-Mandala* is a spare and simple text that can be transformed by the visual and spatial possibilities of staging—a quality reflected in its unusual performance history. It had a unique 'world premiere' at the University of Chicago in the spring of 1988, and in 1993 became the first contemporary Indian play to be produced by a

major regional American theatre company, the Guthrie Theatre
in Minneapolis (I had the privilege of attending both these
premieres). With the Paris-based Nirupama Nityanandan (a member
of Ariane Mnouchkine's Théatre du Soleil) in the role of Rani,
the Chinese-American actor Stan Egan as Appanna and Naga,
and the African-American actress Isabel Monk as Kurudavva, the
Guthrie production captured on a smaller scale the intercultural
resonance associated with a work such as Peter Brook's *Mahabharata*
(1987). In India, the play has been especially attractive to leading
women directors, who have created an audience for it both at
home and abroad. Neelam Mansingh Chowdhry produced it in
Punjabi in 1989, and took her production to the First International
Theatre Festival in Tashkent the same year. Vijaya Mehta directed
the play in Marathi in 1991, and in German for the Berlin Festival
of India in 1992. Amal Allana produced *Nāga-Mandala* in Hindi
in 1998, as had Rajinder Nath in 1991. Given the premodern
setting of the play, its proximity to the life of the average urban
Indian woman is not self-evident, but the polarities of love and
lovelessness, perplexity and fulfilment it assigns to the relationships
of men and women within marriage speak across the particularities
of form and content (especially in performance), and make a
distinctive contribution to the ongoing dialogue on gender.

VI

Bali (1980/2002), the last play included in this volume, represents
a chronological anomaly, and perhaps because of its unusual
dating creates bold new variations on narrative and emotional
patterns that also appear in the plays preceding and following it—
Hayavadana (1971) and *Nāga-Mandala* (1988). *Hittina Hunja*,
the first version of the play published in Kannada in 1980, was
performed in both Kannada and Hindi (in notable productions
by B. V. Karanth and Satyadev Dubey, and less successful versions
by Prema Karanth and Lankesh), but not translated into English
at that time. In 2002, Karnad reworked the play completely in

English for a production at the Leicester Haymarket Theatre in England, and published this version in 2004 alongside another original English play, *The Dreams of Tipu Sultan*. While the majority of Karnad's plays achieve a fixed form through publication in Kannada and subsequent translation into various other languages (especially English), *Bali* has evolved over two decades, and achieved its definitive form not in Kannada but in English. 'I first came across the myth of the Cock of Dough when I was still in my teens,' Karnad comments in the Preface; 'since then, my career as playwright has been littered with discarded drafts of dramatized versions of it. But looking back, I am happy closure eluded me, for the myth continued to reveal unexpected meanings with passing years' (70). This long thematic gestation has a curious equivalence at the level of performance. In Dubey's Hindi production of the early 1980s (which, coincidentally, was titled *Bali*), Naseeruddin Shah and Ratna Pathak Shah had played the central roles of the King and the Queen; in the 2002 English production, they played the older characters of the Mahout and the Queen Mother, giving physical embodiment not only to the passage of time in their own lives as actors but to the intergenerational tensions and class conflicts that undergird the play's meaning.

Like *Hayavadana*, *Bali* has a specific premodern source—the thirteenth-century Kannada epic, *Yashodhara charite*, which can in turn be traced back to two eleventh- and ninth-century Sanskrit epics. Through the same process of 'realistic' fictional elaboration that marks his approach to myth and folklore from *Yayati* onward, Karnad transforms the story of the dough figurine that comes alive at the moment of sacrifice into a mature philosophical exploration of love, jealousy, desire, betrayal, and violence between men and women who are bound by the ties of blood and marriage, or encounter each other in the perfect freedom of anonymity. In comparison with Karnad's earlier work, the novelty and strength of *Bali* lies in the unconventionality of its four characters, and the seriousness with which it yokes intimate personal acts to structures of religious belief and practice. The promise of motherhood within the licit boundaries of marriage is the motivating force in *Nāga-Mandala* and (with qualification) in *Hayavadana*. Both Padmini and Rani are simple, childlike beings: their adulterous relationships are unwilled and temporary, and their desires are fulfilled through supernatural intervention. In *Bali* the queen is childless, and although this lack is an inescapable point of reference in her life, it is not (at least for her) a source of obsessive guilt or shame. Aroused by the mahout's song, she seeks him out for an anonymous coupling that violates the boundaries of caste and class, but when challenged, refuses to profess guilt for her action or to atone for it through a propitiatory ritual. More than any other female character in Karnad's drama, she is a transgressive presence, deprived of conventional feminine roles by chance and circumstance, but self-possessed and cerebral enough not to surrender to the pressures of conformity.

The queen mother is similarly removed from the two-dimensional 'mother-in-law' of myth and folklore. What alienates her from the barren and unfaithful queen is not only a mother's possessiveness and anger, but fundamental differences of belief that insert larger cultural questions into their personal antagonisms. She also, however, accepts her subsidiary status in the life of the younger couple, and in an atypical move, turns her vindictiveness in part against her own son. The familiar narrative of two women vying for the upper hand in relation to a man becomes, in *Bali*, a destructive dance in which there are no winners, only losers. The two male characters in the play, in contrast, are arranged in relations of perfect antithesis and hierarchical reversal: the cultivated, sensitive, and valiant but impotent king versus the crude, amoral, and cowardly but potent mahout with his irresistible song. The dualisms of mind and body, culture and nature that Karnad had addressed in *Hayavadana* reappear in this play, but as unavoidably separate qualities that cannot be brought together. Furthermore, the radical disparities between the mahout and the royal couple underscore not an egalitarian message about the union of a queen and her servant, but the eventual irrelevance of that act to the long-term disequilibrium of the royal marriage.

The true originality of *Bali* is that it assimilates the sexual issues to a historically-nuanced meditation on the nature and psychology of violence. In the Preface, Karnad describes violence as 'the central topic of debate in the history of Indian civilization'—a debate in which Hinduism has been ranged against Jainism and Buddhism (*Two Plays*, 69). Karnad also chooses to address not the public and political carnage of war and conquest (which led, for instance, to emperor Ashoka's conversion to Buddhism), but the legitimation of violence in ritual practices that individuals (such as the queen mother) regard as private acts of faith and worship. The central 'problem' in the play is thus not the queen's adultery but the deep spiritual rift between her Jainism—which aligns itself with compassion, mercy, and non-violence—and the traditional Kshatriya ethos of her husband's family. The king has embraced Jainism in principle, but his instinctive propensity for violence is evident in every scene, whether it is set in the past or the present. When he compels the queen to join him in the symbolic sacrifice so that his desire for atonement may be satisfied, her imagination breathes life into the sacrificial object and leads to her own death. As Karnad notes, the Jain position that 'intended violence condemns one as surely as actual violence' gives the argument a 'complex ethical twist', and creates a solipsistic world without the possibility of real absolution (70). More broadly, the Jain–Hindu debate of the premodern period casts an ironic light on the endemic violence of the postcolonial present in India—a problem addressed directly in both *Tughlaq* and *Talé-Daṇḍa*.

Written and performed over twenty-five years, and connected through *Bali* to his most recent work, the plays in this volume chart the trajectory of Karnad's career as a playwright, and establish some significant correlations of form and content. History as represented in *Tughlaq* is a medium for public and political experience, and a parallel for the present life of the nation; its appropriate mode is realism, and it foregrounds the actions of men. Myth and folklore, the basis for *Hayavadana*, *Bali*, and *Nāga-Mandala*, evoke the private and the personal; they are compatible with the resources of both realism and an essentially theatrical anti-realism (music, mime, magic), and foreground the lives of women. Their fictional characters—articulate individuals as well as types—are involved in a quest for fulfilment and wholeness that leads sometimes to qualified happiness and at other times to death. The plays belonging to the later part of Karnad's career, collected in volume 2, continue these patterns by taking up other periods in Indian history and other mythic episodes, but they also open up a complex new dialogue between languages and initiate entirely current narratives.

APARNA BHARGAVA DHARWADKER
ASSOCIATE PROFESSOR OF THEATRE AND ENGLISH
UNIVERSITY OF WISCONSIN-MADISON

(Some portions of this Introduction are reprinted from my forthcoming book, *Theatres of Independence: Drama, Theory, and Urban Performance in India Since 1947* (University of Iowa Press and Oxford University Press, 2005). For permission to use this material, I would like to thank the University of Iowa Press.)

Works Cited

Jacob, Paul. 'Tughlaq.' *Enact* 105–6 (September–October 1975): n.p.

Karnad, Girish. 'In Search of a New Theatre.' In *Contemporary India: Essays on the Use of Tradition*. Ed. Carla Borden. Delhi: Oxford University Press, 1989.

———. *Three Plays*. Translated by Girish Karnad. Delhi: Oxford University Press, 1994.

———. *Two Plays*. Delhi: Oxford University Press, 2004.

Paul, Rajinder. 'Girish Karnad Interviewed.' *Enact* 54 (June 1971): n.p.

TUGHLAQ

Tughlaq was first presented in English by the Theatre Group of Bombay at the Bhulabhai Desai Auditorium in August 1970. The principal cast was as follows:

KABIR BEDI	Tughlaq
STANLEY PINTO	Aazam
BUBBLES PADAMSEE	Aziz
SABIRA MERCHANT	Step-Mother
PROTAP ROY	Najib
PRADEEP KHAITAN	Barani
GERSON DA CUNHA	Shaikh Imam-ud-din
ZAFAR HAI	Shihab-ud-din
NOEL GODIN	Ratan Singh
KERSEY KATRAK	Shaikh Shams-ud-din
FARROKH MEHTA	Ghiyas-ud-din Abbasid
Directed by	ALYQUE PADAMSEE
Set designed by	PILOO POCHKHANWALA
Music by	KERSEY LORD

for
KRISHNA BASRUR
with affection and admiration

Scene One

AD 1327

The yard in front of the Chief Court of Justice in Delhi. A crowd of citizens—mostly Muslims, with a few Hindus here and there.

OLD MAN: God, what's this country coming to!

YOUNG MAN: What are you worried about, grandfather? The country's in perfectly safe hands—safer than any you've seen before.

OLD MAN: I don't know. I've been alive a long time, seen many Sultans, but I never thought I would live to see a thing like this.

YOUNG MAN: Your days are over, old man. What's the use of Sultans who didn't allow a subject within a mile's distance? This King now, he isn't afraid to be human—

THIRD MAN: But does he have to make such a fuss about being human? Announce his mistakes to the whole world—invite the entire capital?

OLD MAN: And get kicked by an infidel too. It's an insult to Islam.

YOUNG MAN: That's good that! Insult to Islam! So you want to teach him Islam, do you? Tell me, how often did you pray before he came to the throne?

THIRD MAN: That isn't the point.

YOUNG MAN: That's precisely the point. Not even once a week, I
bet. Now you pray five times a day because that's the law and
if you break it, you'll have the officers on your neck. Can you
mention one earlier Sultan in whose time people read the
Koran in the streets like now? Just one?

OLD MAN: What's the use? One must act according to it...

THIRD MAN: All this about the Hindus not paying the jiziya
tax. That's against the Koran, you know. A Mowlvi told me
that—

HINDU: Now, now, don't look at *me* when you say that. We didn't
want an exemption! Look, when a Sultan kicks me in the
teeth and says, 'Pay up, you Hindu dog', I'm happy. I know
I'm safe. But the moment a man comes along and says, 'I
know you are a Hindu, but you are also a human being'—
well, that makes me nervous.

YOUNG MAN: Ungrateful wretch!

OLD MAN: But this wretch is our best friend, Jamal. Beware of the
Hindu who embraces you. Before you know what, he'll turn
Islam into another caste and call the Prophet an incarnation
of his god...

(*The Public Announcer comes out and beats his drum. Silence.*)

ANNOUNCER: Attention! Attention! In the name of the Allah it is
hereby announced that Vishnu Prasad, a Brahmin of Shiknar,
had filed a suit against His Merciful Majesty, that his land had
been seized illegally by the officers of the State and that he
should be given just compensation for the loss of the land and
the privation resulting therefrom. The Kazi-i-Mumalik having considered this matter carefully and in full detail has
declared...

(*He pauses for effect. The audience is tense and the Announcer looks
pleased.*)

...has declared that the Brahmin's claim is just...

(*Commotion in the crowd. The Announcer silences them with a couple of drum beats and continues.*)

...that the Brahmin's claim is just and that His Merciful Majesty is guilty of illegal appropriation of land. The Kazi-i-Mumalik has further declared that in return for the land and in compensation of the privation resulting from its loss the said Vishnu Prasad should receive a grant of five hundred silver dinars from the State Treasury.

(*Renewed commotion. But the Announcer isn't finished yet.*)

His Merciful Majesty has accepted the decision of the Kazi-i-Mumalik as just and in addition to the grant of five hundred silver dinars has offered the said Vishnu Prasad a post in the Civil Service to ensure him a regular and adequate income.

(*Beats the drums again and retires.*)

OLD MAN: What folly is this! May Heaven guide our Sultan.

HINDU: I don't believe a word of it. There's something more to this, that much is obvious—

(*The Announcer comes out followed by Muhammad, the Kazi and the retinue.*)

ANNOUNCER: Attention! Attention! The Warrior in the Path of God, the Defender of the Word of the Prophet—May peace be upon him—,the Friend of the Khalif, the Just, His Merciful Majesty, Sultan Muhammad Tughlaq.

CROWD: Victory—to the King.

MUHAMMAD: My beloved people, you have heard the judgement of the Kazi and seen for yourselves how justice works in my kingdom—without any consideration of might or weakness, religion or creed. May this moment burn bright and light up our path towards greater justice, equality, progress and peace—not just peace but a more purposeful life.

And to achieve this end I am taking a new step in which I hope I shall have your support and cooperation. Later this year the capital of my empire will be moved from Delhi to Daulatabad.

(*The crowd reacts in bewilderment. Muhammad smiles.*)

Your surprise is natural. But I beg you to realize that this is no mad whim of a tyrant. My ministers and I took this decision after careful thought and discussion. My empire is large now and embraces the South and I need a capital which is at its heart. Delhi is too near the border and, as you well know, its peace is never free from the fear of invaders. But for me the most important factor is that Daulatabad is a city of the Hindus and as the capital, it will symbolize the bond between Muslims and Hindus which I wish to develop and strengthen in my kingdom. I invite you all to accompany me to Daulatabad. This is only an invitation and not an order. Only those who have faith in me may come with me. With their help I shall build an empire which will be the envy of the world.

(*Exits with the retinue.*)

OLD MAN: You can go to the Kazi-i-Mumalik for small offences. But who do you appeal to against such madness?

THIRD MAN: This is tyranny! Sheer tyranny! Move the capital to Daulatabad! Such things never happened in his father's days—may his soul rest in peace. Now he has got his father's throne. He isn't happy with that and—

YOUNG MAN: What do you mean?

THIRD MAN: What?

YOUNG MAN: What did you mean by that—when you said he had got his father's throne?

THIRD MAN: Don't try to threaten me, boy. The whole capital saw it.

YOUNG MAN: Saw what?

THIRD MAN: You know what.

YOUNG MAN: Were you there?

THIRD MAN: There were others—my friends—

YOUNG MAN: Hang your friends! Were you there?

THIRD MAN: No!

YOUNG MAN: Well, I was. And I tell you it was an accident.

THIRD MAN: I see.

YOUNG MAN: It was. The elephant suddenly went wild. The crowds must have frightened it. It just ran and dashed against the wooden pandal. And the pandal collapsed.

OLD MAN: Very convenient.

THIRD MAN: And to think the procession had been arranged by the father in his honour!

YOUNG MAN: But the Sultan had gone to the mosque to pray! The old Sultan should never have had the procession at prayer time—You all know it was prayer time and the Sultan never misses a prayer!

HINDU MAN: Yes, yes, we know that. But tell me. How did the elephant know it was time for prayer?

(*Laughter.*)

THIRD MAN: All right, don't trust my word. But do you think a man like Sheikh Imam-ud-din would lie? Well, he said in clear loud words that it was murder. And he said it publicly— I was there!

OLD MAN (*eagerly*): You've seen the Sheikh?

THIRD MAN: Why, of course. Only a week ago. In Kanpur. What a man! What a voice! The audience was spell-bound. And he said the Sultan's guilty of killing his father and brother, he said. He said so many other things too—about Islam and what's happening to it. It was the most inspiring speech I've ever heard. The audience went wild and burnt down half of Kanpur. You think he would talk like that if he wasn't sure?

OLD MAN: They say he looks like the Sultan.

THIRD MAN: No—not very much. People exaggerate, you know. But he has a certain resemblance—some gestures, you know, some mannerisms—

HINDU MAN: Perhaps that's where he gets his habit of making speeches.

THIRD MAN: Watch your words, infidel. Don't you dare mock a saint like him.

(*The Guard comes out of the Court.*)

GUARD: All right, all right. Go home! What are you waiting for? The show's over! Go home—

(*The crowd disperses. Only Aazam remains, hanging around.*)

Well, what do you want?

AAZAM: Nothing, I just wanted to see the Brahmin. He hasn't come out yet, has he?

GUARD: Oh, get away. Wants to see the Brahmin, if you please. Be off—

(*Aazam retreats. The Guard looks into the Court and shouts.*)

Come out—come out. Don't be scared, Your Highness.

(*The Brahmin comes out.*)

Perhaps Your Highness will want an escort to see you safely home! Complaining against the Sultan! Bloody Infidel! Get going, I'm already late.

BRAHMIN: Yes, yes. Certainly. Good-bye.

GUARD: Good-bye.

(*Goes in and shuts the door. The Brahmin starts to go. Aazam follows him and then slowly taps him on the shoulder.*)

AAZAM: Ho...ooo...

(*The Brahmin whirls round and pulls out a dagger as he turns. Aazam jumps back.*)

AAZAM: Oops...

(*They watch each other. Aazam's jaw falls in surprise.*)

AAZAM: Who? Not...not...

BRAHMIN: Aazam?

AAZAM: Aziz? What on earth...
(*Gives a shout of joy, lifts Aziz up and whirls him round and round ecstatically.*)

AZIZ: Let me down—let me down—
(*Aazam lets him down.*)
And hold your tongue. If they find out, I'm finished, man.

AAZAM: But—I don't see you for years and then—this—this?

AZIZ: Shut up!
(*They move off and sit under a tree.*)

AAZAM: I thought something was funny. I mean, a man wins a case against the King himself—you would expect him to come out triumphantly—I mean, holding his head high? Not hide inside! Listen, Brahmins don't carry daggers around like that.
(*Aziz quickly hides the dagger.*)

AZIZ: What are you doing here?

AAZAM: I am where there is a crowd. Look, today's earnings. And you won't believe me if I tell you where they hide their money—

AZIZ: So your bad habits continue, do they?

AAZAM: Not habit. Occupation. Anyway, I'm just a common pickpocket. But you are up to no good either, I can see that. A Muslim dhobi can't become a Brahmin that easily.

AZIZ: For God's sake, keep your voice down. Now look, if I tell you the truth, will you keep it to yourself?

AAZAM: Depends on what I get out of it—All right, you're an old friend. I'll keep quiet for nothing. So?

AZIZ: Did you hear the royal proclamation the other day?

AAZAM: Which one? There are so many.

AZIZ: You know, the one on the second anniversary of his coronation. (*Mimicking a public announcer.*)

'Henceforth people may file a suit against the Sultan himself for the misbehaviour of his officers... No one need have any fear...Justice will be done...' Et cetera. Well, I was at the end of my tether then. There's no future in being a *dhobi* these days. So I did a bit of thinking. There's a Brahmin called Vishnu Prasad whose land had been confiscated recently. I shaved my head and went to him. I said I would buy the land.

AAZAM: Please, a little slowly. I—you know I'm not very bright. But what's the point? I mean the land was confiscated, wasn't it?

AZIZ: Exactly, that's what he said too. But I said, 'Never mind about that'. So he sold me the land—backdating the contract. And I filed my suit. Well, here I am. Five hundred silver dinars for nothing, and a job in His Merciful Majesty's own Civil Service.

AAZAM: But what if he had cut off your head instead?
(*Aziz laughs.*)

Anyway, why did you have to dress up in these ungodly clothes? Couldn't you have come like a proper Muslim?

AZIZ: (*Scandalized.*) But then what would happen to the King's impartial justice? A Muslim plaintiff against a Muslim king? I mean, where's the question of justice there? Where's the equality between Hindus and Muslims? If, on the other hand, the plaintiff's a Hindu...well, you saw the crowds.

AAZAM: Complicated!

AZIZ: It's a bit too subtle for you. Anyway here's my offer. From tomorrow I join the Civil Service. Why don't you come along too? I'll get you a job under me. You know, a Brahmin with a Muslim friend—the Sultan will like that.

AAZAM: No thanks, I'm quite happy—

AZIZ: Come along. It won't be for long. I didn't intend to be a Brahmin all my life! There's money here and we'll make a pile by the time we reach Daulatabad.

AAZAM: And then?

AZIZ: How should I know?

Scene Two

A room in the palace. Muhammad is bent over a chess-board, smiling with suppressed excitement. The Step-Mother enters.

STEP-MOTHER: Muhammad—

MUHAMMAD: Ah, there you are! Absolutely at the right moment. If you had come a minute earlier, the world would have been so much poorer.

STEP-MOTHER: Really? That sounds very important.

MUHAMMAD: But it is. I have just solved the most famous problem in chess. Even al-Adli and as-Sarakhi said it was insoluble. And it's so simple—

STEP-MOTHER: Who were they?

MUHAMMAD: Mother! How can you ask? They were the greatest chess players the world's ever seen.

STEP-MOTHER: What do I know about your chess? You'd better write to Ain-ul-Mulk about it. He'll love it!

MUHAMMAD: Funny you should mention him. I was just thinking of him—but not with reference to chess. You see, my dear friend Ain-ul-Mulk, the companion of my childhood, my fellow champion in chess, is at this very moment marching on Delhi.

STEP-MOTHER: What? What do you mean?

MUHAMMAD: Exactly what I said. He is marching on Delhi with an army of thirty thousand.

STEP-MOTHER: But why, Muhammad?

MUHAMMAD: I don't know. The last letter I wrote to him asked him to be the Governor of the Deccan. I need a strong man there and I thought he would like it.

STEP-MOTHER: But there must be some other reason! (*No reply.*) What are you going to do now?

MUHAMMAD: Do the best I can. But I don't even have six thousand soldiers—Look, I was so happy about this problem and now you've ruined it all. Anyway, you came for something?

STEP-MOTHER: It doesn't matter any more.

MUHAMMAD: But it does, certainly.

STEP-MOTHER: I was worried about your late nights. These days you never seem to go to bed at all. I just wanted to know why.

MUHAMMAD (*smiles*): And you think you've found the answer? Look, if I was that worried about Ain-ul-Mulk why would I waste my time on this?
(*Points to the chess-board.*)

STEP-MOTHER: Then what do you do all night?

MUHAMMAD (*theatrical*): I pray to the Almighty to save me from sleep. All day long I have to worry about tomorrow but it's only when the night falls that I can step beyond all that. I look at the Pleiades and I think of Ibn-ul-Mottazz who thought it was an ostrich egg and Dur-rumma who thought it was a swallow. And then I want to go back to their poetry and sink myself in their words. Then again I want to climb up, up to the top of the tallest tree in the world, and call out to my people: 'Come, my people, I am waiting for you. Confide in me your worries. Let me share your joys. Let's laugh and cry

together and then, let's pray. Let's pray till our bodies melt
and flow and our blood turns into air. History is ours to play
with—ours now! Let's be the light and cover the earth with
greenery. Let's be darkness and cover up the boundaries of
nations. Come! I am waiting to embrace you all!'

But then how can I spread my branches in the stars while
the roots have yet to find their hold in the earth? I wish I could
believe in recurring births like the Hindu; but I have only
one life, one body, and my hopes, my people, my God are all
fighting for it. Tell me, how dare I waste my time sleeping?
And don't tell me to go and get married and breed a family
because I won't sleep.

STEP-MOTHER (*bursts into laughter*): I don't know what to do with
   you. I can't ask a simple question without your giving a royal
   performance. Even Ain-ul-Mulk doesn't seem to stop you—

MUHAMMAD: Mother, suppose I die fighting Ain-ul-Mulk—

STEP-MOTHER: Stop it!

MUHAMMAD: No, really. Suppose I die in the battle. What of it?
   Why should I waste my last few days worrying? I am not
   worried about my enemies. I'm only worried about my
   people.

STEP-MOTHER: Pompous ass! As though other kings didn't do that.

MUHAMMAD: No, they didn't. Look at the past Sultans of Delhi.
   They couldn't bear the weight of their crown. They couldn't
   leave it aside. So they died senile in their youth or were
   murdered.

STEP-MOTHER (*sharply*): Please, Muhammad—

MUHAMMAD: What?

STEP-MOTHER: Nothing—I can't bear to see you joking about
   murder.

MUHAMMAD: Why not?

STEP-MOTHER: I can't. That's all.

(Silence. They are both tense now.)

MUHAMMAD: So you too believe that piece of gossip!

STEP-MOTHER: What gossip?

MUHAMMAD *(mocking)*: What gossip? What scandal? You know perfectly well what I mean.

STEP-MOTHER: Don't be silly. I didn't mean anything of that kind.

MUHAMMAD: But you do believe it? And why shouldn't you? After all my own mother believes it. The whole court believes it. My Amirs believe it. Why shouldn't my step-mother believe it?

STEP-MOTHER *(flaring up)*: Shut up, fool! I've told you I won't have you calling me that?

MUHAMMAD *(suddenly calm, but with deliberate viciousness)*: I know. But you are my step-mother!
(Silence. Enter the Door-Keeper.)

DOOR-KEEPER: In the name of Allah. Vizier Muhammad Najib and Zia-ud-din Barani to see you, Your Majesty.

MUHAMMAD: Send them in.
(The Door-Keeper goes out. The Step-Mother lowers the veil on her face. Najib and Barani enter.)

NAJIB, BARANI: In the name of Allah.

MUHAMMAD: Come in, come in. I was just saying to Mother...

STEP-MOTHER: Muhammad, why don't you tell them about your chess?

MUHAMMAD: Because they aren't interested. Barani is a historian—he's only interested in playing chess with the shadows of the dead. And Najib's a politician—he wants pawns of flesh and blood. He doesn't have the patience to breathe life into these bones. One needs Ain-ul-Mulk for that. So Najib, how far have we reached?

NAJIB: I'm doing my best, Your Majesty. But I don't think we'll get more than six thousand. The odds against us are very heavy...

BARANI: May I know what odds, Your Majesty?

NAJIB: ...but another equally important problem has cropped up, Your Majesty. Sheikh Imam-ud-din is in Delhi.

MUHAMMAD: Aha! Then we should take his blessings before we leave.

NAJIB: Yes, Your Majesty, and get rid of him.

BARANI: What a terrible thing to say about a holy man like that!

MUHAMMAD (*smiles to the Step-Mother, explaining*): Najib is upset because the Sheikh criticizes me publicly—demands that I abdicate. The Sheikh thinks I'm incompetent.

NAJIB: It's worse than that. He has become a backbone of the rebels. As for what else he says, you may ask Barani.

MUHAMMAD: So you've heard him, Barani. What's he like? Is it true he looks like me?

BARANI (*flustered*): A little, Your Majesty. But—how did Najib know I had heard the Sheikh? Forgive me, Your Majesty, but I don't like being spied upon.

NAJIB: It's my job to know. That's why I asked you to come here with me now.

MUHAMMAD: Surely a historian doesn't need an invitation to watch history take shape! Come, what does he say?

BARANI: It's as Your Majesty said...He says the Sultan is a disgrace to Islam.

MUHAMMAD: That's all? I could find worse faults in me. What else?

(*Silence.*)

NAJIB: He says Your Majesty has forfeited the right to rule, by murdering your father and brother at prayer.

(*The Step-Mother and Barani react sharply, but Muhammad is still. A short pause.*)

MUHAMMAD (*quietly*): Did he say that?

BARANI (*almost in a whisper*): Yes, Your Majesty.

MUHAMMAD: So now they talk about it openly, do they?

BARANI: He said it in the heat of the moment, Your Majesty. I'm sure he didn't mean it. Your Majesty must ignore these little things.

MUHAMMAD: Do you really think parricide is a little thing? And fratricide? And the pollution of prayer? It's not what people say, Barani, it's their crooked minds that horrify me. Look at my own mother—she won't talk to me now—not because father died but because my brother died in the accident. He was more amenable to her whims and he would have made a better king for her. So she believes I killed them. Do you know, I've just found out that even this step-mother of mine thinks I am a murderer.

(*Silence.*)

NAJIB (*quietly*): What about the Sheikh, Your Majesty?

MUHAMMAD (*in a tired voice*): Let him babble. He is a saint, it's his privilege.

NAJIB: But we must do something. In Kanpur, they're still rioting and he started it. Now he's here—in the capital.

BARANI: But His Majesty is right. The people have been told that they have a right to criticize the Sultan, to voice their grievances openly. Surely this is the time to show that the Sultan means it—that they were not empty words. The people will surely respond to His Majesty's courage, honesty and justice...

NAJIB (*groans*): Courage, honesty and justice! My dear Barani, we are dealing with a political problem!

BARANI: I know and that's where they count most. Because that's where the Kingdom of Islam which the Prophet—may peace

be upon him—has gifted us must blossom. Oh! You won't
understand it. Your Hindu childhood has twisted your
attitudes beyond repair.

NAJIB: Do you know why I gave up Hinduism? Because it didn't
speak of the salvation of society. It only talked of the soul—
my individual soul—while a poor, frenzied world screamed
in agony around. So I became a Muslim. Islam is worried
about this world, I said, it'll bring the Kingdom of Heaven
on earth. But I know now—it won't work. There's only the
present moment and we must grasp it firmly.

MUHAMMAD (*ironic but affectionate*): So what does the present
moment demand now?

BARANI: It's obvious, Your Majesty. He wants the Sheikh dead.

NAJIB: Nonsense! That'll make him a martyr. You can't kill the
dead. If we kill him now, we're finished. We might as well
surrender to Ain-ul-Mulk.

BARANI (*startled*): Surrender to whom?

MUHAMMAD: Ain-ul-Mulk. He is marching on Delhi.

BARANI: I don't believe it! (*Silence.*) But you mustn't act hastily,
Your Majesty. There's obviously been some misunderstand-
ing. (*Earnestly.*) You know Ain-ul-Mulk. He is a good man
and he worships you. You know he isn't the treacherous
type.

MUHAMMAD (*in anguish*): But why now? Can't he see that I've no
time for 'misunderstandings' now? He knows how important
it is for me to concentrate on moving to Daulatabad.

BARANI: But there must be some way of finding out why he's doing
this. Please send an envoy... Send me... I'll go...

NAJIB: What's the point? We can't waste our time on that. A
traitor's a traitor, friend or saint, and he must be crushed.

BARANI: But don't you want to know why?

NAJIB: I do know why. It's obvious.
(*The rest look at him in surprise.*)

MUHAMMAD: It is?

NAJIB: Your Majesty, when you came to the throne, there was anarchy in Avadh and you made Ain-ul-Mulk the Governor there. He crushed the rebels, restored law and order, and the people in Avadh adore him. He's happy there, secure. Then suddenly he gets your letter making him the Governor of the Deccan, asking him to leave immediately. Is it surprising he should suspect a knife in his back?

(*Silence.*)

MUHAMMAD: God, why didn't I think of that?

BARANI: But Najib did, Your Majesty, and didn't warn you.

NAJIB: Would His Majesty have listened to me if I'd warned then? His Majesty loved Ain-ul-Mulk—too much.

BARANI: And you hate him?

NAJIB: Dear Barani, not hate, just suspicion. It's my job to be suspicious and I can't exempt anyone from it.

STEP-MOTHER: No one?

NAJIB: No, Your Highness.

STEP-MOTHER: Not even the Sultan?

NAJIB (*senses a trap, but calmly*): No, not even the Sultan, Your Highness.

STEP-MOTHER (*flaring up*): Muhammad—
(*Muhammad silences her with a gesture of impatience.*)

MUHAMMAD: So, Najib, what do you propose?

NAJIB: I can't think of anything right now, Your Majesty—except that the Sheikh has a striking resemblance to you.
(*Muhammad, startled, stares at Najib.*)

BARANI: What has the Sheikh got to do with this?

MUHAMMAD (*slowly*): You are a devil, Najib! (*Pause. Then briskly.*)

Good. We'll think about that. In the meantime, the army
should be ready to march. We'll start for Kanauj the day after
tomorrow in the evening.

STEP-MOTHER: And who'll look after the administration here,
Muhammad?

MUHAMMAD: Najib will be here.

(*The Step-Mother obviously doesn't like the answer. Najib smiles
ironically but not too openly.*)

Besides I have invited Shihab-ud-din, the Prince of Sampanshahr,
to be here in my absence. You see, the Amir there doesn't like
me very much, so I thought inviting his son would be a nice
friendly gesture.

BARANI: What's all this, Your Majesty? I can't follow a thing. But
my heart trembles for you.

MUHAMMAD: Forgive me if I let you down, Barani, but I must
play this game my own way. Come, Najib, we must see the
Commander-in-Chief. Mother, if you'll excuse us. (*Bows to
her.*)

STEP-MOTHER: Can Barani stay for a while? I want to talk to him.

MUHAMMAD: Why, yes, certainly.

(*Muhammad and Najib go out. Silence.*)

STEP-MOTHER: I don't know what to say, Barani. I mustn't complain against my own son—

BARANI: Your Highness may place full trust in me.

STEP-MOTHER: I know. That's why I asked you to stay. I am worried
about him. You know what he is like. He is such an intelligent
boy and he works so hard for the people. He doesn't even
go to bed these days. (*Pause.*) But he is so impulsive—and
when he gets into one of his moods I don't know what he'll
do next. (*Pause.*) You are a sober man, Barani, level-headed
and honest, and he needs friends like you. I just wanted to ask
you… Oh, God! It all sounds so stupid.

BARANI: I fully understand Your Highness's feelings.

STEP-MOTHER: It's not that. It's just that I don't like so many of his advisers and friends. (*Suddenly.*) Please promise me not to leave him—ever—whatever he does.

BARANI (*overwhelmed to the point of tears*): May God help me to retain such confidence untarnished. I won't leave His Majesty, Your Highness, I promise you. I love him too much to do that.

STEP-MOTHER: Look at him now. He won't show it, but Ain-ul-Mulk has hurt him. And this Sheikh Imam-ud-din—I don't know what he's going to do.

BARANI: It's not for me to advise, Your Highness, but I have to mention it. I am not jealous of Najib and I admire his integrity. But sometimes I am bothered by his influence on the Sultan.

STEP-MOTHER: I know. I am watching. I'll wait for a few days. (*With sudden violence.*) If he goes on like this, I won't wish his fate even on a dog!

(*Barani, driven to tears by her maternal concern, looks up startled by the venom in her voice.*)

ANNOUNCER: Attention! Attention! The Slave of the Lord, the
    Merciful, the ever-Victorious Sultan Muhammad has declared
    that this evening after the prayer a meeting will be organized
    in the yard in front of the Great Mosque. Sheikh Imam-ud-
    din, who is revered all over India as a Saint and as one who
    stands in the Grace of Allah, will address the meeting. He will
    analyse His Merciful Majesty's administration and show
    where His Majesty has inadvertently taken wrong measures—
    measures harmful to the country and the Faith. His Majesty
    himself will be present at the meeting to seek direction from
    the Revered Sheikh, and the citizens of Delhi are requested
    to attend the meeting in large numbers and do likewise.
    Attention! Attention!

Scene Three

The yard in front of the Great Mosque. Muhammad and Sheikh Imam-ud-din and a few odd servants of the palace. No one else. There is a long silence.

MUHAMMAD (*suddenly*): I can't bear this any longer!

IMAM-UD-DIN: Why Your Majesty? You should be happy if no one turns up.

MUHAMMAD: Do you think I would have gone to the trouble of arranging this meeting if I didn't want my people to hear you? I don't want my people to be dumb cattle, Sheikhsahib, and I do not claim to be omniscient myself. I am quite willing to learn from you—even eager.

IMAM-UD-DIN: Will you be as eager when you hear me out, I wonder? You know I am not the type to sweeten my words because the Sultan himself is present.

MUHAMMAD: Don't I know it? The whole of Delhi has heard of the courage and integrity of Sheikh Imam-ud-din. I would not have taken so much trouble for anyone else.

(*Claps. A servant enters and bows.*)
   Go at once and tell the Vizier I want everyone here—all the Khans, Amirs, Sardars—everyone—at once!

IMAM-UD-DIN: But Your Majesty, I haven't come here to speak to a collection of courtiers—

MUHAMMAD: And I'm afraid I can't go now from door to door asking people to come. I should have issued renewed orders at the Court today. We have been waiting for over half an hour—and not a soul has come yet!

IMAM-UD-DIN: They say we look alike, but we don't think alike, do we? What's the point in my addressing a gang of sycophants? I want to speak to the people who are willing to act, who are willing to do something for Islam and the country. If no one comes today, well, no matter. I'll go to the market-place tomorrow and speak there.

(*Muhammad signs to the servant to go. He goes out.*)

MUHAMMAD: Would you believe me if I told you I have never consciously tried to go against the tenets of Islam?

IMAM-UD-DIN: Please, Your Majesty, even you can't believe that! I can quote scores of transgressions. If they weren't wilful, they could only be results of ignorance. But I can't believe that in a scholar of your eminence. Perhaps you are sincere. But if one fails to understand what the Koran says, one must ask the Sayyids and the Ulema. Instead you have put the best of them behind bars in the name of justice.

MUHAMMAD: They tried to indulge in politics—I couldn't allow that. I have never denied the word of God, Sheikhsahib, because it's my bread and drink. I need it most when the surrounding void pushes itself into my soul and starts putting out every light burning there. But I am alone in my life. My kingdom has millions—Muslims, Hindus, Jains. Yes, there is dirt and sickness in my kingdom. But why should I call on God to clean up the dirt deposited by men?

IMAM-UD-DIN: Because only the Voice of God, the Holy Word, can do it. Please listen to me, Your Majesty. The Arabs spread Islam round the world and they struggled and fought for it for seven hundred years. They are tired now, limp and exhausted. But their work must continue and we need someone to take the lead. You could do it. You are one of the most powerful kings on earth today and you could spread the Kingdom of Heaven on earth. God has given you every-thing—power, learning, intelligence, talent. Now you must repay His debt.

MUHAMMAD: No one can go far on his knees. I have a long way to go. I can't afford to crawl—I have to gallop.

IMAM-UD-DIN: And you will do it without the Koran to guide you? Beware, Sultan, you are trying to become another God. It's a sin worse than parricide.

MUHAMMAD (*refusing the bait*): Only an atheist can try to be God. I am God's most humble slave.

IMAM-UD-DIN: Yes. And slaves have often tried to replace their master.

MUHAMMAD: My congratulations, Imam-ud-din Sahib. For a saint you are very good at innuendoes—I know all about slaves. My grandfather was one and he seized power. But that was in mundane politics. The analogy doesn't work here.

IMAM-UD-DIN: Religion! Politics! Take heed, Sultan, one day these verbal distinctions will rip you into two.

MUHAMMAD: Don't I know it? I still remember the days when I read the Greeks—Sukrat who took poison so he could give the world the drink of gods, Aflatoon who condemned poets and wrote incomparably beautiful poetry himself—and I can still feel the thrill with which I found a new world, a world I had not found in the Arabs or even the Koran. They tore me into shreds. And to be whole now, I shall have to kill the part of me which sang to them. And my kingdom too is what I am—torn into pieces by visions whose validity I can't deny. You are asking me to make myself complete by killing the Greek in me and you propose to unify my people by denying the visions which led Zarathustra or the Buddha. (*Smiles*) I'm sorry. But it can't be done.

IMAM-UD-DIN: You are a learned man. You may be able to manage this delicate balance within yourself. But a kingdom needs not one king but a line of rulers. Will they manage this balance? Where are these brilliant successors of yours? Where are these guarantors of your balanced future?

MUHAMMAD: There is none—yet. But I haven't lost hope. I shall find them and teach them to think like me. They are only cattle yet, but I shall make men out of a few of them. Look, Sheikhsahib, in Kanpur you found so many honest men that they burnt down the whole of Kanpur. They are still on the rampage there and your words inspire them. Now you've come to Delhi and there isn't even a fly to listen to you. They are staying away—at home, safe and secure. They don't want you here. Do you know why?

(*Silence.*)

Because they suspect you now. The moment they heard that I, the Sultan, was organizing a meeting in which you, my severest critic, was going to speak—they became suspicious. Why should the Sultan sponsor his worst critic? They have smelt a trap. And wisely they have stayed away.

IMAM-UD-DIN (*stunned*): Was this a trap?

MUHAMMAD: No, I promise you.

IMAM-UD-DIN: But—you knew this would happen?

MUHAMMAD: I didn't *know*. But I half expected it. I know my people.

IMAM-UD-DIN: So they think I'm your spy—and you knew it when you arranged this meeting!

MUHAMMAD: Believe me, Sheikhsahib, I'm sorry I am not disappointed. Yes, they will now decide you are a spy—they'll greet you as a spy in the market-place tomorrow. But now you do see what I mean, don't you? You are revered as a saint and you have risked your life by speaking out against the Sultan. Yet a trick—and they suspect you. It's futile to think

of them as members of the *dar-ul-Islam*. Generations of
devout sultans have twisted their minds and I have to mend
their minds before I can think of their souls.

(*There is a long silence. Then Sheikh Imam-ud-din starts to move
down slowly.*)

IMAM-UD-DIN: My turn to congratulate you. Your experiment was
a brilliant success. Yes, I have learnt my lesson. Thank you—
and good-bye.

MUHAMMAD: Good-bye? You are not going?

IMAM-UD-DIN: You have finished my work for me. You don't want
me to wait longer, do you? For an audience which won't turn
up?

MUHAMMAD: I need your help, Sheikhsahib.

IMAM-UD-DIN: Don't play any more games with me—

MUHAMMAD: There's no time for games. I am desperate. Ain-ul-
Mulk of Avadh is marching on Delhi at this very moment.

IMAM-UD-DIN: What? Your intimate friend and confidant? Why?
No, I don't wish to know why. That's politics and you know
your way there. But why tell me this?

MUHAMMAD: Because I want peace. I am willing to make peace,
but how can I do it? I don't even know why he has turned
against me. He won't even see my official envoys. (*Pause.*) But
he will see you.

(*The Sheikh is about to speak. But Muhammad goes on.*)
He respects you as every Muslim in India does. He will trust
your word. That's why I'm asking you—will you please go as
my envoy and dissuade him from this folly? Please, Sheikhsahib,
I'm not asking you only for my sake, but for all the Muslims
who will die at the hands of Muslims if there is a war.

(*Pause.*)

IMAM-UD-DIN: I don't trust your motives.

MUHAMMAD: What do my motives matter? You can't deny that this war will mean a slaughter of Muslims at the hands of fellow-Muslims. Isn't that enough for the great Sheikh Imam-ud-din? You have attacked me for inaction. You can't turn away now when you are offered a chance. You can't!

IMAM-UD-DIN: I know I can't.

MUHAMMAD: So you agree?

IMAM-UD-DIN: Do you leave me an alternative?

MUHAMMAD (*slowly*): I'll never be able to thank you enough for this.

(*Claps his hands. A servant enters and bows.*)

Bring the robes of honour for the royal envoy. At once!

(*The servant departs.*)

IMAM-UD-DIN: You don't mean the robes are ready?

MUHAMMAD: Forgive me, Sheikhsahib, but I knew you wouldn't refuse.

IMAM-UD-DIN: But what about Ain-ul-Mulk? Won't he also think of me as your spy? It won't take long before he comes to know of this. (*Indicates the empty auditorium.*)

MUHAMMAD: He is not a fool. Besides, he won't know. There isn't time. We have to start before nightfall. Ain-ul-Mulk has already started and we must meet him near the plains of Kanauj.

(*The servant brings the robes of honour and the headdress on a golden plate. Muhammad takes the robe and goes near the Sheikh.*)

IMAM-UD-DIN (*stopping him*): If you want peace, what does it matter where we meet him?

MUHAMMAD: I do want peace. But I can't leave anything to chance. If Ain-ul-Mulk refuses or resorts to treachery, I have to have my army in a safe place. I owe it to my soldiers.

(*Pause.*)

IMAM-UD-DIN: You know, Sultan, I'm just beginning to understand why they say you are the cleverest man in the world.

MUHAMMAD: I am an incompetent fool. Will you accept the robes
now?

IMAM-UD-DIN: Very well.

(*He puts on the robes. Muhammad places the headdress upon him.
They stand facing each other. The dress makes them look even more
alike.*)

I wish I could be more sure of you...

Scene Four

The Palace. Shihab-ud-din is reading a few letters. There is an announcement.

DOOR-KEEPER (*announcing*): Her Highness the Queen Mother. (*Shihab-ud-din leaps up. The Step-Mother enters and he bows to her.*)

SHIHAB-UD-DIN: Welcome, Your Highness. I am most honoured by the visit, but, had Your Highness sent for me, I would have come myself.

STEP-MOTHER: I suddenly felt frightened, Shihab-ud-din. I couldn't bear the tension any longer. Has there been any further news?

SHIHAB-UD-DIN: I'm afraid not, Your Highness. The last bulletin was received a week ago. Your Highness knows the contents. There has been nothing since then. I'm sorry but—

STEP-MOTHER: No, no, please, don't apologize. I don't know what I should have done without you here. You know when Muhammad said he was inviting you to look after Delhi, I didn't understand him at all. I couldn't see why he had to ask you, rather than a local Amir. I know now—he couldn't have chosen a better man.

SHIHAB-UD-DIN: I am most grateful for Your Highness's trust, but I did very little. The credit should go to Vizier Muhammad Najib.

STEP-MOTHER: Oh! Don't talk to me about him. Thanks to you, I didn't have to deal with him.

SHIHAB-UD-DIN: Your Highness's most humble servant.
(*The Door-Keeper enters.*)

DOOR-KEEPER: In the name of Allah. Sardar Ratansingh.

SHIHAB-UD-DIN (*excited*): He is here? Send him in at once.
(*The Door-Keeper goes out.*)

STEP-MOTHER: Who is that?

SHIHAB-UD-DIN: My adopted brother, Your Highness.

STEP-MOTHER: Him! He'll have news of the front then!
(*Ratansingh enters and bows to the Step-Mother. Shihab-ud-din goes to him in great excitement and embraces him.*)

SHIHAB-UD-DIN: Welcome, Ratansingh. What happened?

RATANSINGH: His Majesty is back in Delhi. We arrived a few minutes ago.

STEP-MOTHER: Oh, then I must go.

RATANSINGH: Forgive me, Your Highness, but His Majesty has gone to see the Vizier. He has asked me to inform Your Highness that he will be here any minute.
(*The Step-Mother doesn't like it. But she swallows it.*)

STEP-MOTHER: But I can't understand it. Why didn't he send word he was coming? Why this secrecy?

RATANSINGH (*hesitates*): I don't think it was meant to be secret, Your Highness. It's just that His Majesty seems much affected by the death of Sheikh Imam-ud-din.

STEP-MOTHER: What? Sheikh Imam-ud-din dead?

RATANSINGH: Yes, Your Highness. He was killed in the battle.
(*Her face goes white.*)

SHIHAB-UD-DIN: But what was the Sheikh doing in the battle?

DOOR-KEEPER (*off-stage*): The Warrior in the path of God, the Victorious, the Mighty, His Majesty the Sultan.

(*Muhammad enters with Najib and Barani.*)

SHIHAB-UD-DIN (*bows*): In the name of Allah. May He shower greater successes on Your Majesty.

MUHAMMAD: That's no way to welcome, Shihab-ud-din. Come— (*They embrace.*)
I am grateful to you for looking after my people in my absence.

SHIHAB-UD-DIN: Your Majesty's humble slave.

STEP-MOTHER: Muhammad, what's this about Sheikh Imam-ud-din?

(*Muhammad freezes. Then slowly.*)

MUHAMMAD: Did you have to mention it now? It was a terrible sight. They brought his body into my tent and I felt—as though it was I who was lying dead there and that he was standing above me looking at me. I should have been there— in his place.

(*Pause.*)

BARANI: It's a great loss to Islam.

STEP-MOTHER: And what about Ain-ul-Mulk? I hope he's dead too.

MUHAMMAD: I let him go.

(*General surprise.*)

STEP-MOTHER: You didn't! You couldn't have!

NAJIB: I hate to say it on this happy occasion, Your Majesty, but that would be really tossing another torch into the chaos in Avadh.

BARANI: Your Highness must forgive me, but His Majesty deserves congratulations on his courage. He has shown there are things more valuable than vengeance.

NAJIB: Not that again!

MUHAMMAD: I didn't just set him free, Najib. I gave him back the Kingdom of Avadh, *and* I promised not to send him to the Deccan.

NAJIB: We are helpless if Your Majesty insists on... (*Stops.*)

STEP-MOTHER: Why, Muhammad? Why did he deserve such special treatment?

MUHAMMAD: I'll tell you what happened. You remember the chess problem I solved the other day? Well, when they brought Ain-ul-Mulk before me, I said: 'Look, I have solved the famous problem set by al-Adli!' He didn't say a word. I drew a sketch on the floor and showed him the solution. He said he liked it, then looked harder for a couple of minutes and said: 'No, there's a flaw here.' And he actually showed me where I had gone wrong! Think of that! I had spent days on that wretched problem and he spots a flaw within half a minute. I had to forgive him.

BARANI: You are a great man, Your Majesty,...

MUHAMMAD (*laughing*): And you are a good man, Barani, and that's more important. Look at Najib—look at the expression on his face! He can't even believe I can be generous.

NAJIB: I am suspicious by nature, Your Majesty; fortunately my duty also demands it of me.

MUHAMMAD: We must go now. Najib, Delhi will observe a day of mourning tomorrow for Sheikh Imam-ud-din. And there will be no festivities to celebrate the victory. When men like him die, it's a sin to be alive. Come, Mother. Good-bye, Shihab-ud-din and many, many thanks.

(*All except Shihab-ud-din and Ratansingh go. A brief silence.*)

RATANSINGH: I have never seen an honest scoundrel like your Sultan. He murders a man calmly and then flagellates himself in remorse.

SHIHAB-UD-DIN: What are you talking about?

RATANSINGH: I'm silent.

SHIHAB-UD-DIN: I'm sorry. But you have never liked the Sultan, I don't know why. After all that he has done for the Hindus- -

RATANSINGH: Yes indeed, who can deny that! He is impartial! Haven't you heard about the Doab? He levied such taxes on the poor farmers that they preferred to starve. Now there's a famine there. And of course Hindus as well as Muslims are dying with absolute impartiality.

SHIHAB-UD-DIN: What's that got to do with Sheikh Imam-ud-din?

RATANSINGH: I don't know. But I tell you I'm glad to survive the Sultan's impartiality.

SHIHAB-UD-DIN: Must you spin riddles?

RATANSINGH: And do you really want to know the truth? All right. Because you insisted, I went to fight alongside the Sultan. I went and saw him in Kanauj. He didn't seem too pleased to see me. He actually scowled. A Sultan's scowl is a terrible thing.

SHIHAB-UD-DIN: So?

RATANSINGH: Next day I see what the scowl is doing. Sheikh Imam-ud-din is to go and propose peace to Ain-ul-Mulk. A platoon of soldiers is to accompany him. And I am placed in the front rank of the platoon. You know what that means. The front rank never survives a battle.

SHIHAB-UD-DIN: Go on.

RATANSINGH: The Sheikh is delighted about being the Sultan's peace emissary. He looks gorgeous—all dressed up in royal robes, a royal turban, even royal slippers, and sitting on the royal elephant. In fact, he looks exactly like the Sultan.

SHIHAB-UD-DIN (*suspicious*): And the Sultan? What was he doing?

RATANSINGH: I didn't know it then, but he was hiding behind some hills with the rest of the army. Laying a trap.

SHIHAB-UD-DIN: A trap?

RATANSINGH: So we marched towards Ain-ul-Mulk's army, led by the gorgeous Sheikh on the royal elephant. The elephant halted about a hundred yards away from the enemy. The

Sheikh stood up on it and tried to say something when a trumpeter on our side sounded the charge! The battle was on—Yes, my dear Shihab, Ain-ul-Mulk didn't start the battle. We did!

SHIHAB-UD-DIN: And the Sultan?

RATANSINGH: I couldn't understand what was happening. Neither did the Sheikh, obviously. His face was twisted with fear but he was shouting at the top of his voice asking us to stop. He didn't stand a chance. Arrows poured into him and within minutes he looked a gory human porcupine.

SHIHAB-UD-DIN: And the Sultan? Didn't he do anything?

RATANSINGH: He did! The Sheikh plunged down from the elephant and over his corpse we fled in confusion. The enemy was convinced the Sultan was dead and they pursued us. They walked right into the trap. It was the bloodiest massacre I've even seen... We won! (*Pause.*) Sheikh Imam-ud-din was murdered, you know. In cold blood.

SHIHAB-UD-DIN: Oh my God!

RATANSINGH: This isn't all. There's a longer history to all this, (*Pause.*) Do you want to hear it? (*Pause.*) Listen, in a few days the nobles of the court and the prominent citizens of Delhi are going to hold a secret meeting to discuss... (*Stops.*)

SHIHAB-UD-DIN: What?

RATANSINGH: How should I know? I haven't attended the meeting yet.

SHIHAB-UD-DIN: How do you know about it?

RATANSINGH: Ah! That's Delhi for you! They were looking for recruits and the moment they realized the Sultan had tried to kill me off, they discreetly approached me and invited me. They have asked you too, incidentally. They hope you won't be too apathetic toward the attempted disposal of your adopted brother!

(*Silence.*)

I have accepted the invitation, of course. Would you like to come along too?

(*Silence.*)

Why, Shihab, you look pale!

Scene Five

A house in Delhi. A collection of Amirs, Sayyids, etc. Shihab-ud-din and Ratansingh.

SHIHAB-UD-DIN: I'll be plain with you. If you don't like the present administration, that's your problem. I'm an outsider in Delhi. I've nothing to do with it.

AMIR I: But that's the whole point, don't you see? You're the only man he won't suspect.

SHIHAB-UD-DIN: I hope that's not a point against him.

AMIR II: Besides, the people in Delhi never trust each other. It's the climate. They have to have an outsider to lead them!

SHIHAB-UD-DIN: Lead them in what?

AMIR I: Just consider this. Why is he taking us to Daulatabad? Have you wondered about that? I'll tell you. He wants to weaken the Amirs. You see, we are strong in Delhi. This is where we belong. But Daulatabad is a Hindu city and we'll be helpless there. We'll have to lick his feet.

AMIR III: And it's no use his saying stay behind if you like. We have to be in the capital!

AMIR II: Look at what's happening in Delhi. Just look at it! You can't take a step without paying some tax or another. There's

even a tax on gambling. How are we to live? You can't even
cheat without having to pay tax for it. (*Laughter.*)

SHIHAB-UD-DIN: But he has done a lot of good work. Built
schools, roads, hospitals. He has made good use of the money.

SAYYID: Then why can't he collect it the right way? The Koran
sanctions only four taxes, but...(*Looks at Ratansingh and
stops.*)

RATANSINGH (*smiles*): Carry on, sir. Don't mind me. I'm here
because Shihab's here; otherwise I am invisible!

SAYYID: Well...uhm, he could tax the Hindus. The *jiziya* is
sanctioned by the Koran. All infidels should pay it. Instead
he says the infidels are our brothers...

SHIHAB-UD-DIN (*getting up in disgust*): Come, Ratansingh, let's go.
This is worse than I thought. They don't deserve to kiss the
hem of the Sultan's dress.

(*The others are offended and retreat.*)

RATANSINGH: Ah, well...

(*Gets up. At this point an old man who has been sitting in a corner
all along steps forward.*)

SHEIKH: Shihab-ud-din—

SHIHAB-UD-DIN: I said I am not going to associate...

SHEIKH: Shihab-ud-din, I have never asked anything of anyone
but Allah. Today I implore you. In the name of Allah, help
us.

SHIHAB-UD-DIN (*impressed by the old man's age and sincerity*):
Who are you?

SAYYID (*contemptuously*): Don't you know? He is Sheikh Shams-
ud-din Tajuddarfim?

SHIHAB-UD-DIN: Sheikh Shams-ud-din? Sir, what is a holy man
like you doing in this company?

SHEIKH: Yes, you are right. I should shut myself up in a mosque
and devote myself to Allah. I shouldn't get mixed up in the

treacherous games of politicians. I know and I had hoped my
life would be like that. But Allah isn't only for me, Shihab-
ud-din; He's for everyone who believes in him. While tyranny
crushes the faithful into dust, how can I continue to hide in
my hole? Haven't you heard what's happening to the leaders
of Islam today? Sheikh Haidari is in prison. Sheikh Hood in
exile...

SHIHAB-UD-DIN: I know. But they dabbled in politics.

SHEIKH: Is it so reprehensible to be concerned about people? Is
it a crime to speak out for oneself and one's family? What
politics did Sheikh Imam-ud-din indulge in? That he was
open, frank and honest?

SHIHAB-UD-DIN: I don't know enough about that. But to me it
seems clear that if the Sultan is to be blamed for that death,
so are all the citizens of Delhi. I sometimes feel the Sheikh
must have almost wished for death after what happened in
Delhi.

AMIR I: What did happen in Delhi?

SHIHAB-UD-DIN: You know that better than me! He came here to
speak to the people and not a soul turned up to hear him.
Not one of you had the courage to come to the meeting
and now you have the cheek to blame the Sultan for his
death.

(*The others whisper and chuckle in derision.*)

SHEIKH: So you don't know what actually happened behind the
scenes?

SHIHAB-UD-DIN: Behind the scenes?
(*More derisive laughter.*)

SHEIKH: Yes, behind the scenes. It's true the Sultan invited the
whole of Delhi to hear the Sheikh. Yet, on that very afternoon,
soldiers went from door to door threatening dire consequences
if anyone dared to attend the meeting.
(*Silence.*)

SHIHAB-UD-DIN (*slowly*): Does the Sultan know this?
(*More laughter.*)

SHEIKH: They were his orders! And do you know, while the Sultan
stood in front of the Great Mosque with the Sheikh and got
more and more agitated at the empty auditorium, his soldiers
were hiding in the streets around, stopping those who tried
to come? You don't believe it? Look here...
(*Unbuttons his shirt and shows a wound on his shoulder.*)
I tried to force my way to the Great Mosque and this is what
I got for it. Who else would do this to an old man?

RATANSINGH: There, you see! That explains why he had to invite
you from Sampanshahr to look after Delhi in his absence.
There's confidence for you!

SHIHAB-UD-DIN (*doggedly*): Perhaps. But it's done me no harm.

RATANSINGH: Of course not. Had he meant to harm you, you
wouldn't be here to talk about it!

SHEIKH: Will you only think about yourself, Shihab-ud-din? You
are the strong, the powerful in this country. You have the
capacity to set things right. Won't you worry a little about the
people? The citizens of Delhi don't wish to go to Daulatabad,
but they are weak. Will you do nothing for them? How many
people like Sheikh Imam-ud-din have to die before you'll be
ready to act?
(*No reply.*)

AMIR I: We have to act now—while the army here is still tired and
disorganized. We have to do something while you're here. If
you won't join us, will you at least promise not to fight against
us?

SHIHAB-UD-DIN: I know too much now to remain neutral.

RATANSINGH (*with a sudden burst of anger*): Then why not join
them? Even my infidel blood boils when I think of Sheikh
Imam-ud-din and Sheikh Shams-ud-din here. You accuse the
people of Delhi of cowardice and yet you won't raise a finger

to correct an obvious wrong. (*Gets up.*) Come, let's go to the palace. The problem of justice won't bother us there.

AMIR I: You must help us, Shihab-ud-din.

SHEIKH: Islam needs your help.

SHIHAB-UD-DIN: What do you want me to do? You don't need me. You need my father. He is the strong man and even the Sultan is afraid of him. But you're in a hurry. I can only swell your numbers—little else.

RATANSINGH: Don't be stupid, Shihab. Don't tell me you still think the Amirs want to fight the Sultan in the open.

(*Shihab-ud-din looks up at him sharply. Ratansingh smiles and turns to the rest.*)

You see what it is. Shihab is an intelligent young man but he's just too nice! You see his father...

SHIHAB-UD-DIN: Don't, Ratan...

RATANSINGH: Come on, everyone knows about it! His father is supposed to have killed my father by treachery and usurped the kingdom. Shihab can't forget that. He wants to make up for it. That's why I'm here, as his adopted brother. And that's why he just can't stand the mention of treachery. (*To Shihab-ud-din.*) Don't overdo it. You'll have to face it some day. After all, what did the Sultan do to Sheikh Imam-ud-din?

SAYYID: It's not going to be easy. We can't afford to make mistakes.

AMIR II: I know. I have been trying to think of some way. But it just gives me a headache.

(*A long silence.*)

RATANSINGH: I have a plan. It's perfect.

SHIHAB-UD-DIN: Yes?

RATANSINGH: Yes. The Sultan, as you know, is a fanatic about prayer. He has made it compulsory for every Muslim to pray five times a day.

SAYYID: That's his only saving grace.

RATANSINGH: Quite! Even the soldiers have to pray, and while they pray, they are not allowed to carry arms. Which means that at the time of prayer, the whole palace is unarmed.

(*Long pause.*)

AMIR II: It takes a Hindu to notice that! (*Half terrified by the simplicity of it all.*) So?

RATANSINGH: Next Tuesday the Amirs here will be seeing the Sultan for the Durbar-i-Khas. See that you prolong the meeting till the prayer hour. Pray with him. You'll only need an extra couple of hundred soldiers outside the palace. The muezzin's call to prayer will be the signal for attack!

(*There is an uncomfortable silence.*)

AMIR II (*quietly*): Fantastic!

SAYYID: But kill someone during prayer...

AMIR I: And a Muslim too...

RATANSINGH: Where's your Holy Koran? The tyrant doesn't deserve to be considered among the faithful. And then, he killed his own father during prayer time, after all.

AMIR I: That's true. But...

RATANSINGH: That's my plan. Think of a better one if you can.

AMIR I: But we'll have to smuggle arms into the palace.

AMIR II: That can be arranged.

AMIR I: You are sure?

AMIR II: Of course, I'm sure. I think this is a brilliant plan.

AMIR III: It is simple.

(*They all talk animatedly.*)

SHEIKH: No, we can't have it!

(*Sudden silence as they all turn to Sheikh Shams-ud-din*).

SHIHAB-UD-DIN: Why, pray?

SHEIKH: You can't pollute the time of prayer. It's a sacred time. We can't stain it with the blood of a Mussulman.

AMIR II: O come, we can always make up later. Do penance for it.

SHEIKH: But prayer isn't penance. Remember we are here to save Islam, not to insult it.

AMIR I: Don't get excited. Islam will benefit in the long run.

SHEIKH (*to Shihab-ud-din, pleading*): You can't agree to this, Shihab-ud-din. You are the only sensible person here. You can't agree to this sacrilege. You can't do this to Islam...

SHIHAB-UD-DIN: Does your Islam work only at prayer? You have persuaded me to do what I had sworn never to do—*you*, Your Holiness. I'm sure the Lord will not mind an interrupted prayer. (*To the others.*) All right, let's get down to the details. We have to work everything out carefully. (*Suddenly.*) Must we do this, Ratan? Must we?

Scene Six

The palace. Muhammad, Najib and Barani. Silence for a while. Muhammad is restless and paces up and down.

BARANI: Why are you both so quiet?

NAJIB: Oh, shut up!

MUHAMMAD: Please, Najib.
(Silence again. The Door-Keeper enters.)

DOOR-KEEPER: In the name of Allah. The Amirs have come for the Durbar-i-Khas.

MUHAMMAD: Send them in.
(The Door-Keeper goes out. Barani and Najib stand up. The Amirs enter along with Shihab-ud-din. They greet each other.)

AMIR I: In the name of Allah.
(Najib smiles to himself.)

MUHAMMAD (*with obvious warmth*): Come in, come in. Please take your seats. I am glad you have all come on time. I want to finish the Durbar-i-Khas as soon as possible. I have promised the Imam I'll be at the mosque for today's prayer. That doesn't give us much time, I'm afraid. Are there any special problems any of you wish to raise?
(No reply.)

Excellent! I have only two topics myself. Not much to discuss there, but naturally I want to inform the Durbar-i-Khas before announcing them to the public. First, I am very happy to inform you that Abbasid Ghiyas-ud-din Muhammad has accepted my invitation to visit our capital.

(*Silence.*)

AMIR I: Who is he, Your Majesty?

AMIR II: I'm afraid I have never heard of that name...

MUHAMMAD: Well, that's nothing to be ashamed of. Abbasid Ghiyas-ud-din Muhammad is not exactly famous. He is a member of the hallowed family of the Abbasid Khalifs.

(*Silence while the Amirs digest this bit of news which obviously makes no sense to them.*)

BARANI: It's good news that a descendant of the last Khalif is visiting us, Your Majesty.

SHIHAB-UD-DIN: May I compliment His Majesty on his wisdom?

MUHAMMAD: Wisdom? What a strange word to use. Why wisdom? A visit by the descendant of the Khalif could show how faithful I am or how religious or even perhaps, how modest. But why do you say 'wisdom'? Do you think I am inviting him to placate the stupid priests?

SHIHAB-UD-DIN: I didn't mean to...

MUHAMMAD: You know, since Sheikh Imam-ud-din died I have been asking myself just one question. I am a king. I wear the royal robes. I have honoured myself with the title of Sultan. But what gives me the right to call myself a King?

(*The Amirs are baffled.*)

Am I a king only because I am the son of a king? Or is it because I can make the people accept my laws and the army move to my commands? Or can self-confidence alone justify it? I ask you—all of you—what would you have me do to become a real king in your eyes?

(*Silence.*)

NAJIB (*disapproving*): Your Majesty—

MUHAMMAD: You are all silent. The others only tell me what I should not do but not what I should. Until I know what else to do, Shihab-ud-din, I have to go on clutching the sceptre in my fist. But I am not happy and I am turning to tradition and history now and seeking an answer there—in the blessings of the Abbasid Khalif.

AMIR I: The sins of Delhi will be washed clean by the visit of so great a man.

MUHAMMAD: You bring tears to my eyes. But the great man isn't coming to Delhi. We shall be in Daulatabad by then.

SHIHAB-UD-DIN: I implore Your Majesty not to move the capital to Daulatabad. I am not from Delhi myself and have no stake in it. But I know the people of Delhi are very unhappy about the move. I have seen—

MUHAMMAD: What am I to do, Shihab-ud-din? I have explained every reason to them, shown how my empire cannot flourish with Delhi as its capital. But how can I explain tomorrow to those who haven't even opened their eyes to the light of today? Let's not waste more time over that. They'll see the point soon. It's getting late and I must come to the more important news. From next year, we shall have copper currency in our empire along with the silver dinars.

AMIR I: Whatever for? I mean what does one do with a copper coin?

MUHAMMAD: Exchange it for a silver coin! A copper coin will have the same value as a silver dinar.

SHIHAB-UD-DIN: But I don't understand, Your Majesty. How can one expect a copper coin to have the same value as a silver one?

MUHAMMAD: It's a question of confidence. A question of trust! The other day I heard that in China they have paper currency—

paper, mind you—and yet it works because the people accept it. They have faith in the Emperor's seal on the pieces of paper.

AMIR I (*whispers to the next man*): I told you he's mad!

MUHAMMAD: What was that?

AMIR I: I was just saying people here won't accept copper currency.

MUHAMMAD: Then why not say it aloud? Because people are afraid, will you mistrust me too? Laugh at me if you like, criticize me, but please don't distrust me. I can order you all to obey me but tell me, how do I gain your full trust? I can only beg for it. (*Pleading.*) I have hopes of building a new future for India and I need your support for that. If you don't understand me, ask me to explain myself and I'll do it. If you don't understand my explanations, bear with me in patience until I can show you the results. But please don't let me down, I beg you. I'll kneel before you if you wish, but please don't let go of my hand.

(*He kneels before them. The Amirs almost recoil at this sudden gesture.*)

SHIHAB-UD-DIN (*embarrassed*): But, Your Majesty, it's not for a king to beg. He must command. We are your ever-willing servants.

MUHAMMAD: Is this your voice alone, Shihab-ud-din, or do the rest of the Amirs agree with you?

AMIRS: Of course we all do—no question of it—Your Majesty should trust us...

MUHAMMAD: Thank you!

(*Gets up, walks up to the throne, picks up a copy of the Koran lying on it.*)

Will you all then take an oath on the Koran to support me in my measures?

(*A long tense silence.*)

SHIHAB-UD-DIN: Does His Majesty distrust me so much that he needs an oath on the Koran from us?

(*Muhammad turns to him in a sudden burst of rage, then controls himself and replaces the Koran on the throne. Silence again. The Door-Keeper enters.*)

DOOR-KEEPER: In the name of Allah. It's the hour of prayer, Your Majesty.

(*Muhammad stands silent for a while. The atmosphere is very charged.*)

MUHAMMAD (*very slowly*): We'll all pray here.

(*The Door-Keeper bows and exits. At the same moment, the Muezzin's voice is heard calling the faithful to the prayer.*)

MUEZZIN (*off-stage*): Alla-Ho-Akbar! Alla-Ho-Akbar!
Alla-Ho-Akbar! Alla-Ho-Akbar
Ashahado La Elaha Illilah
Ashahado La Elaha Illilah
Ashahado Anna Muhammadur Rasool Illah
Ashahado Anna Muhammadur Rasool Illah
Haiyah Alis Salaat—Haiyah Alis Salaat
Haiyah Salil Falaa—Haiyah Salil Falaa
Alla-Ho-Akbar! Alla-Ho-Akbar
La Elaha Illilah...

(*As soon as the Muezzin's call begins, Muhammad unbuckles his sword and places it on the throne. About a dozen servants enter with pots of water, in which those on the stage wash their hands, faces, heads and feet. Another servant brings about a dozen mats on a plank and takes them round. Each person picks up a mat and spreads it facing west. They start praying. Muhammad leads the prayer. Half-way through the prayer a commotion is heard off-stage. Taking that as a cue, Shihab-ud-din and the Amirs get up and pull out their daggers.*)

BARANI (*frightened*): What's this? What's this?

(*The Amirs step towards the throne, near which Muhammad is praying. Suddenly from behind the curtain near the throne about*) *twenty Hindu soldiers rush in with spears and surround the Amirs. One or two Amirs try to run out but the soldiers bar their way. The Amirs stand frozen in fear, then slowly throw down their daggers. The soldiers drag them away—all except Shihab-ud-din. While all this is going on, Muhammad goes on praying unconcerned. Only after finishing the prayer does he step down from the throne. Silence for a while.)*

SHIHAB-UD-DIN: How did you guess?

MUHAMMAD: Do you really want to know?

SHIHAB-UD-DIN: You aren't worried about hurting my feelings, are you?

MUHAMMAD: There was a letter in my letter-room today. A strange letter—strange because, unlike all the others, it didn't abuse me and it was signed. (*Pause.*)

By Ratansingh.

SHIHAB-UD-DIN (*smiles*): Do you really think I'll believe that? It's the oldest trick in the world.

MUHAMMAD: Why should I lie to a dead man?
(*Takes out the letter from his robe and holds it before Shihab-ud-din. Shihab-ud-din looks crushed and frightened.*)

SHIHAB-UD-DIN (*almost to himself*): But does he say why he is doing this to me?

NAJIB: He has disappeared—without a trace!

MUHAMMAD: Let me ask you something. Why did you go against me? What wrong have I done you?

SHIHAB-UD-DIN: What's the point? You won't understand it anyway.

MUHAMMAD: Won't I? Or could it be that you don't know?

SHIHAB-UD-DIN (*suddenly violent*): Get on with your killing, Muhammad. Or does your hand refuse to rise against me? Beware! You won't be able to trap me with your wiles. I am not Ain-ul-Mulk to live crushed under your kindness.

(Muhammad slowly takes out his dagger. Shihab-ud-din is getting more and more frightened. He is almost screaming now as he speaks.)
You want to solve all problems in the flash of a dagger, don't you? But you can't stop this uprising now. My father distrusts you and I've already written to him, about everything here... everything...

NAJIB: Sorry, but Ratansingh has sent those letters to us.

SHIHAB-UD-DIN *(screaming)*: Where will you hide my corpse? How will you gag my voice? Kill me—but you won't stop this—this will go on—

MUHAMMAD: I could have killed you with a word. But I like you too much.

(Stabs him. Then almost frenzied, goes on stabbing him. Hits out at Shihab-ud-din's dead body with a ferocity that makes even the soldiers holding the body turn away in horror.)

BARANI: Your Majesty—he's dead!

(Muhammad stops, then flings the dagger away in disgust.)

MUHAMMAD *(anguished)*: Why must this happen, Barani? Are all those I trust condemned to go down in history as traitors? What is happening? Tell me, Barani, will my reign be nothing more than a tortured scream which will stab the night and melt away in the silence?

(He is trembling. At a sign from Najib, the soldiers lay the body down on a mat and go away. Muhammad stares at the body.)
Najib, see that every man involved in this is caught and beheaded. Stuff their bodies with straw and hang them up in the palace-yard. Let them hang there for a week. No, send them round my kingdom. Let every one of my subjects see them. Let everyone see what... *(Chokes.)*

BARANI: What will that achieve, Your Majesty? What's the use? *(Pause.)*

NAJIB: We must do something about Shihab-ud-din's father. He is a powerful man and he won't like this.

MUHAMMAD (*regaining control of himself*): Don't worry about him. Make a public announcement that there was a rebellion in the palace and that the nobles of the court tried to assassinate the Sultan during prayer. Say that the Sultan was saved by Shihab-ud-din who died a martyr's death defending him. The funeral will be held in Delhi and will be a grand affair. Invite his father to it and see that he is treated with the respect due to the father of a loyal nobleman.

BARANI: Oh God! Aren't even the dead free from your politics?

NAJIB: Your Majesty, if this incident is to be kept a secret, we'll have to hang everyone who was here—even the Hindu guards. They remained loyal to Your Majesty but they have seen it all and are bound to talk. It does mean more corpses. But then, that'll only make the show more impressive.

MUHAMMAD: Najib. I want Delhi vacated immediately. Every living soul in Delhi will leave for Daulatabad within a fortnight. I was too soft, I can see that now. They'll only understand the whip. Everyone must leave. Not a light should be seen in the windows of Delhi. Not a wisp of smoke should rise from its chimneys. Nothing but an empty graveyard of Delhi will satisfy me now.

BARANI: May Heaven protect us!

MUHAMMAD: Call on Heaven while you can, Barani—you may not get another chance. What hopes I had built up when I came to the throne! I had wanted every act in my kingdom to become a prayer, every prayer to become a further step in knowledge, every step to lead us nearer to God. But our prayers too are ridden with disease and must be exiled. There will be no more praying in the kingdom, Najib. Anyone caught praying will be severely punished. Henceforth let the moment of prayer walk my streets in silence and leave without a trace.

NAJIB: But that would only be playing into the hands of the

Ulema, Your Majesty. I suggest we say there'll be no more
prayers till Ghiyas-ud-din Abbasid, the descendant of the
Khalif, visits us. God alone knows when he'll come. Besides,
it'll make a beautiful little paradox!

(*Muhammad does not reply. Najib goes out. Barani sobs. Muhammad
stands staring at Shihab-ud-din's corpse. Barani gets up, takes the
silken cloth from the throne and starts spreading it on the corpse.
But Muhammad casts the cloth aside.*)

MUHAMMAD: Don't cover him, Barani. I want my people to see
his wounds.

ANNOUNCER: Attention! Attention! The Merciful Sultan Muhammad has ordered—that within the next month every citizen of Delhi must leave for Daulatabad. No one should remain behind in Delhi. Anyone who attempts to stay behind or to go elsewhere will be severely punished. All arrangements have been made to ensure the comfort of citizens on the way to Daulatabad. All the needs of the citizens, regarding food, clothing or medicine, will be catered to by the State. It is hoped that every citizen will use these amenities to the full and be in Daulatabad as soon as possible. Attention! Attention!

Scene Seven

A camp on the Delhi-Daulatabad route. Aziz, still dressed as a Brahmin, and Aazam. A Hindu woman is kneeling in front of Aziz.

HINDU WOMAN: Please let me go, sir... My child... Please have mercy on it...only for a day, sir...

AZIZ: I told you I can't. No one can be allowed out of sight until we reach Daulatabad. I'm sorry, but I have my orders.

HINDU WOMAN: But I'll return tomorrow... I swear by my child I will... It's dying. Your Excellency, I have to take it to a doctor...

AZIZ: But what can I do? There's the hakim's tent. Go to him. He'll give you some medicine. (*In a low voice.*) I've told you what you can do. I could try and bribe my senior officials, but you'll have to pay for it.

HINDU WOMAN: But I haven't got a paisa on me, Your Excellency. And what will I give the doctor? My husband's also ill, sir, please, I hold your feet—please let me go.

AZIZ: I can't waste any more time on you. There's a lot of work here. Stop screaming and get back to your tent—I said, get back to your tent!

(*The Hindu woman goes out, weeping.*)

AAZAM: Poor thing! Why don't you let her go? The doctor may help her.

AZIZ: Have you seen the child? No witch-doctor can save it now. My niece had that illness and went out like a light. It's a waste of good money and she's going to need every paisa of it. I'm doing her a favour! And watch out for paise, Aazam; they're going to cost a lot soon.

(*Footsteps are heard off-stage. Aziz buries his head into his books. A family comes in. A man with a woman and six kids. They come and stand. Aziz continues to read. Aazam, embarrassed, wanders around without looking at them. The family waits patiently.*)

Three more families! They must be walking on their knees. (*Looks up and stares at the man.*) So you've come at last, have you? Perhaps you went to visit your in-laws on the way. Don't you know the orders? You were supposed to be here well before sunset.

MAN: What was I to do, Your Excellency? There were two corpses there on the road. Poor things! They must have walked till their hearts gave out. I thought, sinner that I am, I would at least give them a decent burial.

AAZAM: Poor souls. From which camp were they, do you think?

AZIZ: I hope you checked whether they were Muslims before burying them.

MAN: Who's to do all that, Your Excellency? I did what I could.

AZIZ: And what if they were Hindus, pray? You know they don't bury their dead. You'll be in trouble if someone finds out. Actually I ought to send you back to dig them up again. It's against the orders to insult or cause harm to Hinduism—

MAN: I just didn't think of it, Your Excellency. Sinner that I am, I thought I would lighten the burden of my sins by giving them a resting place.

AZIZ: Leave the corpses alone in future. What did you do in Delhi, sinner that you are?

MAN: I am a Kafir, Your Excellency. I have to guard the dead
    bodies in the palace yard—those executed by the Sultan, you
    know. I have to guard them for a week, ten at a time, sir, and
    then dump them in the canal outside the city. There again
    I have to guard them against thieves.

AZIZ: Thieves? Ugh!

MAN: Isn't it terrible, Your Excellency? But there it is. That's what
    men have come to. The relatives of the dead have to pay us
    before taking the bodies. Well, if the orders had been obeyed
    I would have built a house by now. But no, they won't pay—
    even for the dead! They come at night and steal them. Not just
    the poor. Even the rich folk—the most respectable people of
    Delhi! I could tell you a name or two and you wouldn't believe
    it. It is terrible. People won't stop at anything once they get
    into the habit of thieving, that's certain.

(*Aziz looks at Aazam and laughs. Aazam grimaces.*)

AZIZ: So this is your family. All eight here?

MAN: Yes, sir.

AZIZ: Get on with you there. There's a tent kept for you. Yes!
    Whatever happens to the others, people like you mustn't die.
    The Sultan will need a lot more like you soon. So what are
    you going to do till the Sultan arrives in Daulatabad? Another
    couple of children?

MAN: Well, we have decided to get married first, Your Excellency.

AAZAM (*in disgust*): Oh God!

MAN (*apologetic*): Couldn't find time for it in Delhi, sir.

AAZAM: Go away. Go away!

(*The family goes off.*)

    God, what a dirty man! I am feeling sick.

AZIZ: I like such people. They are the real stoics.

AAZAM: I just keep thinking of that poor woman. Why don't you
    let her see the doctor? I'm sure she'll come back. Look, if you

want money, tell me. There are enough rich men in this camp. I'll get some in to time.

AZIZ: Don't you do anything of the kind! You'll ruin us both if they catch you.

AAZAM: We'll be ruined anyway ultimately. If not today, then tomorrow. What other future's there for us? One day my fingers will slow down. I'll get caught. Then, no arms! No legs! A torn mat and a begging bowl, that's all.

AZIZ: You are a hopeless case, you know. Pathetic! You've been in Delhi for so many years and you're as stupid as ever. Look at me. Only a few months in Delhi and I have discovered a whole new world—politics! My dear fellow, that's where our future is—politics! It's a beautiful world—wealth, success, position, power—and yet it's full of brainless people, people with not an idea in their head. When I think of all the tricks I used in our village to pinch a few torn clothes from people—if one uses half that intelligence here, one can get robes of power. And not have to pinch them either—demand them! It's a fantastic world!

(*The Hindu woman is heard wailing.*)

AAZAM: That's that Hindu woman. Her child's dead. She'll complain against you now. If you go on like this, Aziz, we'll soon keep the Kafir company in Daulatabad.

AZIZ: Don't call me Aziz. I've told you. As for her, I've only obeyed my orders. Besides I'm a Brahmin and she won't complain against a Brahmin to a Muslim officer. That'll send her straight to hell. In any case—and listen to this carefully— we won't stay in the Sultan's service for long. I heard some rumours in Delhi. The Sultan's going to introduce copper coins soon. And a copper coin will have the same value as a silver dinar. What do you say to that?

AAZAM (*making a face*): Eyah! There's no fun in stealing copper coins.

AZIZ: Shut up! Just listen to what I'm telling you—you are not going to pinch any coins, you are going to make them. Make counterfeit coins, you understand? If your fingers are getting restless, use them there. (*Noise off-stage.*) Ha! There's the next lot!

(*Buries his head in his books.*)

Scene Eight

AD 1332

The fort at Daulatabad. Two sentries—one young, the other past his middle-age. Night.

YOUNG MAN: What time do you think it is, grandfather?

OLD MAN: Must be just past midnight.

YOUNG MAN: Only that? Good God! When I was in the army, less than two seconds seemed to divide the lamp-lighting hour from the daybreak. Now the night scarcely moves.

OLD MAN: It's only when you wait for the morning that the night stands still. A good sentry must forget that morning even exists.

YOUNG MAN (*looking down the side of the fort*): What a fantastic fort! I have a good head but even I feel giddy when I look down. And isn't that long white thing the road from Daulatabad to Delhi?

OLD MAN: Yes.

YOUNG MAN: They say it's the widest road in the world. But it looks no bigger than a thin snake from here.

OLD MAN: And five years ago that snake bit a whole city to death.

YOUNG MAN: What a fort! What a magnificent thing! I met a foreign visitor the other day and he said he has been round the world and not seen any fort as strong as this anywhere. No army could take this.

OLD MAN: No, invariably, forts crumble from the inside.

YOUNG MAN: You don't love this fort very much, do you, grandfather?

OLD MAN: I am a man of the plains, son. I find it hard to breathe in this eagle's nest.

YOUNG MAN: You are from Delhi?

OLD MAN: Yes.

YOUNG MAN: Was it hard, coming from Delhi to here?

OLD MAN: I survived. But my family was more fortunate. They died on the way.

YOUNG MAN (*sympathetically*): I am sorry. The arrangements must have been very bad.

OLD MAN: Oh no. The merciful Sultan had made perfect arrangements. But do you know, you can love a city like a woman? My old father had lived in Delhi all his life. He died of a broken heart. Then my son Ismail. He was six years old— would have been ten now! The fine dust that hung in the air, fine as silk, it covered him like a silken shroud. After him, his mother.

(*Silence. The young man is embarrassed.*)

YOUNG MAN: Tell me more about this fort, grandfather. Is it true there is a strange and frightening passage within this fort? Dark, they say, like the new moon night.

OLD MAN: Yes, it's a long passage, a winding tunnel, coiled like an enormous hollow python inside the belly of the fort. And we shall be far, far happier when that python breaks out and swallows everything in sight—every man, woman, child, and beast.

(*Footsteps off-stage.*)

YOUNG MAN (*raising his spear*): Who is that?

MUHAMMAD: Muhammad.

YOUNG MAN: Muhammad? What Muhammad?

OLD MAN: Shut up, fool. It's the Sultan.

(*Muhammad walks in—almost in a trance.*)

BOTH: In the name of Allah!

MUHAMMAD (*to the old man*): Go and tell Barani I want to see him.

(*The old man bows and retires.*)

YOUNG MAN: I beg Your Majesty's pardon for my impertinence. I didn't realize...

MUHAMMAD: Don't worry. You were doing your duty.

(*Goes to the edge of the wall and looks down.*)

YOUNG MAN: Your Majesty must forgive my impudence, but I beg Your Majesty not to go too near the edge of the fort. It's a very steep fall.

MUHAMMAD (*smiles*): You are new here, aren't you?

YOUNG MAN: Yes, I am, Your Majesty. I was in the army all these years. They sent me here yesterday. I am very sorry if I've said anything wrong, Your Majesty.

MUHAMMAD: Don't apologize at every word. If you stay here long enough you'll anyway learn to ooze spittle before everyone. Be yourself at least until then. How old are you?

YOUNG MAN: Nineteen, Your Majesty.

MUHAMMAD: Nineteen. Nice age! An age when you think you can clasp the whole world in your palm like a rare diamond. I was twenty-one when I came to Daulatabad first, and built this fort. I supervised the placing of every brick in it and I said to myself, one day I shall build my own history like this, brick by brick.

One night I was standing on the ramparts of the old fort here. There was a torch near me flapping its wild wings and scattering golden feathers on everything in sight. There was a half-built gate nearby trying to contain the sky within its cleft. Suddenly something happened—as though someone had cast a spell. The torch, the gate, the fort and the sky—all melted and merged and flowed in my blood-stream with the darkness of the night. The moment shed its symbols, its questions and answers, and stood naked and calm where the stars throbbed in my veins. I was the earth, was the grass, was the smoke, was the sky. Suddenly a sentry called from far. 'Attention!' Attention! And to that challenge the half-burnt torch and the half-built gate fell apart.

No, Young man, I don't envy you your youth. All that you have to face and suffer is still ahead of you. Look at me. I have searched for that moment since then and here I am still searching for it. But in the last four years, I have seen only the woods clinging to the earth, heard only the howl of wild wolves and the answering bay of street dogs. Another twenty years and you'll be as old as me. I might be lying under those woods there by then. Do you think you'll remember me then?

(*No answer.*)

Come, why are you silent?

YOUNG MAN (*scared*): Your Majesty must forgive me, Your Majesty. But I don't understand what Your Majesty is saying.

MUHAMMAD (*incensed*): You don't understand! You don't understand! Why do you live? Why do you corrupt the air with your diseased breath? (*Suddenly calm.*) I'm sorry. It's my turn to apologize. It isn't your fault. You are also one of them.

(*Uncomfortable silence. Barani enters.*)

BARANI: In the name of Allah. Your Majesty sent for me?

(*Muhammad waves the sentries away.*)

MUHAMMAD: I couldn't bear the walls any more. When I came here I felt I needed an audience—someone to confess my self-pity to. You were asleep?

BARANI: No, Your Majesty. I was reading a book by Imam Abu Hanifa.

MUHAMMAD: Fortunate! You can read when you don't feel sleepy. I can't sleep. I can't read. Even Rumi, who once used to transport me, has become simply a web of words. Do you know, five years ago I actually used to pray to God not to send me any sleep? I can't believe it now.

BARANI: Why don't you see a hakim, Your Majesty?

MUHAMMAD: What can a hakim do? You are a historian, Barani, you are the man to prescribe remedies for this. Have you heard the latest news? Fakr-ud-din has risen against me in Bengal.

BARANI: Oh, I'm...

MUHAMMAD: Yes. And there's been another uprising in the Deccan. In Ma'bar, Ehsanshah has declared himself independent. Bahal-ud-din Gashtasp is collecting an army against me. The drought in Doab is spreading from town to town—burning up the country. Only one industry flourishes in my kingdom, only one—and that's of making counterfeit copper coins. Every Hindu home has become a domestic mint; the traders are just waiting for me to close my eyes; and in my whole kingdom there are only two people I can trust—Ain-ul-Mulk and Shihab-ud-din's father. What should I do, Barani? What would you prescribe for this honeycomb of diseases? I have tried everything. But what cures one disease just worsens another.

BARANI: I am a humble historian, Your Majesty: it's not for me to prescribe. But since Your Majesty has done me the honour of confiding in me, may I make a suggestion? It is a difficult thing to suggest to a king and I beg you to forgive me if it hurts. But you are a learned man, Your Majesty, you are known the world over for your knowledge of philosophy and poetry. History is not made only in statecraft; its lasting results are produced in the ranks of learned men. That's where you belong, Your Majesty, in the company of learned men. Not in the market of corpses.

MUHAMMAD: You want me to retire from my throne? (*Laughs.*) Barani, if you were capable of irony, I would have thought you were laughing at me. But, as usual, you mean it, which makes it harder. I wish it was as easy as that. I have often thought of that myself—to give up this futile see-saw struggle and go to Mecca. Sit there by the Kaaba and search for the peace which Daulatabad hasn't given me. What bliss! But it isn't that easy. It isn't as easy as abandoning the patient in the wilderness because there's no cure for his disease. Don't you see—this patient, racked by fever and crazed by the fear of the enveloping vultures, can't be separated from me? Don't you see that the only way I can abdicate is by killing myself? I could have done something if the vultures weren't so close. I could have crawled forward on my knees and elbows. But what can you do when every moment you expect a beak to dig into you and tear a muscle out? What can you do? Barani, what vengeance is driving these shapes after me?

BARANI: Your Majesty...

MUHAMMAD: You know what my beloved subjects call me? Mad Muhammad! Mad Muhammad! (*Suddenly pleading.*) How can I become wise again, Barani?

BARANI: Your Majesty, there was a time when you believed in love, in peace, in God. What has happened to those ideals? You won't let your subjects pray. You torture them for the smallest offence. Hang them on suspicion. Why this bloodshed? Please stop it, and I promise Your Majesty something better will emerge out of it.

MUHAMMAD: But for that I'll have to admit I've been wrong all along. And I know I haven't. I have something to give, something to teach, which may open the eyes of history but I have to do it within this life. I've got to make them listen to me before I lose even that!

(*The old man comes in running.*)

OLD MAN: In the name of Allah—a calamity, Your Majesty—the Nayab Vizier has sent word—

MUHAMMAD: What is it?

OLD MAN: Vizier Muhammad Najib is dead. His body was found in his bed. The Nayab Vizier says it is murder...

Scene Nine

A hide-out in the hills. Aziz and Aazam are stretched out on the floor.

AAZAM: It's so hot—I'm fed up, I'm fed up of life, I'm fed up of the whole bloody world.

AZIZ: Why don't you just go and commit suicide?

AAZAM: Tried once. Went and jumped into a well. But the cold water cheered me up so much that I had a good swim and went back home. I don't think I could try again.

AZIZ: You'll never learn to do a thing properly.

AAZAM: But how come I steal properly? I have never made a mistake while stealing. Why am I a thief, Aziz? Why aren't we like other people? Have a nice home, till a farm and live happily?

AZIZ: How many happy people have you met? Besides, a man must commit a crime at least once in his lifetime. Only then will his virtue be recognized!

AAZAM: Aw, shut up!

AZIZ: No, truly. Listen. If you remain virtuous throughout your life no one will say a good thing about you, because they won't need to. But start stealing—and they'll say: 'What a nice boy he was! But he's ruined now...' Then kill and they will beat their breasts and say: 'Heavens! He was only a petty thief all these days. Never hurt anyone. But alas!' Then rape a woman and the chorus will go into hallelujahs: 'He was a saint, a real saint and look at him now...'

AAZAM: Well, you have robbed and killed. Now all you have to do to become a saint is rape.

AZIZ: Presently, presently. No hurry. What's the point in raping for sheer lust? That's a mug's game. First one must have power—the authority to rape! Then everything takes on meaning.

AAZAM (*giggles*): So you want power, do you? What do you want to be, a Sultan?

AZIZ: Laugh away, stupid. You'll soon see. It all depends on whether Karim will bring the goods.

AAZAM (*seriously*): But no, Aziz, why are you so dissatisfied? We have such a nice establishment here. We take enough money from travellers and the other robbers are scared to death of you. There's no limit to what we can amass here.

AZIZ: I am bored stiff with all this running and hiding. You rob a man, you run, and hide. It's all so pointless. One should be able to rob a man and then stay there to punish him for getting robbed. That's called 'class'—that's being a real king!

AAZAM: May Allah shower His blessings on Your Majesty! Is there a post for your humble slave at the court?

AZIZ: Oh, yes! You are brainless. So you'll make a good noble-man—an Amir.

AAZAM (*in disgust*): Eah! I don't like that. I don't think I could be anything but a common pickpocket. What about a court thief? (*Aziz bursts into laughter.*)

AZIZ: That's beautiful, Aazam! A court thief! I'd never thought of that. It opens up all sorts of possibilities... There's Karim now!

(*Karim comes in with a man, bound and gagged.*)
  You are late. Are you sure this is the right man?

KARIM: No need to worry.

AZIZ: Excellent. Here you are. (*Gives him a purse.*) I'll send for
  you if there's any more work.
  (*Karim salaams and exits.*)

AAZAM: Who is this animal?

AZIZ: Wait and see. Untie him first.
(*Aazam unties the man. Aziz stares at him and an expression of
horror spreads on his face.*)
  My God! I'll kill that ass Karim! He's brought the wrong man!

MAN: I told him so. I told him who I was. I told him clearly. The
  rascal wouldn't listen. Tied me up. Me! Let the Sultan hear
  of this outrage. He'll whip you to death.

AZIZ, AAZAM: The Sultan?

AZIZ: We beg your pardon, sir. There's been a mistake. Karim was
  supposed to bring someone else—a Turk merchant. But—
  may we know who you are?

MAN: You'll soon know, you scoundrels. I am Ghiyas-ud-din
  Abbasid. The descendant of Khalif Abbasid. I am the Guest
  of Honour of His Majesty.

AAZAM: Ya Allah!
(*Aziz and Aazam prostrate themselves in front of him.*)

GHIYAS-UD-DIN: You'll pay for this! I've come all the way from
  Arabia and not a soul dared touch me. They trembled at the
  mention of my name. And now this outrage! You'll hear more
  about this—

AZIZ: Forgive us, Your Worship. It was a mistake. There's been
  a slip somewhere. It's just that you are alone—I mean the
  Sultan's Guest of Honour—from the Holy Family of the
  Khalifs—

GHIYAS-UD-DIN: Mind your own business, slave. I'll have an

entourage as soon as the Sultan knows I've arrived. He is
sending a special convoy from Daulatabad.

AZIZ: Then perhaps Your Worship will allow us to make amends
for this sacrilege by following you? We'll be your slaves till
you reach Daulatabad.

GHIYAS-UD-DIN: Hm! You may redeem yourself that way. Get up.
No need to prostrate yourself so long. Yes, I do need guides.
It's an unfamiliar country and the people here are treacherous.
The moment they know you are a foreigner they're out to rob
you. Yes, you'll do till the entourage arrives.

AZIZ: But haven't you been here before, Your Worship? Haven't
you seen the Sultan?

GHIYAS-UD-DIN: I haven't. But I shall soon.

(*In the meantime, Aazam has spread a mat on which Ghiyas-ud-
din sits imperially. Aazam offers him some fruits to eat.*)

AZIZ: Forgive me if I am talking beyond my station, Your Worship.
But I must warn you that the Sultan is in a suspicious frame
of mind, we hear. There have been a lot of deaths since he
came to Daulatabad.

GHIYAS-UD-DIN: Yes, I've heard all that. I'm not worried.

AZIZ: Recently he flogged a man to death, had his body filled with
straw and strung up in the market place—all because the man
claimed to be a descendant of the Prophet—may peace be
upon him.

GHIYAS-UD-DIN: You talk too much. What's your name?

AZIZ: Aziz, Your Worship, and this is Aazam. I realize I sound
impertinent, Your Worship. We are happy to follow you to
Daulatabad, be your slaves to make up for our sacrilege. But
Your Worship will forgive us for being worried about our
necks—

GHIYAS UD DIN: You don't need to worry. I have got the Sultan's
letter with me—and the ring he sent as a mark of recognition.

(*Shows the ring.*) I know there are no precious stones in it.
But that would have attracted too much attention.

AZIZ: The Sultan is a wise man. But Your Worship has no friends
or acquaintances in Daulatabad?

GHIYAS-UD-DIN (*irritated*): You ask too many questions for a slave.
No, no friends there. You just hold your tongue and follow me.
(*Aziz laughs. Ghiyas-ud-din looks at him, suddenly suspicious. Aziz
bursts into loud laughter and jumps up.*)

AZIZ: Caught him, Aazam! He fell into my trap like a mouse. This
is the goods, Aazam, this is it! I had heard he was here—
without a paisa on him but boasting of his good fortune—

GHIYAS-UD-DIN: What do you mean?

AZIZ: In five minutes, you won't need to know any meanings.

AAZAM (*frightened*): Don't kill him, Aziz, please don't! He's the
Khalif's grandson—

GHIYAS-UD-DIN (*frightened*): Kill me? But why? What'll you gain
by killing me? I've nothing—you know that—I'll get nothing
till I reach Daulatabad—I'm a poor man. Why kill me?

AAZAM: He is right, Aziz.

GHIYAS-UD-DIN: It's the truth, I swear. That's how I've come here
alive—no one could get anything out of me. What do you
want from me? Look, if you come with me to Daulatabad, I'll
see you'll get something too—

AZIZ: I am not going with you. I am going in your place.

AAZAM: Aziz, listen—

AZIZ: Shut up! Don't waste your breath! We'll never get an
opportunity like this again. Arabia must be full of the Khalif's
descendants. They were a fertile lot, the Khalifs. Now the
Sultan's picked this rat up from the gutters for some game
of his own. Who will worry about this fool when people are
dying without food in Daulatabad? Get out now. Get out.
You'll just make things worse.

(*Aazam goes out.*)

GHIYAS-UD-DIN: Don't kill me, please, I'll kiss your feet. Take everything—my ring, letters, everything. I'll go back. I'll go back to my village. I won't bother you. Please don't kill me. I'll kiss your feet. Please let me go. (*Embraces his legs.*)

AZIZ: No!

GHIYAS-UD-DIN: No? No! No! I knew it. I knew something like this would happen. It was too good to be true—to grow up in filth, live in filth—and then a letter from nowhere. A hope— a ray of light. Now my fate will change, I thought, now I'll be happy. Now things will start afresh. So I started. But I knew it was too good—good things don't come like that— they don't stay—

(*He gives Aziz a sudden push. Aziz falls down on the floor. Ghiyas-ud-din runs out.*)

AZIZ (*shouts without getting up*): Stop him, Aazam. Stop him. (*Jumps up and runs out. Noise of a scuffle.*)

AZIZ (*off-stage*): That's it, Aazam! Bravo!

GHIYAS-UD-DIN (*off-stage*): Don't kill me, please.

(*A scream. Then silence. Aazam comes in running. He is covered with blood. He is sweating, trembling and weeping. After a while Aziz comes in, with Ghiyas-ud-din's turban on his head.*)

AZIZ: Why are you crying, you clown?

AAZAM: Don't talk to me—God! God! Why did I stop him? Why didn't I let him go?

(*Aziz opens Ghiyas-ud-din's bundle.*)

AZIZ: You are a funny creature. You have seen enough corpses to last you seven lives. You have stuffed them with straw, practised obscenities on them. And still you can't see a man die. (*Takes out a robe and puts it on.*) How do I look, eh? The great-grandson of the Khalif!

(*Aazam looks away. Aziz slaps him on the back.*)

Laugh, you fool, laugh. Celebrate! What are you crying for? Look, look at the palace doors. They are opening for us. Dance, dance, you son of an ass—
(*Sings.*)
Grandson of the Khalif! Great grandson of the Khalif! Great-great-great-grandson of the Khalif!
(*Sings and dances in a circle, clapping his hands. Aziz looks at him angrily. Then slowly his face breaks into a smile and soon he is laughing.*)

Scene Ten

The Palace. Muhammad is looking out of the window. The Step-Mother comes in.

STEP-MOTHER: Muhammad, do you know what's happening outside?

MUHAMMAD: Yes.

STEP-MOTHER: Why are you doing it?

MUHAMMAD: What else can I do? I said the new copper coins would have the same value as the silver dinars. Now I can't go against my own orders.

STEP-MOTHER: But this is sheer folly! The Vizier says there are five hundred carts out there and they are all full of counterfeit coins. Are you going to exchange them all for silver?

MUHAMMAD: There's nothing else for it. I should have expected this but didn't—that was my fault. If I don't withdraw the coins now, the whole economy will be in shambles. It's in a bad enough state already.

STEP-MOTHER: Five hundred carts on the first day! And what about tomorrow and the day after? You are just legalizing robbery—

MUHAMMAD: It's all their wealth. I can't let my whim ruin them.

STEP-MOTHER: And how is a treasury full of counterfeit coins going to help them? Will that revive your economy?

MUHAMMAD: Don't worry, Mother. The coins aren't going into the treasury. They'll all be heaped in the new rose garden.

STEP-MOTHER: What's the matter with you? You spent years planning that rose garden and now—

MUHAMMAD: Now I don't need a rose garden. I built it because I wanted to make for myself an image of Sadi's poems. I wanted every rose in it to be a poem. I wanted every thorn in it to prick and quicken the senses. But I don't need these airy trappings now; a funeral needs no separate symbol.

STEP-MOTHER: Then why don't you stop the funeral? Why this unending line of corpses? Muhammad, I have been hearing rumours lately. The Amirs and Khans are apparently getting upset because you are hounding them about Najib.

MUHAMMAD: I am not hounding them. I merely want to find out who murdered Najib.

STEP-MOTHER: Is it true five of them have fled?

MUHAMMAD: Not five—four. The fifth committed suicide. Amir Jalal-ud-din.

STEP-MOTHER: Oh God!

MUHAMMAD: He told his wife he knew who had killed Najib. One of his servants overheard the conversation.

STEP-MOTHER (alarmed): Please, don't go on like this. Please. Najib's dead. Finished. You can't drive the nobles to rebellion for his sake?

MUHAMMAD: Don't you think it strange that an Amir like Jalal-ud-din should kill himself in order to save the murderer? It must be someone very special.

STEP-MOTHER: I'm glad Najib's dead. He was leading you astray. It's because you wouldn't trust anyone as much as him that the kingdom's in this state! The Ulema are against you; the noblemen are against you; the people hate you. It's all his fault. I'm glad he's dead. He should have died a long time ago.

MUHAMMAD: Najib wasn't loyal to me; he was loyal to the throne. The day he turned against me I would have known I'd made a mistake.

STEP-MOTHER: Why not forget him? What good is it to the throne—

MUHAMMAD: I must know who killed him and why.

STEP-MOTHER: Muhammad, how long are you going to torment yourself like this?

MUHAMMAD: Not for long. The Amirs will return. If they don't, I'll be sorry for their families.

STEP-MOTHER: You frighten me, Muhammad, you really do. Please stop this. Muhammad—please—for my sake.
(*No reply.*)
Won't you? I appeal to you.
(*No reply.*)
All right. I killed him. I had him murdered.

MUHAMMAD (*exploding*): For God's sake, don't joke about it! And don't try to be noble and save me from the moronic Amirs and Khans. This isn't a small thing.

STEP-MOTHER: I am perfectly serious. I had him poisoned.

MUHAMMAD: Stop it! Why are you tormenting me now? Don't you see how you're burning out my guts with your infantile dramatics?

STEP-MOTHER: Why shouldn't I have killed him? It was easier than killing one's father or brother. It was better than killing Sheikh Imam-ud-din.

MUHAMMAD: I killed them—yes—but I killed them for an ideal. Don't I know its results? Don't you think I've suffered from the curse? My mother won't speak to me—I can't even look into a mirror for fear of seeing their faces in it. I had only three friends in the world—you, Najib and Barani. And now you want me to believe you killed Najib. Why are you doing this to me?

STEP-MOTHER: It's only seven years ago that you came to the throne. How glorious you were then, how idealistic, how full of hopes. Look at your kingdom now. It's become a kitchen of death—all because of him. I couldn't bear it any longer.

MUHAMMAD: But you don't know that for the past few months he had been advising me against violence, do you? He wanted me to hold back my sword for the stability of the throne.

STEP-MOTHER: Then why didn't you?

MUHAMMAD: Because I couldn't. Not now. Remember Shihab-ud-din of Sampanshahr? He was the first man I killed with my own hands. And I had a glimmer then of what now I know only too well. Not words but the sword—that's all I have to keep my faith in my mission. Why should Najib be sacrificed for that?

STEP-MOTHER: You had your share of futile deaths. I have mine now.

MUHAMMAD (*shouting*): No, they were not futile. They gave me what I wanted—power, strength to shape my thoughts, strength to act. Strength to recognize myself. What did your little murder give you?

(*Suddenly freezes. Stares at her. Then quietly.*)

Woman, woman, so you are also one of them! So that's what you too wanted! Mother is annoyed she can't control me. And now you too are trying the same game, aren't you? Get rid of Najib, so you could control me?

STEP-MOTHER: I want nothing for myself. You are my life, Muhammad. You know that. If I had wanted power, I wouldn't have confessed.

MUHAMMAD: You needn't have confessed. I would have found out on my own. Or else, the Amirs would have rebelled. And then, what power? Clever you. You thought I wouldn't punish you, didn't you? Because I love you more than I have loved anyone in my life. That was the price of your love, wasn't it? (*Suddenly in agony.*) Mother! Why did you have to do it?

STEP-MOTHER (*puts her hand on his shoulder*): Listen to me—

MUHAMMAD: Don't touch me! There's only one punishment for treachery—death!
(*Claps twice.*)

STEP-MOTHER: Don't be a fool, Muhammad. I'm telling you for your own sake. My death won't make you happy. You have enough ghosts to haunt you. Don't add mine to it.

MUHAMMAD: The others died unjustly. You deserve to die—
(*Two soldiers enter.*)
You are worse than an adulteress. But I can't think of a worse punishment for you. Take her to prison.
(*The Step-Mother stands petrified. The soldiers are also baffled.*)
(*Screaming.*) Take her away!
(*The soldiers hold her. She tries to break away.*)
Tell the Nayab Vizier I want her stoned to death publicly tomorrow morning.

STEP-MOTHER (*finding her voice*): Not that, Muhammad, don't do that to me—please.

MUHAMMAD: That's how an adulteress dies. Take her away.

STEP-MOTHER: Muhammad, please—
(*She is dragged away. Muhammad stands looking stunned. Then suddenly he falls to his knees and clutches his hands to his breast.*)

MUHAMMAD: God, God in Heaven, please help me. Please, don't let go of my hand. My skin drips with blood and I don't know how much of it is mine and how much of others. I started in Your path, Lord, why am I wandering naked in this desert now? I started in search of You. Why am I become a pig

rolling in this gory mud? Raise me. Clean me. Cover me with
Your Infinite Mercy. I can only clutch at the hem of Your
cloak with my bloody fingers and plead. I can only beg—have
pity on me. I have no one but You now. Only You. Only
You...You...You...You...

(*Enter Barani.*)

BARANI: In the name...

(*Stops. Muhammad raises his head.*)

MUHAMMAD: Come in, Barani. You've come at the right moment.
You have saved me from treason, you know. I was trying to
pray! Think of that—no one in my kingdom is allowed to
pray and I was praying. Against my own orders! But what else
could I do, Barani? My legs couldn't hold me up any longer.

BARANI (*smiles*): You needn't worry, Your Majesty. I'm here
because I insisted on bringing the joyful tidings myself—

MUHAMMAD: Joy? It's such a long time since I heard that word.

BARANI: We have just received a letter from your Governor. The
good news is that we can all pray now, Your Majesty.

MUHAMMAD: What's the use? I was trying to pray—but I could
only find words learnt by rote, which left no echo in the heart.
I am teetering on the brink of madness, Barani, but the
madness of God still eludes me. (*Shouting.*) And why should
I deserve that madness? I have condemned my mother to
death and I'm not even sure she was guilty of the crime...

ANNOUNCER: Attention! Attention! Muhammad Tughlaq who craves only for the mercy of Allah and for the blessings of the Khalifs, hereby announces that His Worship Ghiyas-ud-din Muhammad, son of His Worship Abdul Kahir, grandson of His Worship Yusuf, great-grandson of His Worship Abdul Aziz, great-great-grandson of His Imperial Holiness Abbasid Al-Mustansir, the Khalif of Baghdad, will bless and purify Daulatabad by arriving here tomorrow afternoon. And Muhammad is sure that the citizens of this city will collect in large numbers to welcome this Saviour.

This is a holy day for us—a day of joy! And its glory will be crowned by the fact that the Public Prayer, which has been mute in our land these five years, will be started again from next Friday. Henceforth every Muslim shall pray five times a day as enjoined by the Holy Koran and declare himself a Faithful Slave of the Lord. Attention! Attention!

Scene Eleven

A plain outside the fort of Daulatabad. Crowds of citizens.

FIRST MAN: Prayer! Prayer! Who wants prayers now?

SECOND MAN: Ask them to give us some food.

FIRST MAN: There's no food. Food's only in the palace. It's prayers for us.

SECOND MAN: The Amirs have food.

FIRST MAN: We starve and they want us to pray. They want to save our souls.

THIRD MAN: Is it true the Sultan has opened up his granary?

SECOND MAN: There was not a grain in it! Not a skin of paddy.

FIRST MAN: And they want us to pray.

THIRD MAN: The other day my younger brother came here from our village. He says it's much worse there. We are better off here, he says. They have to pay twenty grains of silver for a fistful of wheat. And the scenes he saw on his way here! Ugh!

SECOND MAN (*getting annoyed*): Hm...

THIRD MAN: He says the roads are lined with skeletons. A man starved to death right in front of his eyes. In Doab, people are eating barks off the trees, he says. Yes, and women have to make do with skins of dead horses.

SECOND MAN: Shut up.

THIRD MAN: In Baran—that's where Barani, the Sultan's friend, comes from you know—they have to eat burnt strips of skin, he says. No one knows what animals—

SECOND MAN: Why don't you shut up?
(*The crowd listens, tensely.*)

THIRD MAN: He says we are much better off here. Not them. On his way here he saw people crowding round a butcher's shop. You know why? To catch the blood spurting from the slaughtered beasts and drink it!

SECOND MAN: Shut up, you butcher—
(*He attacks the third man. There's a fight. The second man throws the third man down,˙sits on his chest and beats him. He is crying even as he beats. The others watch.*)

FIRST MAN: Why do they need prayer?
(*Music and the announcers are heard from the two sides of the stage.*)

ANNOUNCER I: Attention! Attention! The Slave of the Lord, the Upholder of the Word of the Prophet—may peace be upon him—the Friend of the Khalif, the Faithful, Muhammad Tughlaq—

ANNOUNCER II: Attention! Attention! The Protector of the Faith, the Descendant of the Holy Khalif al-Mustansir, Amir-ul-Mominin Ghiyas-ud-din Muhammad—
(*Aziz, Aazam and their entourage enter from one side. Exactly at the same moment, Muhammad and his entourage step down from the fort. There is tense silence. Muhammad stares at Aziz as though he is not quite sure what is happening. The Hindu woman of Scene Seven steps out of the crowd and stares at Aziz. Her husband pulls her back. Muhammad steps forward and embraces Aziz.*)

MUHAMMAD: Welcome to our city, Your Holiness, welcome to our poor land. My kingdom rejoices at the arrival of your gracious presence. We have waited for years for this joyful moment. Our streets have waited in silence for the moment when the call to the holy prayer will echo through in them again. And each year has been a century. We have waited long, Your Holiness, and our sins have become shadows that entwine round our feet. They have become our dumbness and deprived us of prayer. They have become the fiery sun and burnt up our crops. Now the moment has come for me and my people to rejoice. Only you can save me now, Your Holiness, only the dust of your feet on my head can save me now—

(*Falls to his feet. The crowd gasps. Then everyone kneels.*)

AZIZ: Amen.

(*Muhammad gets up. They embrace again. They depart to the accompaniment of the announcements.*)

HINDU WOMAN: It's him! It's him—

THIRD MAN: Who?

HINDU WOMAN: He killed my child! Those eyes—I'll never forget them—he killed my child...(*Screams.*) He killed my child...(*Keeps on screaming.*)

FIRST MAN: What's it?

SECOND MAN: I didn't hear. Something about a child—

ANOTHER MAN: She says someone killed her child—

FIRST MAN: Who killed the child?

SECOND MAN: I didn't hear properly. Probably the Sultan—

FIRST MAN: Who else will kill her child?

THIRD MAN: It's murder, that's what it is. To ask us to live without food. My daughter died without food. She was murdered.

FIRST MAN: How long are we going to starve like this?

SECOND MAN: Just a fistful of rice—a piece of meat would be enough—

FIRST MAN: We don't want any prayer. We want food—

SEVERAL VOICES: Yes, food—we want food—not prayers—

A SOLDIER: Quiet! Quiet!

FIRST MAN (*shouting*): Kill us, kill us. Don't starve us to death. Kill us quickly...

SECOND MAN: They'll kill us, will they? Let's see who kills whom? Bring them down.

ALL: Bring him down—let's see—So they'll give us poison instead of food, will they? Kill him—kill him—Show him what we can do—

(*Confusion. Some of them mob the soldier and beat him. A group of soldiers arrives and starts beating them, ordering them to keep quiet. The riots begin.*)

Scene Twelve

The Palace. Aziz is eating some fruit. Aazam enters.

AAZAM: Aziz—

AZIZ: Shut up! I've told you not to call me by that name.

AAZAM: I'm fed up of these games, Aziz, I'm going.

AZIZ: Going? Where?

AAZAM: I don't know. But I've bribed two servants of the palace. They are to bring two horses. They'll be here with the horses inside of half an hour. So hurry up.

AZIZ: Fool, now you've probably made them suspicious. I've told you a hundred times nothing can happen to us here. You're asking for the butcher's block.

AAZAM: Have you seen the city? The people are like mad dogs. They have been screaming, burning houses, killing and marauding for a whole week now. Have you ever stepped out of the palace?

AZIZ: Of course not.

AAZAM: I have. Twice.

AZIZ: Twice! Is your skull filled with dung? Twice! How did you go out?

AAZAM: There's a secret passage. I discovered it the day we came here. I have been through it. Twice. And do you know what the city is like? In the northern part, the houses are like forts, the streets narrow as the little finger. And they are choked with dead bodies. Corpses and flies. It stank so much I almost fainted—I can't stand it any longer, Aziz. Today the people are a little quieter. They are tired; besides, they have to dispose of the bodies. Tomorrow they'll start again...

AZIZ: Now look. Why don't you think? Just once—once in your lifetime? How do you know the servants won't betray you? Listen to me. Stay in the palace. It's the safest place now.

AAZAM: Safe? This palace? Ha! The Sultan's mad. How can you trust him? Don't you know how he can slaughter people? How can you trust this lord of skins? It's better to trust servants. Listen. You know there are those heaps of counterfeit coins in the garden outside my window?

AZIZ: I hope they haven't scared you. After all, quite a lot of them are our handiwork.

AAZAM: On the night we came here, I was so nervous I couldn't sleep. So I was standing by the window, looking at those heaps. They looked like giant ant-hills in the moonlight. Suddenly I saw a shadow moving among them. I stared. It was a man wandering alone in the garden. He went to a heap, stood there for half an hour, still as a rock. Then he dug into the heaps with his fists, raised his fists and let the coins trickle out. It was frightening. And you know who it was? Your Sultan. He does that every night—every single night—it's like witchcraft—

AZIZ: So you are running away because the Sultan has insomnia? What about all that you were hoping to achieve? And what happens to me if you go? How will Ghiyas-ud-din Abbasid explain the disappearance of his disciple?

AAZAM: You come with me too, Aziz. I can't go alone. I've tied all our presents in a bundle. It's a huge bundle. Will last us for ever. You are a clever man, Aziz. I know I am a fool. I can't

survive without you... It's time. The horses will probably
have come. Let's go. Come on...

AZIZ: I order you to stay, Aazam.

AAZAM: I can't. I can't. I'll die of fright here.

AZIZ: All right then. Go. Get out, you traitor.

AAZAM: What else can I do? I wish you would come too. Look.
We'll forget all this wealth, these courts, this luxury and live
in peace. Please come...please, Aziz, I'll kiss your feet—

(*No reply.*)

I'm going, Aziz...

(*No reply.*)

Good-bye.

(*Goes out.*)

AZIZ: Idiot!

Scene Thirteen

Another part of the Palace. Muhammad and Barani.

MUHAMMAD: May I know why, Barani?

BARANI: It's as I said. Your Majesty, I have just received a letter from Baran and it says my mother's dead. I couldn't be by her side in the last moments of her life. I must be there at least for her funeral.

MUHAMMAD: What did she die of, do you know?

BARANI: I don't know, Your Majesty. The letter didn't say anything more.

MUHAMMAD: I see. (*Pause.*) And you will return to the court after the funeral, won't you?

BARANI (*evasive*): I don't know, Your Majesty.

MUHAMMAD: If you are only going for the funeral, why shouldn't you be able to come back?

BARANI (*desperately*): I don't know.

MUHAMMAD: Don't you? Because I do. She died in the riots, didn't she, when my soldiers butchered everyone in sight—old men, women, children, everyone? So you see, even I know what is happening in my kingdom. I may be responsible for that massacre, I accept. But have I really fallen so low that even you have to lie to me?

BARANI (*almost crying*): I don't know. I don't know. Please don't ask me. I beg of you.

(*Silence. A soldier enters running.*)

SOLDIER: In the name of Allah. A terrible thing—Your Majesty, I don't know how to—

MUHAMMAD: What is it now?

SOLDIER: Your Majesty, Aazam Jahan, the friend of His Holiness Ghiyas-ud-din Abbasid, is dead.

BARANI: Dead?

SOLDIER: Murdered, Your Majesty. I was on sentry duty at the mouth of the secret tunnel from the palace. I heard a scream. I ran to the spot. It was Aazam Jahan. He was lying in a pool of blood.

BARANI: Heaven have mercy on us!

MUHAMMAD: Was anyone else there?

SOLDIER: Two horsemen, Your Majesty. They had a big bundle with them. But before I could even shout, they were gone. I didn't even see their faces—

MUHAMMAD: Did he say anything before he died?

SOLDIER: No, Your Majesty. He was alive for a while. When I went near I thought—I thought—

MUHAMMAD: Yes?

SOLDIER: I thought he was laughing—giggling. But of course it could be just—his dying breath—

(*There is a long silence. Muhammad stares at the soldier, stunned and incredulous.*)

MUHAMMAD: Not a word of this to anyone. Not even to His Holiness Ghiyas-ud-din Abbasid. No one in the palace must know. You understand?

SOLDIER: Yes, Your Majesty.

MUHAMMAD: Go back to your place. And ask the doorman to fetch His Holiness—at once.

SOLDIER: Yes, Your Majesty.
(*Goes out.*)

MUHAMMAD (*almost to himself*): Don't you think it absurd that a man who has just come from Arabia should prefer the bloody streets to the palace?

BARANI: But I don't understand, Your Majesty, I can't understand how—

MUHAMMAD: You wanted to see history form in front of your eyes, didn't you? Just wait a few moments, and you'll see not just the form but the coiled intestines of it.

BARANI (*wounded*): Your Majesty is a learned man and has every right to laugh at a poor fool like me. But I implore Your Majesty to understand I am not going because my life here has been futile. I have spent seven years in your presence and the greatest historians of the world would have given half their lives to see a year in it. Your Majesty has given me a gift—

MUHAMMAD: Must there be a farewell speech before you go? You want to go. Go. That's all there is to it.
(*Silence.*)

BARANI (*suddenly remembering*): But the public prayer! It's to start within half-an-hour! It wouldn't be right to start it when the palace is in mourning. Your Majesty must—

MUHAMMAD: No, no, no! This is the first public prayer in my kingdom after a silence of five years! We are praying because a holy man like Ghiyas-ud-din Abbasid has come to our land and blessed us! We can't let anything stop that! (*Laughs.*) Oh Barani, Najib should have been here now. He would have loved this farce.

(*Aziz enters with soldiers. Barani and Muhammad bow. The soldiers bow and retire.*)

AZIZ (*blessing them*): May Heaven guide Your Majesty.

MUHAMMAD: I hope Your Holiness is well.

AZIZ: Who would have grounds for complaint when the generosity of Your Majesty looks after him?

MUHAMMAD: I hope Your Holiness has not been too inconvenienced by the riots. I was busy and couldn't attend to your needs personally. And now that I see you, I stand a bearer of evil tidings. We have just received some tragic news. (*Pause.*) Aazam Jahan's body has been found outside the palace. He was murdered.

AZIZ: May Allah save our souls. What's happening to this world? What's Man coming to if even an innocent like Aazam Jahan isn't to be spared the sword?

MUHAMMAD: Who are you?

(*Silence. For a moment no one speaks. Aziz is obviously frightened.*) Who are you? How long did you hope to go on fooling us with your masquerade?

BARANI: But Your Majesty—

MUHAMMAD: Answer me. Don't make me lose my temper.

AZIZ: I am a dhobi from Shiknar. My first name was Aziz. There have been many others since then.

BARANI: But—what about His Holiness?

MUHAMMAD: Do you know the punishment for killing a saint like Ghiyas-ud-din Abbasid? And for deceiving me and my subjects?

AZIZ (*bolder*): No, Your Majesty, though I have never underestimated Your Majesty's powers of imagination. But it would be a gross injustice if I were punished, Your Majesty.

BARANI: What's happening here?

AZIZ: 'Saint' is a word more appropriate for people like Sheikh Imam-ud-din. I doubt if Your Majesty would have used it for Ghiyas-ud-din Abbasid. I know I am a dhobi and he was a descendant of the Khalif. But surely Your Majesty has never associated greatness with pedigree.

MUHAMMAD: Be careful, dhobi. Don't overreach yourself.

AZIZ: I daren't. But may I say that since Your Majesty came to the throne, I have been your most devout servant? I have studied every order, followed every instruction, considered every measure of Your Majesty's with the greatest attention. I insist I am Your Majesty's true disciple.

MUHAMMAD: Don't try to flatter me. I am accustomed to it.

AZIZ: It's hardly flattering you, Your Majesty, to say I am your disciple. But I have watched Your Majesty try to explain your ideas and acts to the people. And I have seen with regret how few have understood them.

BARANI (*who is just beginning to comprehend*): Your Majesty, this scoundrel is trying to spread a net of words around you. It's dangerous even to talk to him. He must be punished forthwith.

AZIZ: Come, sir, let's be sensible. You know His Majesty will never do that to me.

MUHAMMAD: Won't I?

AZIZ: Forgive me. But Your Majesty has publicly welcomed me as a saint, started the public prayers after a lapse of five years in my honour, called me a Saviour. Your Majesty has even— forgive me for pointing it out, I wasn't responsible for it— fallen at my feet, publicly.

BARANI: Villain—

AZIZ: But I am not a common blackmailer, Your Majesty. I stand here on the strength of my convictions and my loyalty to you.

MUHAMMAD: What do you want to say?

AZIZ: I was a poor starving dhobi, when Your Majesty came to the throne and declared the brotherhood of all religions. Does the Sultan remember the Brahmin who brought a case against him and won? I was that Brahmin.

MUHAMMAD: Was the disguise necessary?

AZIZ: I believe so. (*Pause.*) Soon after that Your Majesty introduced the new copper currency. I succumbed to its temptation.

BARANI: God...God...

AZIZ: There was enough money in that business, but too much competition. Soon it became unprofitable, so we took the silver dinars and went to Doab and bought some land there for farming.

BARANI: But this is nonsense! There has been famine there for five years...

MUHAMMAD: That's exactly his point. They got the land dirt-cheap and collected the State subsidy for farmers. When they were discovered, they ran into the hills and became robbers. (*With mock humility to Aziz.*) Am I right?

AZIZ: Dare I contradict what the whole world knows about His Majesty's acumen? But Your Majesty missed out an important stage in my life. Your officers track down criminals with the zest of a tribe of hunters and there was only one way to escape them. We joined them. We had to shift the corpses of all the rebels executed by the State and hang them up for exhibition. Such famous kings, warriors and leaders of men passed through our hands then! Beautiful strong bodies and bodies eaten-up by corruption—all, all were stuffed with straw and went up to the top of the poles.

One day, suddenly, I had a revelation. This was all human life was worth, I said. This was the real meaning of the mystery of death—straw and skin! With that enlightenment, I found Peace. We left the camp and headed for the hills.

MUHAMMAD: Yes, that was a rather important stage.

AZIZ: One day I heard about a beggar who claimed to be Ghiyas-ud-din Abbasid and was on his way to the capital—I couldn't resist the temptation of seeing my master in person. I admit I killed Ghiyas-ud-din and cheated you. Yet I am Your

Majesty's true disciple. I ask you, Your Majesty, which other man in India has spent five years of his life fitting every act, deed and thought to His Majesty's words?

BARANI: This man should be buried alive this minute!

AZIZ: I only acted according to His Majesty's edicts.

MUHAMMAD (*exploding*): Hold your tongue, fool! You dare pass judgement on me? You think your tongue is so light and swift that you can trap me by your stupid clowning? Let's see how well it wags when hanging from the top of a pole. I haven't cared for the bravest and wisest of men—you think I would succumb to you, a dhobi, masquerading as a saint?

AZIZ (*quietly*): What if I am a dhobi, Your Majesty? When it comes to washing away filth, no saint is a match for a dhobi.

(*Muhammad suddenly bursts into a guffaw. There is a slight hysterical tinge to the laughter.*)

MUHAMMAD (*laughing*): Checkmate! Checkmate! I don't think I have ever seen such insolence. This man's a genius—all right, tell me. What punishment should I mete out to you for your crimes?

AZIZ: Make me an officer of your State, Your Majesty.

MUHAMMAD: That would be punishing myself—not you.

AZIZ: All these years I have been a beggar, wasting my life, and I'm not proud of that. I beg Your Majesty to give me a chance to show my loyalty. I'm ready to die for my Sultan.

MUHAMMAD: I don't know why I am acting like a fool. Yet perhaps a State office really would be the best punishment for you. You'll have to return to Arabia after Aazam Jahan's funeral, and disappear on the way. Can you do it?

AZIZ: It certainly won't be the first time I've done that.

MUHAMMAD: Good, then go to the Deccan. I'll give you a letter for Khusrau Malik appointing you as an officer under him. He'll look after you.

AZIZ: What can I say? How can I express my gratitude? In the name of the Prophet—may peace be upon him, I swear—

MUHAMMAD: Don't overdo it. It's time for the prayer. Remember, you are still His Holiness Ghiyas-ud-din Abbasid and you have to be there to lead the prayer. Be off now.

AZIZ: Your Majesty's most faithful servant.

(*Bows and retires. Muhammad slowly moves to the throne. He looks tired, dispirited. There is silence for a while. Barani can't contain himself any longer.*)

BARANI: But why? Why?

MUHAMMAD: All your life you wait for someone who understands you. And then—you meet him—punishment for wanting too much!... As he said, 'One day suddenly I had a revelation'.

BARANI: By all the history I know, I swear he'll stab you in the back. This is sheer folly. He is a ruthless scoundrel and Your Majesty knows he won't keep trust. Once he has power in the Deccan, his ambition will know no barriers. He is bound to find unlimited scope for his villainy there. He is bound to rebel against the Sultan. How can you not see that, Your Majesty?

MUHAMMAD: I forgave Ain-ul-Mulk once and you were on my side then.

BARANI: But how can one mention Ain-ul-Mulk in the same breath as this rascal?

MUHAMMAD: Last week I received a letter from Ain-ul-Mulk. He has invited me and my subjects to his capital to stay there until the famine here subsides.

BARANI: He is a great man, a great friend of yours—

MUHAMMAD: A friend? How are you so sure it's his friendship that invites us to his capital? You know that, since the day he killed Sheikh Imam-ud-din, he has lost his hold on people. His maulvis won't support him, his people don't trust him. He needs my support now. How do you know he isn't inviting me to strengthen himself?

BARANI: Then... Your Majesty isn't accepting the invitation?

MUHAMMAD: There is only one place to go back to now. Delhi. Back to Delhi, Barani, I have to get back to Delhi with my people.

BARANI: But why—why are you doing this to yourself and your people? Your subjects starve for you—struggle for you— die for you—and you honour this murderer? What's the logic in it? It's criminals like him that deserve to die. Death would be too simple a punishment for him. It wouldn't be enough if you flogged the skin off his back. It wouldn't be enough if you had his tongue pulled out. It wouldn't even be enough if you had him put in a sack and tied to a running horse—

MUHAMMAD: Bravo! I doubt if even that dhobi could have thought of so many tortures—

(*Barani shudders as though he were slapped in the face.*)

If justice were as simple as you think or logic as beautiful as I had hoped, life would have been so much clearer. I have been chasing these words now for five years and now I don't know if I am pursuing a mirage or fleeing a shadow. Anyway, what do all these subtle distinctions matter in the blinding madness of the day? Sweep your logic away into a corner, Barani, all I need now is myself and my madness—madness to prance in a field eaten bare by the scarecrow of violence. But I am not alone, Barani. Thank Heaven! For once I am not alone. I have a Companion to share my insanity now— the Omnipotent God! (*Tired.*) When you pass your final judgement on me, don't forget Him.

BARANI: Who am I to pass judgement on you, Your Majesty? I have to judge myself now and that's why I must go and go immediately. I am terrified when I think of all the tortures

I recommended only a moment ago. I am a weak man, Your
Majesty. I don't have your strength to play with violence and
yet not be sucked in by it. Your Majesty warned me when I
slipped and I am grateful for that. I ask Your Majesty's
permission to go while I'm still safe.

(*Waits for an answer. There's no answer. Muhammad is sitting on
the throne with his eyes closed.*)

Your Majesty—

(*No answer.*)

Your Majesty—

MUHAMMAD (*opening his eyes*): Yes?

BARANI: Is Your Majesty not feeling well?

MUHAMMAD: I am suddenly feeling tired. And sleepy. For five
years sleep had avoided me and now suddenly it's flooding
back. Go, Barani. But before you go—pray for us.

(*Closes his eyes again. Barani bows and exits, obviously in tears.
There is silence on the stage for a while, and then a servant comes
in.*)

SERVANT: In the name of...

(*He sees that Muhammad is asleep and goes out. Muhammad's
head falls forward on his chest in deep sleep. The servant re-enters
with a shawl which he carefully wraps round the Sultan. He is about
to go out when the Muezzin's call to prayer is heard. The servant
turns to wake the Sultan, then after a pause, goes out without doing
so.*)

MUEZZIN (*off-stage*): Alla-Ho-Akbar!   Alla-Ho-Akbar!
    Alla-Ho-Akbar! Alla-Ho-Akbar!
    Ashahado La Elaha Illilah
    Ashahado La Elaha Illilah
    Ashahado Anna Muhammadur Rasool Illah
    Ashahado Anna Muhammadur Rasool Illah
    Haiyah Alis Salaat—Haiyah Alis Salaat
    Haiyah Salil Falaa—Haiyah Salil Falaa

Alla-Ho-Akbar! Alla-Ho-Akbar!

La Elaha Illilah...

(*As the Muezzin's call fades away, Muhammad suddenly opens his eyes. He looks around, dazed and frightened, as though he can't comprehend where he is.*)

HAYAVADANA

NOTE

Hayavadana was originally written in Kannada and I must express my thanks to the Homi Bhabha Fellowships Council for the fellowship which enabled me to write the play.

The central episode in the play—the story of Devadatta and Kapila—is based on a tale from the *Kathasaritsagara*, but I have drawn heavily on Thomas Mann's reworking of the tale in *The Transposed Heads* and am grateful to Mrs Mann for permission to do so.

My special thanks are also due to Mr Rajinder Paul who persuaded me to translate the play into English and first published this translation in his journal, *Enact*.

In translating this play, I have not tried to be consistent while rendering the songs into English. Some have been put in a loose verse form while, for others, only a straightforward prose version has been given.

GIRISH KARNAD

Hayavadana was first presented in English by the Madras Players at the Museum Theatre, Madras on 7 December 1972. The cast was as follows:

S. RAMACHANDER	The Bhagavata
A.V. DHANUSHKODI	Actor I/Devadatta
S. KRISHNASWAMY	Hayavadana
E. RAGHUKUMAR	Actor II/Kapila
A. RATNAPAPA	Padmini
VISHALAM EKAMBARAM	Doll I
BHAGIRATHI NARAYANAN	Doll II
LAKSHMI KRISHNAMURTY	Kali
AMAN MITTAL	Child
Directed by	LAKSHMI KRISHNAMURTY
	YAMUNA PRABHU
Music by	B.V. KARANTH

for
S_____

Act One

The stage is empty except for a chair, kept centre-stage, and a table on stage right—or at the back—on which the Bhagavata and the musicians sit.
At the beginning of the performance, a mask of Ganesha is brought on stage and kept on the chair. Pooja is done. The Bhagavata sings verses in praise of Ganesha, accompanied by his musicians.
Then the mask is taken away.

> O Elephant-headed Herambha
> whose flag is victory
> and who shines like a thousand suns,
> O husband of Riddhi and Siddhi,
> seated on a mouse and decorated with a snake,
> O single-tusked destroyer of incompleteness,
> we pay homage to you and start our play.

BHAGAVATA: May Vighneshwara, the destroyer of obstacles, who removes all hurdles and crowns all endeavours with success, bless our performance now. How indeed can one hope to describe his glory in our poor, disabled words? An elephant's head on a human body, a broken tusk and a cracked belly—whichever way you look at him he seems the embodiment of imperfection, of incompleteness. How indeed can one fathom the mystery that this very Vakratunda-Mahakaya, with his

crooked face and distorted body, is the Lord and Master of
Success and Perfection? Could it be that this Image of Purity
and Holiness, this Mangalamoorty, intends to signify by his
very appearance that the completeness of God is something
no poor mortal can comprehend? Be that as it may. It is not
for us to understand this Mystery or try to unravel it. Nor
is it within our powers to do so. Our duty is merely to pay
homage to the Elephant-headed god and get on with our
play.

This is the city of Dharmapura, ruled by King Dharmasheela
whose fame and empire have already reached the ends of the
eight directions. Two youths who dwell in this city are our
heroes. One is Devadatta. Comely in appearance, fair in
colour, unrivalled in intelligence, Devadatta is the only son
of the Revered Brahmin, Vidyasagara. Having felled the
mightiest pundits of the kingdom in debates on logic and
love, having blinded the greatest poets of the world with his
poetry and wit, Devadatta is as it were the apple of every eye
in Dharmapura.

The other youth is Kapila. He is the only son of the
ironsmith, Lohita, who is to the King's armoury as an axle
to the chariotwheel. He is dark and plain to look at, yet in
deeds which require drive and daring, in dancing, in strength
and in physical skills, he has no equal.

(*A scream of terror is heard off-stage. The Bhagavata frowns,
quickly looks in the direction of the scream, then carries on.*)

The world wonders at their friendship. The world sees these
two young men wandering down the streets of Dharmapura,
hand in hand, and remembers Lava and Kusha, Rama and
Lakshmana, Krishna and Balarama.

(*Sings.*) Two friends there were
—one mind, one heart—

(*The scream is heard again. The Bhagavata cannot ignore it any
more.*)

Who could that be—creating a disturbance at the very outset

of our performance? (*Looks.*) Oh—It's Nata, our Actor. And
he is running. What could have happened, I wonder?

(*The Actor comes running in, trembling with fear. He rushes on to
the stage, runs round the stage once, then sees the Bhagavata and
grabs him.*)

ACTOR: Sir, Bhagavata sir—

BHAGAVATA (*trying to free himself*): Tut! Tut! What's this? What's
this?

ACTOR: Sir...oh my God!—God!—

BHAGAVATA: Let me go! I tell you, let go of me!
(*Freeing himself.*) Now what's this? What...

ACTOR: I—I—I—Oh God! (*Grabs him again.*)

BHAGAVATA: Let me go!
(*The Actor moves back.*)

What nonsense is this? What do you mean by all this shouting
and screaming? In front of our audience too! How dare you
disturb...

ACTOR: Please, please, I'm—sorry... But—but...

BHAGAVATA (*more calmly*): Now, now, calm down! There's nothing
to be afraid of here. I am here. The musicians are here.
And there is our large-hearted audience. It may be that
they fall asleep during a play sometimes. But they are ever
alert when someone is in trouble. Now, tell us, what's the
matter?

ACTOR (*panting*): Oh—Oh—My heart... It's going to burst...

BHAGAVATA: Sit down! Sit. Right! Now tell me everything quietly,
slowly.

ACTOR: I was on my way here...I was already late...didn't want
to annoy you... So I was hurrying down when...Ohh!
(*Covers his face with his hands.*)

BHAGAVATA: Yes, yes. You were hurrying down. Then?

ACTOR: I'm shivering! On the way...you see...I had drunk a lot of water this morning...my stomach was full...so to relieve myself...

BHAGAVATA: Watch what you are saying! Remember you are on stage...

ACTOR: I didn't do anything! I only wanted to...so I sat by the side of the road—and was about to pull up my dhoti when...

BHAGAVATA: Yes?

ACTOR: A voice—a deep, thick voice... It said: 'Hey, you there—don't you know you are not supposed to commit nuisance on the main road?'

BHAGAVATA: Quite right too. You should have known that much.

ACTOR: I half got up and looked around. Not a man in sight—no one! So I was about to sit down again when the same voice said...

BHAGAVATA: Yes?

ACTOR: 'You irresponsible fellow you, can't you understand you are not to commit nuisance on the main road?' I looked up. And there—right in front of me—across the fence...

BHAGAVATA: Who was there?

ACTOR: A horse!

BHAGAVATA: What?

ACTOR: A horse! And it was talking.

BHAGAVATA: What did you have to drink this morning?

ACTOR: Nothing, I swear. Bhagavata sir, I haven't been near a toddy-shop for a whole week. I didn't even have milk today.

BHAGAVATA: Perhaps your liver is sensitive to water.

ACTOR (desperate): Please believe me. I saw it clearly—it was a horse—and it was talking.

BHAGAVATA (resigned): It's no use continuing this nonsense. So you saw a talking horse? Good. Now go and get made up...

ACTOR: Made up? I fall to your feet, sir, I can't...

BHAGAVATA: Now look here...

ACTOR: Please, sir...

(*He holds up his hand. It's trembling.*)

You see, sir? How can I hold up a sword with this? How can I fight?

BHAGAVATA (*thinks*): Well then. There's only one solution left. You go back...

ACTOR: Back?

BHAGAVATA: ...back to that fence, have another look and make sure for yourself that whoever was talking, it couldn't have been that horse.

ACTOR: No!

BHAGAVATA: Nata...

ACTOR: I can't!

BHAGAVATA: It's an order.

ACTOR (*pleading*): Must I?

BHAGAVATA: Yes, you must.

ACTOR: Sir...

(*The Bhagavata turns to the audience and starts singing.*)

BHAGAVATA: Two friends there were
—one mind, one heart—
Are you still here?

(*The Actor goes out looking at the Bhagavata, hoping for a last minute reprieve. It doesn't come.*)

Poor boy! God alone knows what he saw—and what he took it to be! There's Truth for you... Pure Illusion.

(*Sings.*) Two friends there were
—one mind, one heart—

(*A scream in the wings. The Actor comes rushing in.*)

Now look here...

ACTOR: It's coming. Coming...

BHAGAVATA: What's coming?

ACTOR: Him! He's coming... (*Rushes out.*)

BHAGAVATA: Him? It? What's coming? Whatever or whoever it is,
the Actor has obviously been frightened by its sight. If even
a hardened actor like him gets frightened, it's more than likely
that our gentle audience may be affected too. It's not proper
to let such a sight walk on stage unchallenged. (*To the wings.*)
Hold up the entry-curtain!

(*Two stage-hands enter and hold up a half-curtain, about six feet
in height—the sort of curtain used in Yakshatgana or Kathakali.
The curtain masks the entry of Hayavadana, who comes and stands
behind it.*)

Who's that?

(*No reply. Only the sound of someone sobbing behind the curtain.*)
How strange! Someone's sobbing behind the curtain. It looks
as though the Terror which frightened our Actor is itself now
crying!

(*To the stage-hand.*) Lower the curtain!

(*The curtain is lowered by about a foot. One sees Hayavadana's
head, which is covered by a veil. At a sign from the Bhagavata, one
of the stage-hands removes the veil, revealing a horse's head. For
a while the horse-head doesn't realize that it is exposed to the gaze
of the audience. The moment the realization dawns, the head ducks
behind the curtain.*)

BHAGAVATA: A horse! No, it can't be!

(*He makes a sign. The curtain is lowered a little more—just enough
to show the head again. Again it ducks. Again the curtain is lowered.
This goes on till the curtain is lowered right down to the floor.
Hayavadana, who has a man's body but a horse's head, is sitting
on the floor hiding his head between his knees.*)

Incredible! Unbelievable!

(*At a sign from the Bhagavata, the stage-hands withdraw. The
Bhagavata goes and stands near Hayavadana. Then he grunts to
himself as though he has seen through the trick.*)

Who are you?

(*Hayavadana lifts his head, and wipes the tears away. The Bhagavata beckons to him to come centre-stage.*)

Come here!

(*Hayavadana hesitates, then comes forward.*)

First you go around scaring people with this stupid mask. And then you have the cheek to disturb our show with your clowning? Have you no sense of proportion?...Enough of this nonsense now. Take it off—I say, take off that stupid mask!

(*Hayavadana doesn't move.*)

You won't?—Then I'll have to do it myself!

(*Holds Hayavadana's head with both his hands and tries to pull it off. Hayavadana doesn't resist.*)

It is tight. Nata—My dear Actor...

(*The Actor comes in, warily, and stands open-mouthed at the sight he sees.*)

Why are you standing there? Don't you see you were taken in by a silly mask? Come and help me take it off now.

(*The Actor comes and holds Hayavadana by his waist while the Bhagavata pulls at the head. Hayavadana offers no resistance, but can't help moaning when the pain becomes unbearable. The tug-of-war continues for a while. Slowly, the truth dawns on the Bhagavata.*)

Nata, this isn't a mask! It's his real head!

(*The Actor drops Hayavadana with a thud. Hayavadana gets up and sits as before, head between knees.*)

Truly, surprises will never cease! If someone had told me only five minutes ago that there existed a man with a horse's head, I would have laughed out in his face.

(*To Hayavadana.*) Who are you?

(*Hayavadana gets up and starts to go out. The Actor hurriedly moves out of his way.*)

Wait! Wait! That's our green room there. It's bad enough that you scared this actor. We have a play to perform today, you know.

(*Hayavadana stands, dejected.*)

   (*Softly.*) Who are you?

(*No reply.*)

   What brought you to this? Was it a curse of some *rishi*? Or was it some holy place of pilgrimage, a *punyasthana*, which you desecrated? Or could it be that you insulted a *pativrata*, dedicated to the service of her husband? Or did you...

HAYAVADANA: Hey...

BHAGAVATA (*taken aback*): Eh?

HAYAVADANA: What do you mean, Sir? Do you think just because you know the *Puranas* you can go about showering your Sanskrit on everyone in sight? What temple did I desecrate? What woman did I insult? What...

BHAGAVATA: Don't get annoyed...

HAYAVADANA: What else? What *rishi*? What sage? What? Whom have I wronged? What have I done to anyone? Let anyone come forward and say that I've caused him or her any harm. I haven't—I know I haven't. Yet...

(*He is on the point of beginning to sob again.*)

BHAGAVATA: Don't take it to heart so much. What happened? What's your grief? You are not alone here. I am here. The musicians are here. And there is our large-hearted audience. It may be that they fall asleep during a play sometimes...

HAYAVADANA: What can anyone do? It's my fate.

BHAGAVATA: What's your name?

HAYAVADANA: Hayavadana.

BHAGAVATA: How did you get this horse's head?

HAYAVADANA: I was born with it.

BHAGAVATA: Then why didn't you stop us when we tried to take if off? Why did you put up with our torture?

HAYAVADANA: All my life I've been trying to get rid of this head. I thought—you with all your goodness and *punya*... if at least you manage to pull it off...

BHAGAVATA: Oho! Poor man! But, Hayavadana, what can anyone do about a head one's born with? Who knows what error committed in the last birth is responsi...

HAYAVADANA (*annoyed*): It has nothing to do with my last birth. It's this birth which I can't shake off.

BHAGAVATA: Tell us what happened. Don't feel ashamed.

HAYAVADANA (*enraged*): Ashamed? Me? Why should I...

BHAGAVATA: Sorry. I beg your pardon. I should have said 'shy'.

HAYAVADANA (*gloomy*): It's a long story.

BHAGAVATA: Carry on.

HAYAVADANA: My mother was the Princess of Karnataka. She was a very beautiful girl. When she came of age, her father decided that she should choose her own husband. So princes of every kingdom in the world were invited—and they all came. From China, from Persia, from Africa. But she didn't like any of them. The last one to come was the Prince of Araby. My mother took one look at that handsome prince sitting on his great white stallion—and she fainted.

ACTOR: Ah!

HAYAVADANA: Her father at once decided that this was the man. All arrangements for the wedding were made. My mother recovered—and do you know what she said?

ACTOR, BHAGAVATA: What?

HAYAVADANA: She said she would only marry that horse!

ACTOR: What?

HAYAVADANA: Yes. She wouldn't listen to anyone. The Prince of Araby burst a blood-vessel.

ACTOR: Naturally.

HAYAVADANA: No one could dissuade her. So ultimately she was married off to the white stallion. She lived with him for fifteen years. One morning she wakes up—and no horse! In its place stood a beautiful Celestial Being, a *gandharva*. Apparently this Celestial Being had been cursed by the god Kubera to be born a horse for some act of misbehaviour. After fifteen years of human love he had become his original self again.

BHAGAVATA: I must admit several such cases are on record.

HAYAVADANA: Released from his curse, he asked my mother to accompany him to his Heavenly Abode. But she wouldn't. She said she would come only if he became a horse again. So he cursed her...

ACTOR: No!

HAYAVADANA: He cursed her to become a horse herself. So my mother became a horse and ran away prancing happily. My father went back to his Heavenly Abode. Only I—the child of their marriage—was left behind.

BHAGAVATA: It's a sad story.

ACTOR: Very sad.

HAYAVADANA: What should I do now, Bhagavata Sir? What can I do to get rid of this head?

BHAGAVATA: Hayavadana, what's written on our foreheads cannot be altered.

HAYAVADANA (*slapping himself on the forehead*):
But what a forehead! What a forehead! If it was a forehead like yours, I would have accepted anything. But this!...I have tried to accept my fate. My personal life has naturally been blameless. So I took interest in the social life of the Nation—Civics, Politics, Patriotism, Nationalism, Indianization, the Socialist Pattern of Society... I have tried everything. But where's my society? Where? You must help me to become a complete man, Bhagavata Sir. But how? What can I do?

(*Long silence. They think.*)

BHAGAVATA: Banaras?

HAYAVADANA: What?

BHAGAVATA: If you go to Banaras and make a vow in front of the god there...

HAYAVADANA: I've tried that. Didn't work.

BHAGAVATA: Rameshwaram?

HAYAVADANA: Banaras, Rameshwaram, Gokarn, Haridwar, Gaya, Kedarnath—not only those but the *Dargah* of Khwaja Yusuf Baba, the Grotto of Our Virgin Mary—I've tried them all. Magicians, mendicants, maharshis, fakirs, saints and sadhus— sadhus with short hair, sadhus with beards—sadhus in saffron, sadhus in the altogether—hanging, singing, rotating, gyrating—on the spikes, in the air, under water, under the ground—I've covered them all. And what did I get out of all this? Everywhere I went I had to cover my head with a veil— and I started going bald. (*Pause. Shyly.*) You know, I hate this head, but I just can't help being fond of this lovely, long mane. (*Pause.*) So—I had to give the miss to Tirupati.

(*Long silence.*)

BHAGAVATA: Come to think of it, Hayavadana, why don't you try the Kali of Mount Chitrakoot?

HAYAVADANA: Anything you say.

BHAGAVATA: It's temple at the top of Mount Chitrakoot. The goddess there is famous for being ever-awake to the call of the devotees. Thousands used to flock to her temple once. No one goes now, though.

HAYAVADANA: Why not?

BHAGAVATA: She used to give anything anyone asked for. As the people became aware of this, they stopped going.

HAYAVADANA: Fools!

BHAGAVATA: Why don't you try her?

HAYAVADANA (*jumps up*): Why not? I'll start at once...

BHAGAVATA: Good. But I don't think you should go alone. It's a wild road. You'll have to ask a lot of people, which won't be easy for you. So...
(*To the Actor.*) You'd better go with him.

ACTOR: Me?

BHAGAVATA: Yes, that way you can make up for having insulted him.

HAYAVADANA: But, Bhagavata Sir, may I point out that his roadside manners...

ACTOR: There! He's insulting me now! Let him find his own way. What do I care?

BHAGAVATA: Come, come, don't let's start fighting now. (*To Hayavadana.*) Don't worry. There's no highway there. Only a cart-track at best.
(*To the Actor.*) You've no reason to feel insulted. Actually you should admire him. Even in his dire need, he doesn't lose his civic sense. Be off now.

HAYAVADANA (*to the Actor*): Please, don't get upset. I won't bother you, I promise.
(*To the Bhagavata.*) I am most grateful...

BHAGAVATA (*blessing him*): May you become successful in your search for completeness.
(*The two go.*)
Each one to his own fate. Each one to his own desire. Each one to his own luck. Let's now turn to our story.
(*He starts singing. The following is a prose rendering of the song.*)

BHAGAVATA (*sings*): Two friends there were—one mind, one heart. They saw a girl and forgot themselves. But they could not understand the song she sang.

FEMALE CHORUS (*sings*): Why should love stick to the sap of a single body? When the stem is drunk with the thick yearning

of the many-petalled, many-flowered lantana, why should it
be tied down to the relation of a single flower?

BHAGAVATA (*sings*): They forgot themselves and took off their
bodies. And she took the laughing heads, and held them high
so the pouring blood bathed her, coloured her red. Then she
danced around and sang.

FEMALE CHORUS (*sings*): A head for each breast. A pupil for each
eye. A side for each arm. I have neither regret nor shame. The
blood pours into the earth and a song branches out in the
sky.

(*Devadatta enters and sits on the chair. He is a slender, rather good-
looking person with a fair complexion. He is lost in thought. Kapila
enters. He is powerfully built and darker.*)

KAPILA (*even as he is entering*): Devadatta, why didn't you come
to the gymnasium last evening? I'd asked you to. It was such
fun...

DEVADATTA (*preoccupied*): Some work.

KAPILA: Really, you should have come. The wrestler from Gandhara—
he's one of India's greatest, you know—he came. Nanda and
I were wrestling when he arrived. He watched us. When I
caught Nanda in a crocodile-hold, he first burst into applause
and said...

(*Notices that Devadatta isn't listening and stops. Pause.*)

DEVADATTA (*waking up*): Then?

KAPILA: Then what?

DEVADATTA (*flustered*): I mean...what did Nanda do?

KAPILA: He played the flute.

DEVADATTA (*more confused*): No...I mean...you were saying
something about the wrestler from Gandhara, weren't you?

KAPILA: He wrestled with me for a few minutes, patted me on the
back and said, 'You'll go far.'

DEVADATTA: That's nice.

KAPILA: Yes, it is... Who's it this time?

DEVADATTA: What do you mean?

KAPILA: I mean—who—is—it—this—time?

DEVADATTA: What do you mean who?

KAPILA: I mean—who is the girl?

DEVADATTA: No one. (*Pause.*) How did you guess?

KAPILA: My dear friend, I have seen you fall in love fifteen times in the last two years. How could I not guess?

DEVADATTA: Kapila, if you've come to make fun of me...

KAPILA: I am not making fun of you. Every time, you have been the first to tell me about it. Why so reticent this time?

DEVADATTA: How can you even talk of them in the same breath as her? Before her, they're as...

KAPILA: ...as stars before the moon, as the glow-worms before a torch. Yes, yes, that's been so fifteen times too.

DEVADATTA (*exploding*): Why don't you go home? You are becoming a bore.

KAPILA: Don't get annoyed. Please.

DEVADATTA: You call yourself my friend. But you haven't understood me at all.

KAPILA: And have you understood me? No, you haven't. Or you wouldn't get angry like this. Don't you know I would do anything for you? Jump into a well—or walk into fire? Even my parents aren't as close to me as you are. I would leave them this minute if you asked me to.

DEVADATTA (*irritated*): Don't start on that now. You've said it fifty times already.

KAPILA: ...And I'll say it again. If it wasn't for you I would have been no better than the ox in our yard. You showed me that there were such things as poetry and literature. You taught me...

DEVADATTA: Why don't you go home? All I wanted was to be by myself for a day. Alone. And you had to come and start your chatter. What do you know of poetry and literature? Go back to your smithy—that's where you belong.

KAPILA (*hurt*): Do you really want me to go?

DEVADATTA: Yes.

KAPILA: All right. If that's what you want.

(*He starts to go.*)

DEVADATTA: Sit down.

(*This is of course exactly what Kapila wants. He sits down on the floor.*)

And don't speak...

(*Devadatta gets down on the floor to sit beside Kapila. Kapila at once leaps up and gestures to Devadatta to sit on the chair. Devadatta shakes his head but Kapila insists, pulls him up by his arm. Devadatta gets up.*)

You are a pest.

(*Sits on the chair. Kapila sits down on the ground happily. A long pause.*)

DEVADATTA (*slowly*): How can I describe her, Kapila? Her forelocks rival the bees, her face is...

(*All this is familiar to Kapila and he joins in, with great enjoyment.*)

BOTH: ...is a white lotus. Her beauty is as the magic lake. Her arms the lotus creepers. Her breasts are golden urns and her waist...

DEVADATTA: No. No!

KAPILA: Eh?

DEVADATTA: I was blind all these days. I deceived myself that I understood poetry. I didn't. I understood nothing.

Tanvee shyama—

BOTH: ...*shikharidashana pakvabimbadharoshthee—Madhyekshama chakitaharinee prekshana nimnanabhih.*

DEVADATTA: The Shyama Nayika—born of Kalidasa's magic description—as Vatsyayana had dreamt her. Kapila, in a single appearance, she has become my guru in the poetry of love. Do you think she would ever assent to becoming my disciple in love itself?

KAPILA (*aside*): This is new!

DEVADATTA (*his eyes shining*): If only she would consent to be my Muse, I could outshine Kalidasa. I'd always wanted to do that—but I thought it was impossible... But now I see it is within my reach.

KAPILA: Then go ahead. Write...

DEVADATTA: But how can I without her in front of me? How can I concentrate when my whole being is only thinking of her, craving for her?

KAPILA: What's her name? Will you at least tell me that?

DEVADATTA: Her name? She has no name.

KAPILA: But what do her parents call her?

DEVADATTA (*anguished*): What's the use? She isn't meant for the likes of me...

KAPILA: You don't really believe that, do you? With all your qualities—achievements—looks—family—grace...

DEVADATTA: Don't try to console me with praise.

KAPILA: I'm not praising you. You know very well that every parent of every girl in the city is only waiting to catch you...

DEVADATTA: Don't! Please. I know this girl is beyond my wildest dreams. But still—I can't help wanting her—I can't help it. I swear, Kapila, with you as my witness I swear, if I ever get her as my wife, I'll sacrifice my two arms to the goddess Kali, I'll sacrifice my head to Lord Rudra...

KAPILA Ts! Ts! (*aside*): This is a serious situation. It does look as though this sixteenth girl has really caught our Devadatta in her net. Otherwise, he isn't the type to talk of such violence.

DEVADATTA: I mean it! What's the use of these hands and this head if I'm not to have her? My poetry won't live without her. The *Shakuntalam* will never be excelled. But how can I explain this to her? I have no cloud for a messenger. No bee to show the way. Now the only future I have is to stand and do penance in Pavana Veethi...

KAPILA: Pavana Veethi! Why there?

DEVADATTA: She lives in that street.

KAPILA: How do you know?

DEVADATTA: I saw her in the market yesterday evening. I couldn't remove my eyes from her and followed her home.

KAPILA: Tut! Tut! What must people have thought?

DEVADATTA: She went into a house in Pavana Veethi. I waited outside all evening. She didn't come out.

KAPILA: Now tell me. What sort of a house was it?

DEVADATTA: I can't remember.

KAPILA: What colour?

DEVADATTA: Don't know.

KAPILA: How many storeys?

DEVADATTA: I didn't notice.

KAPILA: You mean you didn't notice anything about the house?

DEVADATTA: The door-frame of the house had an engraving of a two-headed bird at the top. I only saw that. She lifted her hand to knock and it touched the bird. For a minute, the bird came alive.

KAPILA (*jumps up*): Then why didn't you tell me before? You've been wasting precious time...

DEVADATTA: I don't understand...

KAPILA: My dear Devadatta, your cloud-messenger, your bee, your pigeon is sitting right in front of you and you don't even know it? You wait here. I'll go, find out her house, her name...

DEVADATTA (*incredulous*): Kapila—Kapila...

KAPILA: I'll be back in a few minutes...

DEVADATTA: I won't ever forgot this, Kapila...

KAPILA: Shut up!...And forget all about your arms and head. This job doesn't need either Rudra or Kali. I'm quite enough.
(*Goes out.*)

DEVADATTA: Kapila—Kapila... He's gone. How fortunate I am to have a friend like him. Pure gold. (*Pause.*) But should I have trusted this to him? He means well—and he is a wizard in his smithy, in his farm, in his fields. But here? No. He is too rough, too indelicate. He was the wrong man to send. He's bound to ruin the whole thing. (*Anguished.*) Lord Rudra, I meant what I said. If I get her, my head will be a gift to you. Mother Kali, I'll sacrifice my arms to you. I swear...
(*Goes out. The Bhagavata removes the chair. Kapila enters.*)

KAPILA: This is Pavana Veethi—the street of merchants. Well, well, well. What enormous houses! Each one a palace in itself. It's a wonder people don't get lost in these houses.
(*Examines the doors one by one.*)
   Now. This is not a double-headed bird. It's an eagle—This? A lotus. This is—er—a lion. Tiger. A wheel! And this? God alone knows what this is. And the next? (*In disgust.*) A horse!—A rhinoceros—Another lion. Another lotus!—Where the hell is that stupid two-headed bird? (*Stops.*) What was the engraving I couldn't make out? (*Goes back and stares at it. Shouts in triumph.*) That's it! Almost gave me the slip! A proper two-headed bird. But it's so tiny you can't see it at all unless you are willing to tear your eyes staring at it. Well now. Whose house could this be? (*Looks around.*) No one in sight.

Naturally. What should anyone come here for in this hot sun? Better ask the people in the house.

(*Mimes knocking. Listens. Padmini enters humming a tune.*)

PADMINI: ...Here comes the rider—from which land does he come?...

KAPILA (*gapes at her. Aside*): I give up, Devadatta. I surrender to your judgement. I hadn't thought anyone could be more beautiful than the wench Ragini who acts Rambha in our village troupe. But this one! You're right—she is Yakshini, Shakuntala, Urvashi, Indumati—all rolled into one.

PADMINI: You knocked, didn't you?

KAPILA: Er—yes...

PADMINI: Then why are you gaping at me? What do you want?

KAPILA: I—I just wanted to know whose house this was.

PADMINI: Whose house do you want?

KAPILA: This one.

PADMINI: I see. Then who do you want here?

KAPILA: The master...

PADMINI: Do you know his name?

KAPILA: No.

PADMINI: Have you met him?

KAPILA: No.

PADMINI: Have you seen him?

KAPILA: No.

PADMINI: So. You haven't met him, seen him or known him. What do you want with him?

KAPILA (*aside*): She is quite right. What have I to do with him? I only want to find out his name...

PADMINI: Are you sure you want this house? Or were you...

KAPILA: No. I'm sure this is the one.

PADMINI (*pointing to her head*): Are you all right here?

KAPILA (*taken aback*): Yes—I think so.

PADMINI: How about your eyes? Do they work properly?

KAPILA: Yes.

PADMINI (*showing him four fingers*): How many?

KAPILA: Four.

PADMINI: Correct. So there's nothing wrong with your eyes. As for the other thing, I'll have to take you on trust. Well then. If you are sure you wanted this house, why were you peering at all those doors? And what were you mumbling under your breath?

KAPILA (*startled*): How did you know?

PADMINI: I am quite sane...and I've got good eyes.

KAPILA (*looks up and chuckles*): Oh, I suppose you were watching from the terrace...

PADMINI (*in a low voice, mysteriously*): Listen, you'd better be careful. We have any number of thefts in this street and people are suspicious. Last night there was a man standing out there for nearly two hours without moving. And today you have turned up. It's just as well I saw you. Anyone else would have taken you to the police. Beware! (*Aloud.*) Now tell me. What are you doing here?

KAPILA: I—I can't tell you.

PADMINI: Really! Who will you tell it to?

KAPILA: Your father...

PADMINI: Do you want my father or do you want the master of this house?

KAPILA: Aren't they the same?

PADMINI (*as though explaining to a child*): Listen, my father could be a servant in this house. Or the master of this house could be my father's servant. My father could be the master's father,

brother, son-in-law, cousin, grandfather or uncle. Do you
agree?

KAPILA: Er—yes.

PADMINI: Right. Then we'll start again. Whom should I call?

KAPILA: Your father.

PADMINI: And if he's not in?

KAPILA (*lost*): Anyone else.

PADMINI: Which anyone?

KAPILA: Perhaps—your brother.

PADMINI: Do you know him?

KAPILA: No.

PADMINI: Have you met him?

KAPILA: No.

PADMINI: Do you know his name?

KAPILA (*desperate*): Please, please—call your father or the master
or both, or if they are the same, anyone... please call someone!

PADMINI: No. No. That won't do.

KAPILA (*looking around; aside*): No one here. Still I have to find
out her name. Devadatta must be in agony and he will never
forgive me if I go back now. (*Aloud.*) Madam, please. I have
some very important work. I'll touch your feet...

PADMINI (*eager*): You will? Really? Do you know, I've touched
everyone's feet in this house some time or the other, but no
one's ever touched mine? You will?

KAPILA (*slapping his forehead as he sinks to the ground*): I'm
finished—decimated—powdered to dust—powdered into tiny
specks of flour. (*To Padmini.*) My mother, can I at least talk
to a servant?

PADMINI: I knew it. I knew you wouldn't touch my feet. One can't

even trust strangers any more. All right, my dear son! I
opened the door. So consider me the door-keeper. What do
you want?

KAPILA (*determined*): All right! (*Gets up.*) You have no doubt
heard of the Revered Brahmin Vidyasagara.

PADMINI: It's possible.

KAPILA: In which case you'll also know of Devadatta, his only son.
A poet. A pundit. Knows the Vedas backwards. Writes the
grandest poetry ever. Long, dark hair. Delicate, fair face. Age
twenty. Height five feet seven inches. Weight...

PADMINI: Wait a minute! What's he to you?

KAPILA: Friend. Greatest in the world! But the main question now
is: What's he going to be to you?

(*Sudden silence.*)

PADMINI (*blushing as the import of the remark dawns on her*):
Mother!

(*Runs in. Kapila stands, staring after her.*)

KAPILA: Devadatta, my friend, I confess to you I'm feeling uneasy.
You are a gentle soul. You can't bear a bitter word or an evil
thought. But this one is fast as lightning—and as sharp. She
is not for the likes of you. What she needs is a man of steel.
But what can one do? You'll never listen to me. And I can't
withdraw now. I'll have to talk to her family...

(*Follows her in.*)

BHAGAVATA: Need one explain to our wise and knowing audience
what followed next? Padmini is the daughter of the leading
merchant in Dharmapura. In her house, the very floor is
swept by the Goddess of Wealth. In Devadatta's house, they've
the Goddess of Learning for a maid. What could then possibly
stand in the way of bringing the families together? (*Marriage
music.*) Padmini became the better half of Devadatta and
settled in his house. Nor did Devadatta forget his debt to
Kapila. The old friendship flourished as before. Devadatta—

Padmini—Kapila! To the admiring citizens of Dharmapura,
Rama—Sita—Lakshmana.

(*Enter Devadatta and Padmini.*)

PADMINI: Why is he so late? He should have been here more than
an hour ago.

(*Looks out of a window.*)

DEVADATTA: Have you packed your clothes properly?

PADMINI: The first thing in the morning.

DEVADATTA: And the mattresses? We may have to sleep out in the
open. It's quite chilly. We'll need at least two rugs.

PADMINI: Don't worry. The servant's done all that.

DEVADATTA: And your shawl? Also some warm clothes...

PADMINI: What's happened to you today? At other times you are
so full of your books, you even forget to wash your hands
after a meal. But today you've been going on and on and on
all morning.

DEVADATTA: Padmini, I've told you ten times already I don't like
the idea of this trip. You should rest—not face such hazards.
The cart will probably shake like an earthquake. It's dangerous
in your condition. But you won't listen.

PADMINI: My condition! What's happened to me? To listen to you,
one would think I was the first woman in this world to
become pregnant. I only have to stumble and you act as
though it's all finished and gone...

DEVADATTA: For God's sake, will you stop it?

PADMINI (*laughs*): Sorry! (*Bites her tongue in repentance.*) I won't
say such things again.

DEVADATTA: You've no sense of what not to say. So long as you
can chatter and run around like a child...

PADMINI (*back at the window*): Where is Kapila?

DEVADATTA: ...and drool over Kapila all day.

PADMINI (*taken aback*): What do you mean?

DEVADATTA: What else should I say? The other day I wanted to read out a play of Bhasa's to you and sure enough Kapila drops in.

PADMINI: Oh! That's biting you still, is it? But why are you blaming me? He was your friend even before you married me, wasn't he? He used to drop in every day even then...

DEVADATTA: But shouldn't he realize I'm a married man now? He just can't go on as before...

PADMINI: Don't blame him. It's my fault. He learnt a bit about poetry from you and I thought he might enjoy Bhasa. So I asked him to come. He didn't want to but I insisted.

DEVADATTA: I know that.

PADMINI: Had I realized you would be so upset, I wouldn't have.

DEVADATTA: I'm not upset, Padmini. Kapila isn't merely a friend— he's like my brother. One has to collect merit in seven lives to get a friend like him. But is it wrong for me to want to read to you alone? Or to spend a couple of days with you without anyone else around? (*Pause.*) Of course, once he came, there wasn't the slightest chance of my reading any poetry. You had to hop around him twittering 'Kapila! Kapila!' every minute.

PADMINI: You aren't jealous of him, are you?

DEVADATTA: Me? Jealous of Kapila? Why do you have to twist everything I say...

PADMINI (*laughs. Affectionately*): Don't sulk now. I was just trying to be funny. Really you have no sense of humour.

DEVADATTA: It's humour for you. But it burns my insides.

PADMINI: Aw, shut up. Don't I know how liberal and largehearted you are? You aren't the sort to get jealous. If I were to fall into a well tomorrow, you wouldn't even miss me until my bloated corpse floated up...

DEVADATTA (*irritated*): Padmini!

PADMINI: Sorry, I forgot. I apologize——I slap myself on the cheeks. (*Slaps herself on both cheeks with her right hand several times in punishment.*) Is that all right? The trouble is I grew up saying these awful things and it's become a habit now. But you are so fragile! I don't know how you're going to go through life wrapped in silk like this! You are still a baby...

DEVADATTA: I see.

PADMINI: Look now. You got annoyed about Kapila. But why? You are my saffron, my marriage thread, my deity. Why should you feel disturbed? I like making fun of Kapila——he is such an innocent. Looks a proper devil, but the way he blushes and giggles and turns red, he might have been a bride.

DEVADATTA (*smiles*): Well, this bride didn't blush.

PADMINI: No one taught this bride to blush. But now I'm learning from that yokel.

(*They both laugh. She casually goes back to the window and looks out.*)

DEVADATTA (*aside*): Does she really not see? Or is she deliberately playing this game with him? Kapila was never the sort to blush. But now, he only has to see her and he begins to wag his tail. Sits up on his hind legs as though he were afraid to let her words fall to the ground. And that pleading in his eyes——can't she really see that? (*Aloud.*) Padmini, Kapila isn't used to women. The only woman he has known in his life is his mother.

PADMINI: You mean it's dangerous to be with him? The way you talk one would never imagine he was your best friend.

DEVADATTA (*incensed*): Why do you have to twist everything I say...

PADMINI (*conciliatory*): What did I say? Listen, if you really don't want to go to Ujjain today, let's not. When Kapila comes, tell him I'm ill.

DEVADATTA: But...you will be disappointed.

PADMINI: Me? Of course not. We'll do as you feel. You remember what the priest said—I'm your 'half' now. The better half! We can go to Ujjain some other time... In another couple of months, there's the big Ujjain fair. We'll go then—just the two of us. All right? We'll cancel today's trip.

DEVADATTA (*trying to control his excitement*): Now—if you aren't going to be disappointed—then—truly—that's what I would like most. Not because I'm jealous of Kapila—No, I'm not, I know that. He has a heart of gold. But this is your first baby...

PADMINI: What do you mean first? How many babies can one have within six months?

DEVADATTA: You aren't going to start again?

PADMINI: No, no, no, I won't say a word.

DEVADATTA (*pinching her cheek*): Bad upbringing—that's what it is. I don't like the idea of your going out in a cart in your present condition, that's all.

PADMINI: Ordinarily I would have replied I had a womb of steel, but I won't—in the present condition.
(*Both laugh.*)
All right. If you are happy, so am I.

DEVADATTA (*happy*): Yes, we'll spend the whole day by ourselves. The servants are going home anyway. They can come back tomorrow. But for today—only you and me. It's been such a long time since we've been on our own.

KAPILA (*off-stage*): Devadatta...

PADMINI: There's Kapila now. You tell him.

(*She pretends to go in, but goes and stands in a corner of the stage, listening. Kapila enters excited.*)

KAPILA: I'm late, ain't I? What could I do? That cartman had kept the cart ready but the moment I looked at it, I knew one of the oxen was no good. I asked him to change it. 'We won't reach Ujjain for another fortnight in this one,' I said. He started...

DEVADATTA: Kapila...

KAPILA: ...making a scene, but I stood my ground. So he had to fetch a new one. These cart-hirers are a menace. If ours hadn't gone to Chitrapur that day...

DEVADATTA: Kapila, we have to call off today's trip.

KAPILA (*suddenly silenced*): Oh!

DEVADATTA (*embarrassed*): You see, Padmini isn't well...

KAPILA: Well, then of course...

(*Silence.*)

I'll return the cart then.

DEVADATTA: Yes.

KAPILA: Or else he may charge us for the day.

DEVADATTA: Uhm.

KAPILA (*aside*): So it's off. What am I to do for the rest of the day? What am I to do for the rest of the week? Why should it feel as though the whole world has been wiped out for a whole week? Why this emptiness? Kapila, Kapila, get a tight hold on yourself. You are slipping, boy, control yourself. Don't lose that hold. Go now. Don't come here again for a week. Devadatta's bound to get angry with you for not visiting. Sister-in-law will be annoyed. But don't come back. Go, Go! (*Aloud.*) Well then—I'll start.

DEVADATTA: Why don't you sit for a while?

KAPILA: No, no. We might upset sister-in-law more then with our prattle.

DEVADATTA: That's true. So come again. Soon.

KAPILA: Yes, I will.

(*Starts to go. Padmini comes out.*)

PADMINI: Why are you sitting here? When are we going to start? We are already late...

(*They look at her, surprised.*)

KAPILA: But if you aren't well, we won't...

PADMINI: What's wrong with me? I'm in perfect health. I had a headache this morning. But a layer of ginger paste took care of that. Why should we cancel our trip for a little thing like that?

(*Devadatta opens his mouth to say something but stays quiet.*)

(*To Kapila.*) Why are you standing there like a statue?

KAPILA: No, really, if you have a headache...

PADMINI: I don't have a headache now!

DEVADATTA: But, Padmini...

PADMINI: Kapila, put those bundles out there in the cart. The servant will bring the rest.

(*Kapila stands totally baffled. He looks at Devadatta for guidance. There's none.*)

Be quick. Otherwise I'll put them in myself.

(*Kapila goes out. Padmini goes to Devadatta. Pleading.*)

Please don't get angry. Poor boy, he looked so lost and disappointed, I couldn't bear to see it. He has been running around for us this whole week.

DEVADATTA (*turning his head away*): Where's the box in which I put the books? Let me take it.

PADMINI: You are an angel. I knew you wouldn't mind. I'll bring it. It's quite light.

(*Goes out.*)

DEVADATTA (*to himself*): And my disappointment? Does that mean nothing to you? (*Aloud.*) Don't. I'll take it. Please, don't lift anything.

(*Goes in after her.*)

BHAGAVATA: Why do you tremble, heart? Why do you cringe

like a touch-me-not bush through which a snake has passed?
The sun rests his head on the Fortunate Lady's flower.
And the head is bidding good-bye to the heart.
(*Kapila, followed by Padmini and Devadatta, enters miming a cart-ride. Kapila is driving the cart.*)

PADMINI: How beautifully you drive the cart, Kapila! Your hands
    don't even move, but the oxen seem to know exactly which
    way you want them to go.
(*Kapila laughs happily.*)
    Shall we stop here for a while? We've been in this cart all day
    . and my legs feel like bits of wood.

KAPILA: Right! Ho—Ho...
(*Pulls the cart to a halt. They get down. She slips but Devadatta
supports her.*)

PADMINI: What a terrible road. Nothing but potholes and rocks.
    But one didn't feel a thing in the cart! You drove it so gently—
    almost made it float. I remember when Devadatta took me
    in a cart. That was soon after our marriage. I insisted on being
    shown the lake outside the city. So we started, only the two
    of us and Devadatta driving—against my advice, I must say.
    And we didn't even cross the city-gates. The oxen took
    everything except the road. He only had to pull to the right,
    and off they would rush to the left! I've never laughed so
    much in my life. But of course he got very angry, so we had
    to go back home straight!
(*Laughs. But Kapila and Devadatta don't join in.*)
    Kapila, what's that glorious tree there? That one, covered with
    flowers?

KAPILA: Oh that! That's called the Fortunate Lady's flower—that
    means a married woman...

PADMINI: I know! But why do they call it that?

KAPILA: Wait. I'll bring you a flower. Then you'll see.
(*Goes out.*)

PADMINI (*watching him, aside*): How he climbs—like an ape.
Before I could even say 'yes', he had taken off his shirt, pulled
his *dhoti* up and swung up the branch. And what an ethereal
shape! Such a broad back: like an ocean with muscles rippling
across it—and then that small, feminine waist which looks so
helpless.

DEVADATTA (*aside*): She had so much to talk about all day, she
couldn't wait for breath. Now, not a word.

PADMINI (*aside*): He is like a Celestial Being reborn as a hunter.
How his body sways, his limbs curve—It's a dance almost.

DEVADATTA (*aside*): And why should I blame her? It's his strong
body—his manly muscles. And to think I had never *ever*
noticed them all these years! I was an innocent—an absolute
baby.

PADMINI (*aside*): No woman could resist him.

DEVADATTA (*aside*): No woman could resist him—and what does
it matter that she's married? What a fool I've been. All these
days I only saw that pleading in his eyes stretching out its
arms, begging for a favour. But never looked in her eyes.
And when I did, took the whites of her eyes for their real
depth. Only now I see the depths. Now I see these flames
leaping up from those depths. Now! So late! Don't turn
away now, Devadatta, look at her. Look at those yellow,
purple flames. Look how she's pouring her soul into his
mould. Look! Let your guts burn out. Let your lungs turn to
ash, but don't turn away. Look and don't scream. Strangle
your agony. But look deep into these eyes—look until those
peacock flames burn out the blindness in you. Don't be a
coward now.

PADMINI (*aside*): How long can one go on like this? How long?
How long? If Devadatta notices...
(*Looks at Devadatta. He is looking at her already and their eyes
meet. Both look away.*)

PADMINI (*aloud*): There he comes. All I wanted was one flower and he's brought a heap.

(*Kapila comes in, miming a whole load of flowers in his arms and hands. He pours them out in front of her.*)

KAPILA: Here you are. The Fortunate Lady's flowers.

PADMINI: And why a 'Fortunate Lady', pray?

KAPILA: Because it has all the marks of marriage a woman puts on. The yellow on the petals. Then that red round patch at the bottom of the petals, like on your foreheads. Then, here, that thin saffron line, like in the parting of your hair. Then— uhm...oh yes—here near the stem a row of black dots, like a necklace of black beads—

PADMINI: What imagination! (*To Devadatta.*) You should put it in your poetry. It's good for a simile.

DEVADATTA: Shall we go? It's quite late.

PADMINI: Let's stay. I have been sitting in that cart for I don't know how long. I didn't know the road to Ujjain was so enchanting.

KAPILA: The others take a longer route. This is a more wooded area, so very few come this way. But I like this better. Besides, it's fifteen miles shorter.

PADMINI: I wouldn't have minded even if it were fifteen miles longer. It's like a garden.

KAPILA: Isn't it? Look there, do you see it? That's the river Bhargavi. The poet Vyasa had a hermitage on its banks. There's a temple of Rudra there now.

DEVADATTA (*suddenly awake*): A temple of Rudra?

KAPILA: Yes, It's beautiful. And—there—beyond that hill is a temple of Kali.

(*Two stage-hands come and hold up a half-curtain in the corner to which he points. The curtain has a picture of Goddess Kali on it. The Bhagavata places a sword in front of it.*)

It was very prosperous once. But now it's quite dilapidated.

DEVADATTA (*as though in a trance*): The temple of Rudra!

KAPILA: Yes, that's old too. But not half as ruined as the Kali temple. We can have a look if you like.

PADMINI: Yes, let's.

DEVADATTA: Why don't you go and see the Kali temple first?

KAPILA: No, that's quite terrible. I saw it once: bats, snakes, all sorts of poisonous insects—and no proper road. We can go to the Rudra temple, though. It's nearer.

PADMINI: Come on. Let's go.

DEVADATTA: You two go. I won't come.

PADMINI (*pause*): And you?

DEVADATTA: I'll stay here and watch the cart.

KAPILA: But there's no fear of thieves here. (*Sensing the tension.*) Or else. I'll stay here.

DEVADATTA: No, no. You two go. I'm also a little tired.

PADMINI (*aside*): He has started it again. Another tantrum. Let him. What do I care? (*Aloud.*) Come, Kapila, we'll go.

KAPILA: But perhaps in your condition...

PADMINI (*exploding*): Why are you two hounding me with this condition? If you don't want to come, say so. Don't make excuses...

KAPILA: Devadatta, it's not very far. You come too.

DEVADATTA: I told you to go. Don't force me, please.

PADMINI: Let's not go. I don't want the two of you to suffer for my sake.

DEVADATTA (*to Kapila*): Go.

KAPILA (*he has no choice*): Come. We'll be back soon.
(*Kapila and Padmini go out.*)

DEVADATTA: Good-bye, Kapila. Good-bye, Padmini. May Lord Rudra bless you. You are two pieces of my heart—Live happily

together. I shall find my eternal happiness in that thought.
(*Agonized.*) Give me strength, Lord Rudra. My father, give me
courage. I'm already trembling, I'd never thought I would be
so afraid. Give me courage, Father, strengthen me.
(*He walks to the temple of Kali. It's a steep and difficult climb. He
is exhausted by the time he reaches the temple. He prostrates himself
before the goddess.*)
Bhavani, Bhairavi, Kali, Durga, Mahamaya, Mother of all
Nature, I had forgotten my promise to you. Forgive me,
Mother. You fulfilled the deepest craving of my life. You gave
me Padmini—and I forgot my word. Forgive me, for I'm here
now to carry out my promise.
(*Picks up the sword.*)
Great indeed is your mercy. Even in this lonely place some
devotee of yours—a hunter perhaps or a tribesman—has left
this weapon. Who knows how many lives this weapon has
sacrificed to you. (*Screaming.*) Here, Mother Kali, here's
another. My head. Take it, Mother, accept this little offering
of my head.
(*Cuts off his head. Not an easy thing to do. He struggles, groans,
writhes. Ultimately succeeds in killing himself.
A long silence. Padmini and Kapila return to the cart.*)
PADMINI (*enters talking*):...he should have come. How thrilling
it was! Heavenly! But of course he has no enthusiasm for
these things. After all...
(*Notices Devadatta isn't there.*)
Where's Devadatta?
(*They look around.*)
He said he'd stay here!
KAPILA (*calls*): Devadatta—Devadatta—
PADMINI: He's probably somewhere around. Where will he go? He
has the tenderest feet on earth. They manage to get blisters,
corns, cuts, boils and wounds without any effort.

KAPILA (*calls*): Devadatta.

PADMINI: Why are you shouting? Sit down. He'll come.

(*Kapila inspects the surrounding area. Gives a gasp of surprise.*) What's it?

KAPILA: His footprints. He has obviously gone in that direction. (*Pause.*) But—that's where the Kali temple is!

PADMINI: You don't mean he's gone there! How absurd!

KAPILA: You stay here. I'll bring him back.

PADMINI: But why do you have to go? There's nothing to fear in this broad daylight!

KAPILA (*hurrying off*): It's very thickly wooded there. If he gets lost, he'll have to spend the whole night in the jungle. You stay here. I'll come back in no time.

(*Runs out.*)

PADMINI (*exasperated*): He's gone! Really, he seems more worried about Devadatta than me.

(*She sits down. Kapila goes to the Kali temple—but naturally faster than Devadatta did. He sees the body and his mouth half opens in a scream. He runs to Devadatta and kneels beside him. Lifts his truncated head and moans.*)

KAPILA: You've cut off your head! You've cut off your head! Oh my dear friend, my brother, what have you done? Were you so angry with me? Did you feel such contempt for me, such abhorrence? And in your anger you forgot that I was ready to die for you? If you had asked me to jump into fire, I would have done it. If you had asked me to leave the country, I would have done it. If you had asked me to go and drown in a river, I would have accepted. Did you despise me so much that you couldn't ask me that? I did wrong. But you know I don't have the intelligence to know what else I should have done. I couldn't think—and so you've pushed me away? No, Devadatta, I can't live without you. I can't breathe without you. Devadatta, my brother, my guru, my friend...

(*Picks up the sword.*)

You spurned me in this world. Accept me as your brother at least in the next. Here, friend, here I come. As always, I follow in your footsteps.

(*Cuts off his head. It's an easier death this time. Padmini, who has been still till now, moves.*)

PADMINI: Where are they? Now Kapila's disappeared too. He couldn't still be searching for him. That's not possible. Devadatta's too weak to have gone far. They must have met. Perhaps they're sitting now, chatting as in the old days. For once, no bother of a wife around. No, more likely Devadatta's sulking. He's probably tearing poor Kapila to shreds by just being silent and grumpy. Yes, that would be more like him.

(*Pause.*)

It's almost dark. And they aren't back. Shameless men—to leave me alone like this here!
No, it's no use sitting here any longer. I had better go and look for them. If I die of a snake-bite on the way, serve them right. Or perhaps, so much the better for them.

(*Walks to the temple, slowly. Rubs her eyes when she reaches there.*)

How dark it is! Can't see a thing. (*Calls.*) Kapila—Kapila— Devadatta isn't here either. What shall I do here? At this time of the night! Alone! (*Listens.*) What's that? Some wild beast. A hyena! It's right outside—what shall I do if it comes in? Ah! It's gone. Mother Kali, only you can protect me now.

(*Stumbles over the bodies.*)

What's this? What's this?

(*Stares at the bodies and then lets out a terrified scream.*)

Oh God! What's this? Both! Both gone! And didn't even think of me before they went? What shall I do? What shall I do? Oh, Devadatta, what did I do that you left me alone in this state? Was that how much you loved me? And you, Kapila, who looked at me with dog's eyes, you too! How selfish you

are, you men, and how thoughtless! What shall I do now?
Where shall I go? How can I go home?
(*Pause.*)
　　Home? And what shall I say when I get there? What shall I
say happened? And who'll believe me? They'll all say the two
fought and died for this whore. They're bound to say it. Then
what'll happen to me? No, Mother Kali, no, it's too horrible
to think of. No! Kapila's gone, Devadatta's gone. Let me go
with them.
(*Picks up the sword.*)
　　I don't have the strength to hack off my head. But what does
it matter how I die, Mother? You don't care. It's the same to
you—another offering! All right. Have it then. Here's another
offering for you.
(*Lifts the sword and puts its point on her breast when, from behind
the curtain, the goddess's voice is heard.*)
VOICE: Hey...
(*Padmini freezes.*)
　　Put it down! Put down that sword!
(*Padmini jumps up in fright and, throwing the sword aside, tries
to run out of the temple. Then stops.*)
PADMINI: Who's that?
(*No reply.*)
　　Who's that?
(*A tremendous noise of drums. Padmini shuts her eyes in terror.
Behind the curtain one sees the uplifted blood-red palms of the
goddess. The curtain is lowered and taken away and one sees a
terrifying figure, her arms stretched out, her mouth wide open with
the tongue lolling out. The drums stop and as the goddess drops her
arms and shuts her mouth, it becomes clear she has been yawning.*)
KALI (*completes the yawn*): All right. Open your eyes and be quick.
　　Don't waste time.
(*Padmini opens her eyes and sees the goddess. She runs and falls
at her feet.*)

PADMINI: Mother—Kali...

KALI (*sleepy*): Yes, it's me. There was a time—many years ago—when at this hour they would have the *mangalarati*. The devotees used to make a deafening racket with drums and conch-shells and cymbals. So I used to be wide awake around now. I've lost the habit. (*Yawns.*) Right. What do you want? Tell me. I'm pleased with you.

PADMINI: Save me, Mother...

KALI: I know. I've done that already.

PADMINI: Do you call this saving, Mother of all Nature? I can't show my face to anyone in the world. I can't...

KALI (*a little testily*): Yes, yes, you've said that once. No need to repeat yourself. Now do as I tell you. Put these heads back properly. Attach them to their bodies and then press that sword on their necks. They'll come up alive. Is that enough?

PADMINI: Mother, you are our breath, you are our bread—and—water...

KALI: Skip it! Do as I told you. And quickly. I'm collapsing with sleep.

PADMINI (*hesitating*): May I ask a question?

KALI: If it's not too long.

PADMINI: Can there ever be anything you don't already know, Mother? The past and the future are mere specks in your palm. Then why didn't you stop Devadatta when he came here? Why didn't you stop Kapila? If you'd saved either of them, I would have been spared all this terror, this agony. Why did you wait so long?

KALI (*surprised*): Is that all you can think of now?

PADMINI: Mother...

KALI: I've never seen anyone like you.

PADMINI: How could one possibly hide anything from you, Mother?

KALI: That's true enough.

PADMINI: Then why didn't you stop them?

KALI: Actually if it hadn't been that I was so sleepy, I would have thrown them out by the scruff of their necks.

PADMINI: But why?

KALI: The rascals! They were lying to their last breaths. That fellow Devadatta—he had once promised his head to Rudra and his arms to me! Think of it—head to him and arms to me! Then because you insisted on going to the Rudra temple, he comes here and offers his head. Nobly too—wants to keep his word, he says—no other reason!

Then this Kapila, died right in front of me—but 'for his friend'. Mind you! Didn't even have the courtesy to refer to me. And what lies! Says he is dying for friendship. He must have known perfectly well he would be accused of killing Devadatta for you. Do you think he wouldn't have grabbed you if it hadn't been for that fear? But till his last breath— 'Oh my friend! My dear brother!'

Only you spoke the truth.

PADMINI: It's all your grace, Mother...

KALI: Don't drag me into it. I had nothing to do with it. You spoke the truth because you're selfish, that's all. Now don't go on. Do what I told you and shut your eyes.

PADMINI: Yes, Mother...

(*Eagerly, Padmini attaches the severed heads to the bodies of the men. But in her excitement she mixes them up so that Devadatta's head goes to Kapila's body and vice versa. Then presses the sword on their necks, does namaskara to the goddess, walks downstage and stands with her back to the goddess, her eyes shut tight.*)

PADMINI: I'm ready, Mother.

KALI (*in a resigned tone*): My dear daughter, there should be a limit even to honesty. Anyway, so be it!

(Again the drums. The curtain is held up again and the goddess disappears behind it. During the following scene, the stage-hands, the curtain as well as the goddess leave the stage.
Padmini stands immobile with her eyes shut. The drums stop. A long silence follows. The dead bodies move. Their breathing becomes loud and laboured. They sit up, slowly, stiffly. Their movement is mechanical, as though blood-circulation has not started properly yet. They feel their own arms, heads and bodies, and look around, bewildered.
Henceforth the person with the head of Devadatta will be called Devadatta. Similarly with Kapila.
They stand up. It's not easy and they reel around a bit.
Padmini is still.)

DEVADATTA: What—happened?

KAPILA: What happened?
(Padmini opens her eyes, but she still doesn't dare to look at them.)

PADMINI: Devadatta's voice! Kapila's voice!
    (Screaming with joy.) Kapila! Devadatta!
(Turns and runs to them. Then suddenly stops and stands paralysed.)

KAPILA: Who...?

DEVADATTA: Padmini?

KAPILA: What—happened? My head—Ooh! It feels so heavy!

DEVADATTA: My body—seems to weigh—a ton.

PADMINI *(running around in confusion)*: What have I done? What have I done? What have I done? Mother Kali, only you can save me now—only you can help me—What have I done? What have I done? What should I do? Mother, Mother...

DEVADATTA *(a little more alive)*: Why are you—crying?

KAPILA: What's—wrong?

PADMINI: What shall I tell you, Devadatta? How can I explain it, Kapila? You cut off your heads. But the goddess gave you

life—but—I—I—in the dark…Mother, only you can protect
me now—Mother! I—mixed up your heads—I mixed them
up! Forgive me—I don't deserve to live—forgive me…

KAPILA (*looking at Devadatta*): You mixed up…

DEVADATTA: …the heads?

(*They stare at each other. Then burst into laughter. She doesn't
know how to react. Watches them. Then starts laughing.*)

DEVADATTA: Mixed-up heads!

KAPILA: Heads mixed-up!

DEVADATTA: Exchanged heads!

KAPILA: Heads exchanged!

DEVADATTA: How fantastic! All these years we were only friends!

KAPILA: Now we are blood-relations! Body-relations! (*Laughing.*)
      What a gift!

DEVADATTA: Forgive you? We must thank you…

KAPILA: We'll never be able to thank you—enough…

DEVADATTA: Exchanged heads!

(*They roar with laughter. Then all three hold hands and run round
in a circle, singing.*)

ALL THREE (*together*):
      What a good mix!
      No more tricks!
      Is this one that
      Or that one this?
      Ho! Ho!

(*They sing this over and over again until they collapse on the
floor.*)

KAPILA: Oooh—I'm finished!

PADMINI: …Dead!

DEVADATTA: Nothing like this could have ever happened before.

PADMINI: You know, seeing you two with your heads off was bad

enough. But when you got up it was terrible! I almost died
of fright...
(*They laugh.*)

KAPILA: No one will believe us if we tell them.

PADMINI (*suddenly*): We won't tell anyone.

DEVADATTA: We'll keep our secrets inside us.

PADMINI: 'Inside us' is right.
(*Laughter.*)

KAPILA: But how can we not tell? They'll know soon...

DEVADATTA: No one'll know.

KAPILA: I'm sure they'll...

DEVADATTA: I'll take any bet.

KAPILA: But how's that possible?

DEVADATTA: You'll see. Why worry now?

PADMINI: Come. Let's go.

KAPILA: It's late.

DEVADATTA: No Ujjain now. We go back home!

KAPILA: Absolutely.

PADMINI: This Ujjain will last us a lifetime. Come.
(*They get up. Every now and then someone laughs and then all
burst out together.*)

PADMINI: Devadatta, I really don't know how we're going to keep
this from your parents. They'll guess as soon as they see you
bare-bodied.

DEVADATTA: They won't, I tell you. They take us too much for
granted.

KAPILA: What do you mean?

DEVADATTA: Who ever pays attention to a person he sees every
day?

KAPILA: I don't mean that...

PADMINI: I'm not so sure. I'm afraid I'll get the blame for it ultimately.

DEVADATTA: Stop worrying! I tell you it...

KAPILA: But what has she got to do with you now?

DEVADATTA (*stops*): What do you mean?

KAPILA: I mean Padmini must come home with me, shouldn't she? She's my wife, so she must...

(*Exclamations from Devadatta and Padmini.*)

PADMINI: What are you talking about, Kapila?

KAPILA (*explaining*): I mean, you are Devadatta's wife. I have Devadatta's body now. So you have to be my wife.

PADMINI: Shut up!

DEVADATTA: Don't blather like an idiot! I am Devadatta...

PADMINI: Aren't you ashamed of yourself?

KAPILA: But why, Padmini? I have Devadatta's body now...

DEVADATTA: We know that. You don't have to repeat yourself like a parrot. According to the Shastras, the head is the sign of a man...

KAPILA (*angry now*): That may be. But the question now is simply this: Whose wife is she? (*Raising his right hand.*) This is the hand that accepted her at the wedding. This the body she's lived with all these months. And the child she's carrying is the seed of this body.

PADMINI (*frightened by the logic*): No, no, no. It's not possible. It's not. (*Running to Devadatta.*) It's not, Devadatta.

DEVADATTA: Of course, it isn't, my dear. He is ignorant. (*To Kapila.*) When one accepts a partner in marriage, with the holy fire as one's witness, one accepts a person, not a body. She didn't marry Devadatta's body, she married Devadatta— the person.

KAPILA: If that's your argument, I have Devadatta's body, so I am Devadatta—the person.

DEVADATTA: Listen to me. Of all the human limbs the topmost—in position as well as in importance—is the head. I have Devadatta's head and it follows that I am Devadatta. According to the Sacred Texts...

KAPILA: Don't tell me about your Sacred Texts. You can always twist them to suit your needs. She married Devadatta's body with the holy fire as her witness and that's enough for me.

DEVADATTA (laughs): Did you hear that, Padmini? He claims to be Devadatta and yet he scorns the Texts. You think Devadatta would ever do that?

KAPILA: You can quote as many Texts as you like, I don't give a nail. Come on, Padmini...

(Takes a step towards her. But Devadatta steps in between.)

DEVADATTA: Take care!

PADMINI: Come, Devadatta. It's no use arguing with this rascal. Let's go.

DEVADATTA: Come on.

KAPILA (stepping between them): Where are you taking my wife, friend?

DEVADATTA: Will you get out of our way or should...

KAPILA: It was you who got in my way.

DEVADATTA (pushing Kapila aside): Get away, you pig.

KAPILA (triumphant): He's using force! And what language! Padmini, think! Would Devadatta ever have acted like this? This is Kapila's violence.

DEVADATTA: Come, Padmini.

KAPILA: Go. But do you think I'll stay put while you run away with my wife? Where will you go? How far can you go? Only to the city, after all. I'll follow you there. I'll kick up a row in the streets. Let's see what happens then.

(*Devadatta stops.*)

PADMINI: Let him scream away. Don't pay him any attention.

DEVADATTA: No. He's right. This has to be solved here. It'll create a scandal in the city.

PADMINI: But who'll listen to him? Everyone will take you for Devadatta by your face.

KAPILA: Ha! You think the people in Dharmapura don't know my body, do you? They've seen me a thousand times in the wrestling pit. I've got I don't know how many awards for body-building. Let's see whom they believe.

PADMINI (*pleading*): Why are you tormenting us like this? For so many years you have been our friend, accepted our hospitality...

KAPILA: I know what you want, Padmini. Devadatta's clever head and Kapila's strong body...

PADMINI: Shut up, you brute.

DEVADATTA: Suppose she did. There's nothing wrong in it. It's natural for a woman to feel attracted to a fine figure of a man.

KAPILA: I know it is. But that doesn't mean she can just go and live with a man who's not her husband. That's not right.

PADMINI (*crying out*): How can we get rid of this scoundrel! Let's go—Let's go anywhere—to the woods—to the desert anywhere you like.

KAPILA: You'll have to kill me before you'll really escape me. You could. I don't have the strength to resist Kapila.

PADMINI (*using a new argument*): But I gave you life—

KAPILA: That was no favour. If you hadn't, you would have been a widow now. Actually he should be grateful to me because my wife saved his life. Instead, he's trying to snatch you away.
(*Padmini moans in agony.*)

DEVADATTA: This way we won't get anywhere, Kapila.

KAPILA: Call me Devadatta.

DEVADATTA: Whatever you are, this is no way to solve the problem.

KAPILA: Of course not. If marriage were a contract, it would be. But how can Padmini's fancy be taken as the solution?

DEVADATTA: Then what is the solution to this problem?
(*They all freeze.*)

BHAGAVATA: What? What indeed is the solution to this problem, which holds the entire future of these three unfortunate beings in a balance? Must their fate remain a mystery? And if so shall we not be insulting our audience by tying a question mark round its neck and bidding it good-bye? We have to face the problem. But it's a deep one and the answer must be sought with the greatest caution. Haste would be disastrous. So there's a break of ten minutes now. Please have some tea, ponder over this situation and come back with your own solutions. We shall then continue with our enquiry.
(*The stage-hands hold a white curtain in front of the frozen threesome, while the Bhagavata and others relax and sip tea.*)

Act Two

The white curtain is removed.

BHAGAVATA: What? What indeed is the solution to this problem, which holds the entire future of these three unfortunate beings in a balance?

Way back in the ages, when King Vikrama was ruling the world, shining in glory like the earth's challenge to the sun, he was asked the same question by the demon Vetala. And the king offered a solution even without, as it were, batting an eyelid. But will his rational, logical answer backed by the Sacred Texts appeal to our audience?

(*Sings.*)

> The future pointed out by the tongue
> safe inside the skull is not acceptable to us.
> We must read the forehead which Brahma
> has disconnected from the entrails.
> We must unravel the net on the palm
> disclaimed by the brain.
> We must plumb the hidden depths of the
> rivers running under our veins.

Yes, that would be the right thing to do.

So our three unfortunate friends went to a great *rishi* in search of a solution to their problem. And the *rishi*—

remembering perhaps what King Vikrama had said—gave the verdict:

(*In a loud, sonorous voice.*)

As the heavenly Kalpa Vriksha is supreme among trees, so is the head among human limbs. Therefore the man with Devadatta's head is indeed Devadatta and he is the rightful husband of Padmini.

(*The three spring to life. Devadatta and Padmini scream with delight and move to one corner of the stage, laughing and dancing. Kapila, brokenhearted, drags his feet to the other corner.*)

DEVADATTA (*embracing Padmini*): My Padmini...my lovely Padmini...

PADMINI: My King—My Master...

DEVADATTA: My little lightning...

PADMINI: The light of my joy...

DEVADATTA: The flower of my palm...

PADMINI: My celestial-bodied Gandharva... My sun-faced Indra...

DEVADATTA: My Queen of Indra's Court...

PADMINI (*caressing his shoulders*): Come. Let's go. Let's go quickly. Where the earth is soft and the green grass plays the swing.

DEVADATTA: Let us. Where the banyan spreads a canopy and curtains off the skies.

PADMINI: What a wide chest. What other canopy do I need?

DEVADATTA: My soft, swaying Padmini. What other swing do I want?

PADMINI: My Devadatta comes like a bridegroom with the jewellery of a new body...

DEVADATTA (*a manly laugh*): And who should wear the jewellery but the eager bride?

PADMINI: Let's go. (*Pause.*) Wait. (*She runs to Kapila.*) Don't be sad, Kapila. We shall meet again, shan't we? (*In a low voice, so Devadatta can't hear.*) It's my duty to go with Devadatta. But remember I'm going with your body. Let that cheer you up. (*Goes back to Devadatta.*) Good-bye, Kapila.

DEVADATTA: Good-bye.

(*They go out, laughing, rubbing against each other. Kapila stands mute for a while. Then moves.*)

BHAGAVATA: Kapila—Kapila...(*No reply.*) Don't grieve. It's fate, Kapila, and...

KAPILA: Kapila? What? Me? Why am I Kapila?
(*Exits.*)

BHAGAVATA: So the roads diverged. Kapila went into the forest and disappeared. He never saw Dharmapura again. In fact, he never felt the wind of any city again. As for Devadatta and Padmini, they returned to Dharmapura and plunged into the joys of married life.

(*Padmini enters and sits. She is stitching clothes, Devadatta comes. He is carrying in his hands two large dolls—which could be played by two children. The dolls are dressed in a way which makes it impossible to decide their sex.*
Devadatta comes in quietly and stands behind Padmini.)

DEVADATTA: Hey!

PADMINI (*startled*): Oh! Really, Devadatta. You startled me. The needle pricked me! Look, my finger's bleeding.

DEVADATTA: Tut—Tut! Is it really? Put it in my mouth. I'll suck it.

PADMINI: No, thanks. I'll suck it myself. (*Sees the dolls.*) How pretty! Whose are these?

DEVADATTA: Whose? Ours, of course! The guest is arriving soon. He must have playmates.

PADMINI: But the guest won't be coming for months yet, silly, and...

DEVADATTA: I know he isn't, but you can't get dolls like these any time you like! These are special dolls from the Ujjain fair.

PADMINI: They are lovely! (*Hugs the dolls.*) They look almost alive—such shining eyes—such delicate cheeks. (*Kisses them.*) Now sit down and tell me everything that happened at the fair. You wouldn't take me with you...

DEVADATTA: How could I—in your condition? I went only because you insisted you wanted to keep your word. But I'm glad I went. A very funny thing happened. There was a wrestling pit and a wrestler from Kamarupa was challenging people to fight him. I don't know what got into me. Before I'd even realized it, I had stripped and jumped into the pit.

PADMINI (*fondling the dolls*): You didn't! You've never ever wrestled before...

DEVADATTA: Didn't think of anything. I felt 'inspired'! Within a couple of minutes, I had pinned him to the ground.

PADMINI (*laughs out*): What would your father say if he heard of this?

DEVADATTA: My few acquaintances there were quite amazed.

PADMINI (*caressing his arm*): That day in the gymnasium you defeated the champion in a sword-fight. Now this! Don't overdo it: people may start suspecting.

DEVADATTA: Of course they won't. I was standing there bare-bodied and not a soul suspected. A friend even asked me if I'd learnt it from Kapila.

PADMINI: You have, after all!
(*They laugh.*)

DEVADATTA: You know, I'd always thought one had to use one's brains while wrestling or fencing or swimming. But this body just doesn't wait for thoughts—it acts!

PADMINI: Fabulous body—fabulous brain—fabulous Devadatta.

DEVADATTA: I have been running around all these days without even proper sleep and yet I don't feel a bit tired. (*Jumps up.*) Come on, we'll have a picnic by the lake. I feel like a good, long swim.

PADMINI (*mocking*): In my condition?

DEVADATTA: I didn't ask you to swim. You sit there and enjoy the scenery. Once our son's born, I'll teach you to swim too.

PADMINI: You go on about it being a son. What if it's a daughter?

DEVADATTA: If she's a daughter like you, I'll teach the two of you together.

PADMINI: Ready!
(*He pulls her to him.*)
      Now—now—what about the picnic?

DEVADATTA: Quite right. First things first.

PADMINI (*pause*): Devadatta...

DEVADATTA: Yes?

PADMINI: Why do you—have to apply that sandal oil on your body?

DEVADATTA: I like it.

PADMINI: I know, but...

DEVADATTA: What?

PADMINI (*hesitating*): Your body had that strong, male smell before—I liked it.

DEVADATTA: But I've been using sandal oil since I was a child!

PADMINI: I don't mean that. But—when we came back from the temple of Kali—you used to smell so manly...

DEVADATTA: You mean that unwashed, sweaty smell Kapila had? (*Incredulous.*) You liked that?

PADMINI (*pause. Then lightly*): It was just a thought. Come on, let's start. We'll be late.
(*They go out. A long silence.*)

DOLL I: Not a bad house, I would say.

DOLL II: Could have been worse. I was a little worried.

DOLL I: This is the least we deserved. Actually we should have got a palace. A real palace!

DOLL II: And a prince to play with. A real prince!

DOLL I: How the children looked at us at the fair! How their eyes glowed!

DOLL II: How their mothers stared at us! How their mouths watered!

DOLL I: Only those beastly men turned up their noses! 'Expensive! Too expensive!'

DOLL II: Presuming to judge us! Who do they think they are!

DOLL I: Only a prince would be worthy of us.

DOLL II: We should be dusted every day...

DOLL I: ...dressed in silk...

DOLL II: ...seated on a cushioned shelf...

DOLL I: ...given new clothes every week.

DOLL II: If the doll-maker had any sense, he'd never have sold us.

DOLL I: If he had any brains, he should never have given us to this man...

DOLL II: ...with his rough labourer's hands.

DOLL I: Palms like wood...

DOLL II: A grip like a vice...

DOLL I: My arms are still aching.

DOLL II: He doesn't deserve us, the peasant.
(*Devadatta comes running in, tosses the dolls in the air, catches them and kisses them.*)

DEVADATTA: My dolls, your prince has arrived! The prince has come!

DOLL I (*in agony*): Brute! An absolute brute!

DOLL II (*in agony*): Beast! A complete beast!

DEVADATTA (*runs to the Bhagavata*): Here, Bhagavata Sir, take these sweets. You must come to the feast tomorrow at our house.

BHAGAVATA: What's it for?

DEVADATTA: Haven't you heard? I've got a son like a gem—a son like a rose—Yippeee...

(*He goes out dancing some* Lezim *steps. A long silence.*)

DOLL I: Is that little satan asleep yet?

DOLL II: Think so. God! It's killing me...

DOLL I: ...crying, all day...

DOLL II: ...making a mess every fifteen minutes.

DOLL I: What have we come to! One should never trust God.

DOLL II: It's our fault. We should have been wary from the moment we saw that child in her dreams.

DOLL I: We should have noticed she was bloating day by day.

DOLL II: We should have suspected foul play then.

DOLL I: It wasn't our fault. How could we know she was hiding this thing inside her?

DOLL II: How she was swelling! Day by day! Week by week! As though someone were blowing air into her...

DOLL I: How ugly she looked...

DOLL II: ...not to her husband, though!

DOLL I: When they were alone, he would place his hand on her belly and say, 'Is he kicking now?'

DOLL II (*seriously*): We should have been on our guard.

DOLL I (*dispirited*): We should.

DOLL II: And then comes this little monster.

DOLL I: ...this lump of flesh...

DOLL II: It doesn't even have proper eyes or ears...

DOLL I: ...but it gets all the attention.

DOLL II (*in disgust*): Ugh...

DOLL I (*sick*): Awk...

(*Devadatta and Padmini enter with the child, for which a wooden doll may be used. They walk across the stage, engrossed in talking to and about the child, and go out.*)

DOLL I: A spider's built its web around my shoulders.

DOLL II: Yesterday a mouse nibbled at my toe.

DOLL I: The other day a cockroach ate my left eye.

DOLL II: Six months—and not a soul has come near us.

DOLL I: Six months—and not a hand has touched us.

DOLL II: Six months and we reach this state. What'll happen in a year's time?

(*Padmini and Devadatta enter.*)

PADMINI: Listen.

DEVADATTA: Yes.

PADMINI: You mustn't say 'no'—at least this time.

DEVADATTA: To what?

PADMINI: We'll take him to the lake.

DEVADATTA: In this cold?

PADMINI: What if it's cold? He's older now. There's no need to mollycoddle him. I grew up running around in heat and cold and rain—and nothing happened to me. I'm all right.

DEVADATTA: No, it's unnecessary trouble for everyone.

PADMINI: What do you mean trouble? What's happened to you these days? You sit at home all day. Never go out. You've forgotten all your swimming and sports.

DEVADATTA: I'm a Brahmin, Padmini. My duty...

PADMINI: I've heard all this!

DEVADATTA: It was fun the first few days because it was new. All that muscle and strength. But how long can one go on like that? I have a family tradition to maintain—the daily reading, writing and studies...

PADMINI: I don't know.

DEVADATTA (*affectionate*): Now look here, Padmini...
(*Puts his hand round her shoulder. She suddenly shudders.*)
Why? What happened?

PADMINI: Nothing—I don't know why—I suddenly had goose flesh.

(*Pause.*)

DEVADATTA (*withdrawing his hand*): Do you know where I've kept the copy of *Dharma Sindhu*? I've been looking for it.

PADMINI: I think I saw it on the shelf. Must be there...

(*Devadatta goes to Doll I, moves it aside and picks up the book. Doll I shudders.*)

DOLL II: Why? What happened?

DOLL I: He touched me, and...

DOLL II: Yes?

DOLL I: His palms! They were so rough once, when he first brought us here. Like a labourer's. But now they are soft— sickly soft—like a young girl's.

DOLL II: I know. I've noticed something too.

DOLL I: What?

DOLL II: His stomach. It was so tight and muscular. Now...

DOLL I: I know. It's soft and loose.

DOLL II: Do you think it'll swell up too?
(*They laugh.*)

DOLL I (*holding its hands in front of its stomach to suggest a swollen belly*): It'll swell a little...

DOLL II (*holding its hands a little farther in front*): —then more...

DOLL I (*even further*): —more and...

DOLL II (*even further*): —and more until...

DOLL I: ...if it's a woman...

DOLL II: ...there'll be a child...

DOLL I: ...and if it's a man...

DOLL II: BANG!

(*They roll with laughter. Padmini comes in with the child. She sings a lullaby.*)

PADMINI: Here comes a rider!
From what land does he come?
Oh his head a turban
with a long pearly tail.
Round his neck a garland
of virgin-white jasmines.
In his fist a sword
with a diamond-studded hilt.
The white-clad rider
rides a white charger
which spreads its tossing mane
against the western sky,
spreads its mane like breakers
against the western sky.
Sleep now, my baby
and see smiling dreams.
There he comes—here he is!
From which land does he come?
But why are the jasmines on his chest
red O so red?
What shine in his open eyes?
Pebbles O pebbles.
Why is his young body
cold O so cold?
The white horse gallops
across hills, streams and fields.
To what land does he gallop?
Nowhere O nowhere.

(*Half-way through the lullaby, Devadatta comes in and sits by Padmini's side, reading. They don't look at each other. At the end of the lullaby, they fall asleep.*)

DOLL I (*in a hushed voice*): Hey.

DOLL II: Yes?

DOLL I: Look.

DOLL II: Where?

DOLL I: Behind her eyelids. She is dreaming.

DOLL II: I don't see anything.

DOLL I: It's still hazy—hasn't started yet. Do you see it now?

DOLL II (*eagerly*): Yes, yes.
(*They stare at her.*)

DOLL I: A man.

DOLL II: But not her husband.

DOLL I: No, someone else.

DOLL II: Is this the one who came last night?

DOLL I: Yes—the same. But I couldn't see his face then.

DOLL II: You can now. Not very nice—rough. Like a labourer's. But he's got a nice body—looks soft.

DOLL I: Who do you think it is?

DOLL II: I—It's fading. (*Urgently.*) Remember the face!

DOLL I: It's fading—Oh! It's gone!

DOLL II: And she won't even remember it tomorrow.
(*Padmini and Devadatta sit up.*)

PADMINI: Are you ill?

DEVADATTA: Why?

PADMINI: You were moaning in your sleep last night.

DEVADATTA: Was I?

PADMINI: Aren't you feeling well?

DEVADATTA: Who? Me? I'm fine.
(*Gets up energetically to show how well he feels. Suddenly grabs his shoulder with a groan.*)

PADMINI: What's wrong? Tell me.

DEVADATTA (*avoiding her eyes*): Nothing. I went to the gymnasium yesterday morning. Then went swimming.

PADMINI: To the gymnasium? After all these years? But why?

DEVADATTA: I just felt like it. That's all. Don't go on about it.

PADMINI (*without irony*): Are you going again today?

DEVADATTA (*flares up*): No, I'm not. And there's no need to laugh. I know I've made a fool of myself by going there. I won't again.
(*Goes out. Long pause.*)

PADMINI: What are you afraid of, Devadatta? What does it matter that you are going soft again, that you are losing your muscles? I'm not going to be stupid again. Kapila's gone out of my life—forever. I won't let him come back again. (*Pause.*) Kapila? What could he be doing now? Where could he be? Could his body be fair still, and his face dark? (*Long pause.*) Devadatta changes. Kapila changes. And me?
(*Closes her eyes.*)

DOLL I: There he is again.

DOLL II: In the middle of the day?

DOLL I (*doubtful*): I'm not sure this is the usual visitor. This one looks rougher and darker.

DOLL II: It's him all right. Look at his face.

DOLL I: He goes to her...

DOLL II: ...very near her...

DOLL I (*in a whisper*): What's he going to do now?

DOLL II (*even more anxious*): What?
(*They watch.*)

DOLL I (*baffled*): But he's climbing a tree!

DOLL II (*almost a wail of disappointment*): He's dived into a river!

DOLL I: Is that all he came for?

DOLL II: It's going...

DOLL I: ...going...

DOLL II: Gone! Wretched dreams! They just tickle and fade away.

(*Padmini wakes up and mimes putting the crying child to sleep.*)

PADMINI (*suddenly vicious*): Change! Change! Change! Change! Change! The sand trickles. The water fills the pot. And the moon goes on swinging, swinging, swinging, from light to darkness to light.

(*Devadatta comes in. He is now completely changed to his original self.*)

DEVADATTA: A pundit's coming to see me. He wants me to explain some verses to him. Can you keep some sweets and lime-juice ready?

PADMINI: Yes. (*Pause.*) Did you hear...? The maid was telling me.

DEVADATTA: What?

PADMINI: Kapila's mother died this morning. (*Pause.*) Poor thing! She'd been bed-ridden all these years, ever since...

DEVADATTA (*snapping at her*): What did you expect me to do about it? (*Then embarrassed.*) Get the lime-juice ready soon.

(*They go out.*)

DOLL I: Each one to his fate!

DOLL II: Each one to her problems!

DOLL I: As the doll-maker used to say, 'What are things coming to!'

DOLL II: Especially last night—I mean—that dream...

DOLL I: Tut! Tut! One shouldn't talk about such things!

DOLL II: It was so shameless...

DOLL I: I said be quiet...

DOLL II: Honestly! The way they...

DOLL I: Look, if we must talk about it, let me tell.

DOLL II: You don't want to talk about it. So.

DOLL I: You don't understand a thing. They...

DOLL II: What do you know? Last night...

DOLL I: Let me! In that dream...

DOLL II: I'm...

DOLL I: Shut up!

DOLL II: You shut up!
(*They start arguing, then fighting. They roll on the ground, on top of each other, biting, scratching, hitting each other. They shout, scream and giggle. As they fight, the giggles become louder and more frantic. Their clothes get torn. At last they lie side by side panting, bursting with little giggles. Then they sit up. Padmini enters, looks at them.*)

PADMINI: Just look at the dolls! The baby's really torn them to rags. How long can we go on with them! (*Calls.*) Listen.

DEVADATTA (*entering*): Yes.

PADMINI: We must get new dolls for our baby. These are in tatters.

DEVADATTA: You're right. I hadn't noticed.

PADMINI: The Ujjain fair is to be held in another four days. Why don't you go and get new dolls there? If you start today you'll be there in time for it. It's unlucky to keep torn dolls at home.

DOLL I (*to Doll II*): Did you hear that? She wants to throw us out...

DOLL II: She wants new dolls.

DOLL I: The whore.

DOLL II: The bitch.

DOLL I: May her house burn down.

DOLL II: May her teeth fall out.

DEVADATTA (*to Padmini*): All right.
(*He picks them up by their collars.*)

DOLL I: See how he picks us up. Like stray puppies.

DOLL II: That ball of flesh will remain here. But it's the dung-heap for us.

DEVADATTA (*to Padmini*): It'll take me more than a week to go to Ujjain and come back. Shall I ask one of the neighbours to get them for us?

DOLL I (*to Devadatta*): You wretch—before you throw us out watch out for yourself.

DOLL II: Cover your wife before you start worrying about our rags.

PADMINI (*to Devadatta*): Who knows what sort of dolls they'll get for us? We must bring things ourselves for our baby.

DEVADATTA: But...

PADMINI: If you don't want to go, say so. Don't...

DEVADATTA: Shall I ask one of the servants to come and sleep here at night while I'm away?

PADMINI: No need. We are not in the middle of a forest.

DOLL I (*to Devadatta*): Watch out, you fool...

DOLL II: Refuse, you idiot...

DEVADATTA: All right. I'll start at once. Take care of yourself.
(*He drags the dolls out.*)

DOLL I: Villain...

DOLL II: Rascal...

DOLL I: Swine...

DOLL II: Bastard...

(*One can hear them screaming curses as he takes them out. Padmini stands watching him go. Then to the child in her arms.*)

PADMINI: My poor child, you haven't yet seen the witching fair of the dark forest, have you? Let's go and see it. How can I describe it to you? There's so much. Long before the sun rises, the shadows of twigs draw *alpanas* on the floor. The stars raise *arati* and go. Then the day dawns and the fun begins. The circus in the tree-tops and the cock-fights in a shower of feathers. And the dances! The tiger-dance, and the peacock-dance, and the dance of the sun's little feet with silver anklets on the river. In the heart of the forest stands the stately chariot of the shield-bearer. It's made of pure gold—rows of egrets pull it down the street, and rows of flames of the forest salute it with torches. Then the night comes, and our poor baby is tired. So we blow gently and out goes the moon. But before we leave, there's one more thing to do. Right outside the fair, watching it from a distance, stands the tree of the Fortunate Lady. It's an old tree, a close friend of ours. We have to say 'hello' to it. All right?

(*She goes out with the child. A long silence. Kapila enters. He too is as he was at the beginning of the play, tough and muscular.*)

BHAGAVATA: Who? Kapila?

KAPILA: Yes.

BHAGAVATA: It's such a long time since we met.

KAPILA: Yes.

BHAGAVATA: Where are you now?

KAPILA: Here.

BHAGAVATA: Here? In this jungle! It's difficult to believe any man could live here.

KAPILA: Beasts do. Why not men?

BHAGAVATA: What do you do?

KAPILA: Live.

BHAGAVATA: Have you had any news from the city?

KAPILA: Long ago. Father sent word asking me to come back. I said, 'I won't come. No need for you to come here either!' That's all.

BHAGAVATA: You mean—you don't know your father died last year? Also your mother...

KAPILA (*expressionless*): No.

BHAGAVATA: And Padmini has a son.

KAPILA: I see.

BHAGAVATA: Why this anger, Kapila?

KAPILA: What anger?

BHAGAVATA: It shows in the way you stand, you move.

KAPILA: All that is your poetry.
(*Moves on.*)

BHAGAVATA: Kapila! Kapila!
(*Kapila goes round the stage once. He mimes picking up an axe and felling a tree. A long silence. Only the soundless image of Kapila cutting the tree.*
Padmini enters, child in arms. She is scared and walks in rapidly. She sees Kapila and stands transfixed. Kapila doesn't see her for a while and when he does, stands paralysed. A long silence.)

KAPILA (*slowly*): You?

PADMINI: Yes.

KAPILA: Here?

PADMINI: My son had never laughed with the river or shivered in the wind or felt the thorn cut his feet. So I brought him out. I lost my way in the woods.

KAPILA: You shouldn't have lost it this far.

PADMINI: The wrong road stuck to my feet; wouldn't let go.

KAPILA: You shouldn't have lost it this far. Wild beasts—robbers—pathless paths—all sorts of dangers.

PADMINI: I asked the villagers. And the pilgrims. And the hunters. And the tribesmen. When there wasn't anyone any more, I asked myself. Everyone saw to it that I didn't lose the wrong road.

(*Pause.*)

KAPILA: Is that your son?

PADMINI: Yes. And yours.

KAPILA: Mine?

PADMINI: Your body gave him to me.

KAPILA: Mine? (*Erupting.*) Not mine. I'm Kapila, Padmini. I didn't accept it that day. But I accept it now, I'm Kapila.

PADMINI (*softly*): And how's Kapila?

(*The Bhagavata sings. The following is a prose rendering of the song.*)

BHAGAVATA: Once I spread my wings, and kicked away the earth and flew up. I covered the seven continents, the ten shores and measured the sky.

Now because you have a child at your breast, a husband on your thighs, the red of rust on the lips of your late-opening mouth, I pick a picture here, and there a card of fate, and live for the grace of a grain—an astrologer's bird.

KAPILA: Can I look at him?

PADMINI: That's why I brought him.

(*Kapila looks at the child.*)

KAPILA: What's wrong with me? You've come so far and I haven't even asked you to sit down. Why don't you go in and take a little rest?

(*She goes in with the child. He stands as in a daze. She comes out without the child.*)

KAPILA: Why...

PADMINI: I don't need any rest.

(*Long silence.*)

KAPILA: How are you?

PADMINI: I'm well. No illness, problems or difficulties.

KAPILA: Your son looks exactly like you.

PADMINI (*a slight pause*): And you.
(*Kapila doesn't reply.*)
   He has the same mole on his shoulder.

KAPILA: What mole?
(*She comes to him and points out the mole on his shoulder.*)

PADMINI: This one. Which other could it be? That's the only one
   you have on your shoulder.

KAPILA: Oh! I hadn't seen it. I don't much look at this body.

PADMINI (*quietly*): Do you despise it that much?
(*No reply.*)
   Why have you tortured it so?
(*Takes his hand in hers.*)
   When this went to you, it was so soft, like a prince's. These
   arms were so slender and fair. Look at them now. Why have
   you done this to yourself?

KAPILA: When this body came to me, it was like a corpse hanging
   by my head. It was a Brahmin's body after all: not made for
   the woods. I couldn't lift an axe without my elbows moaning.
   Couldn't run a length without my knees howling. I had no
   use for it. The moment it came to me, a war started between
   us.

PADMINI: And who won?

KAPILA: I did.

PADMINI: The head always wins, doesn't it?

KAPILA: Fortunately, yes. Now I can run ten miles and not stop
   for breath. I can swim through the monsoon floods and fell
   a banyan. The stomach used to rebel once. Now it digests
   what I give. If I don't, it doesn't complain.

PADMINI: Must the head always win?

KAPILA: That's why I am Kapila now. Kapila! Kapila with a body which fits his face.

PADMINI: What a good mix
No more tricks
Is this one that
Or that one this?
Do you remember the song we sang in the Kali temple?

KAPILA: So?

PADMINI: Nothing. I often remember it. It's almost my autobiography now. Kapila! Devadatta! Kapila with Devadatta's body! Devadatta with Kapila's body! Four men in a single lifetime.

KAPILA (*suddenly*): Why have you come away from him?

PADMINI: What do you want me to say?
(*They freeze.*)

BHAGAVATA: How could I make you understand? If Devadatta had changed overnight and had gone back to his original form, I would have forgotten you completely. But that's not how it happened. He changed day by day. Inch by inch. Hair by hair. Like the trickling sand. Like the water filling the pot. And as I saw him change, I couldn't get rid of you. That's what Padmini must tell Kapila. She should say more, without concealing anything. 'Kapila, if that *rishi* had given me to you, would I have gone back to Devadatta some day exactly like this?' But she doesn't say anything. She remains silent.

KAPILA (*to Padmini*): Why have you come here?

PADMINI: I had to see you.

KAPILA: Why? (*No reply.*) Why? Why did you have to come just when I thought I'd won this long and weary battle? Why did you have to pursue me just when I had succeeded in uprooting these memories? I am Kapila now. The rough and violent Kapila. Kapila without a crack between his head and his shoulders. What do you want now? Another head? Another suicide? Listen to me. Do me a favour. Go back. Back to Devadatta. He is your husband, the father of this child. Devadatta and Padmini! Devadatta and Padmini! A pair coupled with the holy fire as the witness. I have no place there, no peace, no salvation. So go. I beg of you. Go.

(*A long silence.*)

PADMINI: I will. If you want me to.

KAPILA (*almost a moan*): Oh God!

PADMINI: Why?

KAPILA: Nothing. Another memory—when I too was asked to go—Yes, go back. Now.

PADMINI: I will. But can I ask a little favour? My son's tired. He's asleep. He has been in my arms for several days now. Let him rest a while. As soon as he gets up I'll go. (*Laughs.*) Yes, you won, Kapila. Devadatta won too. But I—the better half of two bodies—I neither win nor lose. No, don't say anything. I know what you'll say and I've told myself that a thousand times. It's my fault. I mixed the heads up. I must suffer the consequences. I will. I'm sorry I came. I didn't think before I started. Couldn't. But at least until my child wakes up, may I sit here and look at you? Have my fill for the rest of my life? I won't speak a word.

(*Long pause.*)

KAPILA: What does it matter now whether you stay or go? You've done the damage. I had buried all those faceless memories in my skin. Now you've dug them up with your claws.

PADMINI: Why should one bury anything?

KAPILA: Why shouldn't one? Why should one tolerate this mad dance of incompleteness?

PADMINI: Whose incompleteness? Yours?

KAPILA: Yes, mine. One beats the body into shape, but one can't

beat away the memories trapped in it. Isn't that surprising?
That the body should have its own ghosts, its own secrets?
Memories of touch—memories of *a* touch—memories of a
body swaying in these arms, of a warm skin against this palm—
memories which one cannot recognize, cannot understand,
cannot even name because this head wasn't there when they
happened.

PADMINI: Kapila...

KAPILA (*without anger*): Why did you come? You came. You
touched me. You held my hand, and my body recognized your
touch. I have never touched you, but this body, this
appendage, laughed and flowered out in a festival of memories to which I'm an outcaste.

PADMINI: Poor Kapila!

KAPILA: Don't pity me.

PADMINI: Be quiet, stupid. Your body bathed in a river, swam and
danced in it. Shouldn't your head know what river it was,
what swim? Your head too must submerge in that river: the
flow must rumple your hair, run its tongue in your ears and
press your head to its bosom. Until that's done, you'll
continue to be incomplete.

(*Kapila raises his head and looks at her. She caresses his face, like
a blind person trying to imprint it on her finger-tips. Then she rests
her head on his chest.*)

My Kapila! My poor, poor Kapila! How needlessly you've
tortured yourself.

(*Kapila lifts her up and takes her in.*)

BHAGAVATA: You cannot engrave on water
　　　　　　nor wound it with a knife,
　　　　　　which is why
　　　　　　the river
　　　　　　has no fear
　　　　　　of memories.

FEMALE CHORUS: The river only feels the
                 pull of the waterfall.
                 She giggles, and tickles the rushes
                 on the bank, then turns
                 a top of dry leaves
                 in the navel of the whirlpool, weaves
                 a water-snake in the net of silver strands
                 in its green depths, frightens the frog
                 on the rug of moss, sticks and bamboo leaves,
                 sings, tosses, leaps and
                 sweeps on in a rush—

BHAGAVATA: While the scarecrow on the bank
           has a face fading
           on its mudpot head
           and a body torn
           with memories.

(*Devadatta enters. He is holding a sword in one hand, and in the other, two dolls, made of cloth.*)

BHAGAVATA: Who! Devadatta?

DEVADATTA: Where does Kapila live here?

BHAGAVATA: Uhm—well—Anyway, how are...you...

DEVADATTA: If you don't want to tell me, don't. I can find out for
    myself.

BHAGAVATA: There. Behind those trees.

DEVADATTA: How long has Padmini been here?

BHAGAVATA: About four or five days.

DEVADATTA: Amazing! Even a man like me found the road hard.
    But how quickly she covered it—and with a child in her
    arms.

BHAGAVATA: Devadatta...

(*Devadatta moves on.*)

    Devadatta moves on. There are only two words which make

sense to him now—Kapila and Padmini! Kapila and Padmini! The words sweep him along to the doorstep of Kapila's hut. But suddenly he stops. Until this moment he has been rearing to taste the blood of Kapila. But now he is still and calm.

(*Kapila comes out.*)

KAPILA: Come, Devadatta. I was waiting for you. I've been expecting you since yesterday. I have been coming out every half an hour to see if you'd arrived. Not from fear. Only eager.

(*Padmini comes out and stands watching them.*)

KAPILA (*to Devadatta*): You look exactly the same.

DEVADATTA (*laughs*): You too.

KAPILA (*points to the sword*): What's that?

DEVADATTA (*extending the hand which holds the dolls*): Dolls. For the child. I came home from the fair. There was no one there. So I came here.

(*Padmini steps forward and takes the dolls. But neither speaks. Padmini goes back to her place and stands clutching the dolls to her bosom.*)

KAPILA: Come in and rest a while. There'll always be time to talk later.

(*Devadatta shakes his head.*)

Why? Are you angry?

DEVADATTA: Not any more. (*Pause.*) Did my body bother you too much?

KAPILA: It wasn't made for this life. It resisted. It also had its revenge.

DEVADATTA: Did it?

KAPILA: Do you remember how I once used to envy you your poetry, your ability to imagine things? For me, the sky was the sky, and the tree only a tree. Your body gave me new

feelings, new words. I felt awake as I'd never before. Even
started writing poems. Very bad ones, I'm afraid.
(*They laugh.*)
There were times when I hated it for what it gave me.

DEVADATTA: I wanted your power but not your wildness. You lived
in hate—I in fear.

KAPILA: No, I was the one who was afraid.

DEVADATTA: What a good mix. No more tricks.
(*They laugh.*)
Tell me one thing. Do you really love Padmini?

KAPILA: Yes.

DEVADATTA: So do I.

KAPILA: I know.
(*Silence.*)
Devadatta, couldn't we all three live together—like the
Pandavas and Draupadi?

DEVADATTA: What do you think?
(*Silence. Padmini looks at them but doesn't say anything.*)

KAPILA (*laughs*): No, it can't be done.

DEVADATTA: That's why I brought this. (*Shows the sword.*) What
won't end has to be cut.

KAPILA: I got your body, but not your wisdom.

DEVADATTA: Where's your sword then?

KAPILA: A moment.
(*Goes in. Padmini stands looking at Devadatta. But he looks
somewhere far away.*)

BHAGAVATA: After sharing with Indra
        his wine
        his food
        his jokes
        I returned to the earth
        and saw from far—

a crack had appeared
in the earth's face—
exactly
like Indra's smile

(*Kapila returns with his sword. They take up positions.*)

KAPILA: Are you still in practice?

DEVADATTA: Of course not. But you'd learned well. And you?

KAPILA: I learnt again. But one's older now—slower at learning.

DEVADATTA (*pause*): You realize it's immaterial who's better with a sword now, don't you?

KAPILA: Yes, I do.

DEVADATTA: There's only one solution to this.

KAPILA: We must both die.

DEVADATTA: We must both die.

KAPILA: With what confidence we chopped off our heads in that temple! Now whose head—whose body—suicide or murder—nothing's clear.

DEVADATTA: No grounds for friendship now. No question of mercy. We must fight like lions and kill like cobras.

KAPILA: Let our heads roll to the very hands which cut them in the temple of Kali!

(*Music starts. The fight is stylized like a dance. Their swords don't touch. Even Padmini's reaction is like a dance.*)

BHAGAVATA (*sings*): Like cocks in a pit
                    we dance—he and I,
                    foot woven with foot
                    eye soldered to eye.
                    He knows and I know
                    all there's to be known:
                    the witch's burning thirst
                    burns for blood alone.
                    Hence this frozen smile,

which cracks and drips to earth,
and claw-knives, digging flesh
for piecemeal death.
The *rishi* who said 'Knowledge gives rise to forgiveness' had
no knowledge of death.
(*Kapila wounds Devadatta who falls to his feet and fights. He stabs
Kapila. Both fight on their knees, fall and die.*
A long silence. Padmini slowly comes and sits between the bodies.)

PADMINI: They burned, lived, fought, embraced and died. I stood
silent. If I'd said, 'Yes, I'll live with you both', perhaps they
would have been alive yet. But I couldn't say it. I couldn't say,
'Yes'. No, Kapila, no, Devadatta. I know it in my blood you
couldn't have lived together. You would've had to share not
only me but your bodies as well. Because you knew death you
died in each other's arms. You could only have lived ripping
each other to pieces. I had to drive you to death. You forgave
each other, but again, left me out.

BHAGAVATA (*without leaving his seat*): What is this? It's a sight to
freeze the blood in one's veins. What happened, child? Can
we help you?

PADMINI (*without looking at him*): Yes, please. My son is sleeping
in the hut. Take him under your care. Give him to the hunters
who live in this forest and tell them it's Kapila's son. They
loved Kapila and will bring the child up. Let the child grow
up in the forest with the rivers and the trees. When he's five
take him to the Revered Brahmin Vidyasagara of Dharmapura.
Tell him it's Devadatta's son.

BHAGAVATA: And you?

PADMINI: Make me a large funeral pyre. We are three.

BHAGAVATA: You mean you are performing *sati*? But why, child?

PADMINI (*puts the dolls on the ground*): Give these dolls to my son.
I won't see him. He may tempt me away from my path.

(*At a sign from the Bhagavata, two stage-hands come and place a curtain in front of Padmini.*)

> Kali, Mother of all Nature, you must have your joke even now. Other women can die praying that they should get the same husband in all the lives to come. You haven't left me even that little consolation.

(*Does* namaskara. *The stage-hands lift the curtain, slowly, very slowly, very slowly, as the song goes on. The curtain has a blazing fire painted on it. And as it is lifted, the flames seem to leap up. The female musicians sing a song. The following is a prose rendering of it.*)

FEMALE CHORUS (*sings*): Our sister is leaving in a palanquin of sandalwood. Her mattress is studded with rubies which burn and glow. She is decked in flowers which blossom on tinder-wood and whose petals are made of molten gold. How the garlands leap and cover her, aflame with love.

> The Fortunate Lady's procession goes up the street of laburnums, while the *makarandas* tie the pennants and the jacarandas hold the lights.

> Good-bye, dear sister. Go you without fear. The Lord of Death will be pleased with the offering of three coconuts.

BHAGAVATA (*picks up the dolls and comes downstage*): Thus Padmini became a *sati*. India is known for its *pativratas*, wives who dedicated their whole existence to the service of their husbands; but it would not be an exaggeration to say that no *pativrata* went in the way Padmini did. And yet no one knows the spot where she performed *sati*. If you ask the hunting tribes who dwell in these forests, they only point to a full-blossomed tree of the Fortunate Lady. They say that even now on full moon and on new moon nights, a song rises from the roots of the tree and fills the whole forest like a fragrance.

FEMALE CHORUS (*sings*): Why should love stick to the sap of a single body? When the stem is drunk with the thick yearning

of the many-petalled, many-flowered lantana, why should it
be tied down to the relation of a single flower?

A head for each breast. A pupil for each eye. A side for
each arm. I have neither regret nor shame. The blood pours
into the earth and a song branches out in the sky.

(*When the song ends, the Bhagavata does a namaskara to the
audience. The audience should get a definite feeling that the play
has ended when a scream is heard in the wings.*)

BHAGAVATA: What's that? Oh! Nata, our Actor!

(*Actor II comes rushing out. He doesn't even see the Bhagavata in
his desperate hurry.*)

Why is he running? Where's the National Anthem?

(*Actor II suddenly stops in his tracks.*)

ACTOR II: The National Anthem!

BHAGAVATA: What?

ACTOR II: How did you know?

BHAGAVATA: Know what?

ACTOR II: Please, Bhagavata Sir, how did you know...

BHAGAVATA: Know what?

ACTOR II: About the National Anthem.

BHAGAVATA: What do you mean?

ACTOR II: Please, Sir, I beg of you. I implore you. Don't make fun
of me. How did you know it was the National Anthem...

BHAGAVATA: Why? Haven't you seen an audience...

ACTOR II (*relieved*): Phew! That! Ram Ram!

BHAGAVATA: Why? What happened?

ACTOR II: What happened? Sree Hari! Look...

(*Lifts his hand. It's trembling.*)

BHAGAVATA: Why? What...

ACTOR II: I almost died of fright...

BHAGAVATA: Really?

ACTOR II: I was coming down the road, when I heard someone singing at a distance, at the top of his voice. He was singing, *Jhanda Ooncha Rahe Hamara* (May our flag fly high!) Then he proceeded to *Sare Jahan se Acchha Hindostan Hamara* (Our India is better than the whole world). Then *Rise, Rise my Kannada Land.* Then *Vande Mataram...*

BHAGAVATA: Then?

ACTOR II: I was baffled. A true patriot at this time of the night? I had to find out who it was. A house—a big, thick fence around with not a gap in it. But I managed to find a hole to crawl through. I was just half-way in when I saw...

BHAGAVATA: What?

(*The Actor wipes his brow.*)

Come on, what did you see?

ACTOR II: A horse!

BHAGAVATA (*eager*): A horse?

ACTOR II: Yes. It turned to me and in a deep, sonorous voice said, 'Friend, I'm now going to sing the National Anthem. So please do stand up to attention!'

BHAGAVATA: Listen, Nata, are you sure...

ACTOR II: I swear...

BHAGAVATA: No, no, what I mean is...

(*Commotion in the wings.*)

What's that now?

(*Actor I enters with a boy of about five. The boy is very serious, even sulky. There's not a trace of laughter on his face. He is holding the two cloth dolls which we have already seen, but the dolls are dirtier now. The commotion comes from Actor I, who is so busy trying to make the child laugh—making faces at him, clowning, capering, and shouting—he doesn't notice the Bhagavata.*)

BHAGAVATA (*delighted*): Oh! Nata! You again!

ACTOR I (*turns around and sees the Bhagavata*): Oh, Sir, it's you!

BHAGAVATA: Well well, you'll live to be a hundred.

ACTOR I: Why? What have I done?

BHAGAVATA: I was just thinking of you and you turned up. Just now this Nata (*pointing to Actor II*) was saying he saw a horse-headed man and I wondered if it was Hayavadana. So I remembered you.

ACTOR II: Bhagavata Sir...

ACTOR I (*ignoring Actor II*): There's an actor's fate in a nutshell for you. Always remembered for someone else.

BHAGAVATA: Where's Hayavadana now? Has he come back?

ACTOR I: I don't know, Sir. He chased me away the moment we reached the Kali temple. Wouldn't let me stay there a minute longer.

BHAGAVATA: Oh! I very much hope the goddess granted him what he wanted. (*Sees the child.*) Who's this child?

ACTOR I: Him? Well? (*To the child.*) Go on, tell him.
(*The child remains silent. Doesn't answer any questions.*)

BHAGAVATA: Who are you, child? What's your name? Where are your parents?

ACTOR I: You see? Not a word. Children of his age should be outtalking a dictionary, but this one doesn't speak a word. Doesn't laugh, doesn't cry, doesn't even smile. The same long face all twenty-four hours. There's obviously something wrong with him.
(*Bends before the child and clowns a bit.*)
See? No response—no reactions. When he grows up, he should make a good theatre critic.

ACTOR II (*restless*): Bhagavata Sir...

BHAGAVATA (*to Actor I*): Where did you find him?

ACTOR I: In a tribal village of hunters. On my way back I had to stay a night there and a tribal woman brought him to me. Said, 'This is not our child. It's from the city. Take it back'.

BHAGAVATA: A child of this city? (*Actor I nods.*) How strange! (*Notices the dolls.*) But—but—these dolls...

(*Tries to touch the dolls. The child reacts violently and moves away angry, terrified.*)

ACTOR I: I was about to warn you! Whatever you do, don't touch his dolls! At other times he'll starve and freeze to death rather than say a word. But touch the dolls and he'll bare his fangs. He almost bit off my finger once.

ACTOR II: Bhagavata Sir...

BHAGAVATA (*to Actor I*): But Nata—(*Pause.*) Child, let me see your shoulder.

(*The child moves back.*)

No, no, I won't touch the dolls. I promise you. Just your shoulder.

(*Inspects his shoulder. Then with a cry of triumph.*) Nata...

ACTOR II: Bhagavata Sir...

ACTOR I: Yes...

BHAGAVATA: Look, the mole. It's Padmini's son... There's no doubt about it.

ACTOR I: Padmini? Which...

ACTOR II (*shouting at the top of his voice*): Bhagavata Sir!

(*Actor I and the Bhagavata react.*)

BHAGAVATA: Yes? Why are you shouting?

ACTOR II: I have been calling you for the last half-an-hour...

BHAGAVATA: Yes, yes. What's it?

ACTOR II: You said I'd seen a horse-headed man. I didn't. What I saw was a complete, perfect, proper...

(*A voice is heard off-stage singing the third stanza of 'Jana Gana Mana'.*)

There it is!

(*All stare in the direction of the song. A horse enters the stage singing.*)

HORSE: *Tava Karunaruna' Rage*
              Nidrita Bharata Jage
              Tava Charane Nata Matha
              Jaya Jaya Jaya He Jaya Rajeshwara
(*Comes and stands in front of them.*)
       Hohoo! What's this? Mr Bhagavata Sir! My Actor friend! Well,
       well, well! What a pleasant surprise! Delightful! How are you,
       Sir, how are you?

BHAGAVATA: It's not—not Hayavadana, is it?

HAYAVADANA: Your most obedient servant, Sir.

BHAGAVATA: But what...

ACTOR II: You mean you know this horse?

BHAGAVATA (*bursts into a guffaw*): We're old friends.

ACTOR I (*laughing*): Fellow-pilgrims!

HAYAVADANA: But not fellow-travellers. What?
(*They roar with laughter. Suddenly the boy too starts laughing.
Doubles up with laughter. The dolls fall out of his hand as he claps
his hands.*)

THE BOY (*clapping his hands*): The horse is laughing! The horse
       is laughing!

ACTOR I (*jumping with delight*): The boy is laughing!

HAYAVADANA (*goes to the boy*): Why, my little friend, you may
       laugh, but I may not?

(*The boy is in hysterics.*)

DEVADATTA: That's Padmini's son, Hayavadana.

HAYAVADANA: Padmini? I am not aware of...

BHAGAVATA: You don't know her. But this poor child—he hadn't
       laughed, or cried, or talked in all these years. Now you have
       made him laugh.

HAYAVADANA: Delighted. Delighted.

BHAGAVATA: But tell me: you went to the goddess to become a complete man, didn't you? What happened?

HAYAVADANA: Ah! That's a long story. I went there, picked up a sword which was lying around—very unsafe, I tell you—put it on my neck and said: 'Mother of all Nature, if you don't help me, I'll chop off my head!'

ACTOR I: Then?

HAYAVADANA: The goddess appeared. Very prompt. But looked rather put out. She said—rather peevishly, I thought—'Why don't you people go somewhere else if you want to chop off your stupid heads? Why do you have to come to me?' I fell at her feet and said, 'Mother, make me complete'. She said 'So be it' and disappeared—even before I could say 'Make me a complete man!' I became a horse.

ACTOR I: I am sorry to hear that...

HAYAVADANA: Sorry? Whatever for? The goddess knew what she was doing. I can tell you that. Ha Ha! Being a horse has its points. (*Pause.*) I have only one sorrow.

BHAGAVATA: Yes?

HAYAVADANA: I have become a complete horse—but not a complete being! This human voice—this cursed human voice—it's still there! How can I call myself complete? What should I do, Bhagavata Sir? How can I get rid of this human voice?

BHAGAVATA: I don't know what to advise you, Hayavadana.

HAYAVADANA: That's why I sing all these patriotic songs—and the National Anthem! That particularly! I have noticed that the people singing the National Anthem always seem to have ruined their voices, so I try. But—but—it—it doesn't seem to work. What should I do?

(*He starts to sob.*)

BOY: Don't cry, horse. Don't cry. Stop it now.

HAYAVADANA: No, I won't cry. The boy's right. What's the point of shedding tears?

BOY: Don't cry. You are nice when you laugh.

HAYAVADANA: No, I won't cry. I won't give up trying either. Come, little friend, let's sing the National Anthem together.

BOY: What is that?

BHAGAVATA: How could he? He has been brought up in a forest.

HAYAVADANA: Then sing some other song. Look, if you sing a song, I'll take you round on my back.

BOY (*excited*): Yes—please.

HAYAVADANA: Well, then, what are we waiting for? Get on my back. Quick.

(*The Bhagavata seats the child on the horse's back.*)

BOY: Hiyah—Hiyah—

HAYAVADANA: No, no. You sing first. Then we start.

BHAGAVATA: Sing, son.

(*The boy sings and the horse goes around in a slow trot.*)

BOY: Here comes a rider.
              From what land O what land?
              On his head a turban.
              Sleep now, sleep now.
              Why his chest
              Red O red?
              Why his eyes
              Pebbles O pebbles?
              Why his body
              Cold O cold?
              Where goes the horse?
              Nowhere O nowhere.

(*As the song ends, the horse comes and stands in front of the Bhagavata.*)

HAYAVADANA: Mr Bhagavata Sir...

BHAGAVATA: Yes.

HAYAVADANA: It seems to me the rider described in the song is dead. I am right?

BHAGAVATA: Er—I think so—yes.

HAYAVADANA: Who could have taught this child such a tragic song?

BOY: Mother...

BHAGAVATA: What's there in a song, Hayavadana? The real beauty lies in the child's laughter, in the innocent splendour of that laughter. No tragedy can touch it.

HAYAVADANA: Is that so?

BHAGAVATA: Indeed. What can match a child's laughter in its purity?

HAYAVADANA: To be honest, Mr Bhagavata Sir, I have my doubts about this theory. I believe—in fact I may go so far as to say I firmly believe—that it's this sort of sentimentality which has been the bane of our literature and national life. It has kept us from accepting Reality and encouraged escapism. Still, if you say so, I won't argue. Come, child, let's have another song.

BOY: I don't know...

HAYAVADANA: Then sing the same song again.

BOY: You laugh first.

HAYAVADANA: Laugh again? Let me try. (*Tries to laugh.*) Ha Ha Ha! No, it's not easy to laugh—just like that.

BOY (*mimes whipping*): Laugh—laugh...

HAYAVADANA: All right. All right. I'll try again. Ha! Ha! Ha! Ha!— Huhhuh...Heahhh...

(*His laughter ends up as a proper neigh.*)

ALL: What's that?

BHAGAVATA: Hayavadana—Hayavadana...

HAYAVADANA: Heahhh...

(*His human voice is gone now. He can only neigh and leaps around with great joy.*)

BHAGAVATA: Careful—careful. Don't drop the child...

(*But the horse is too happy to listen. It prances around, neighing gleefully. The boy is also enjoying himself, singing bits of the song and urging the horse on.*)

BHAGAVATA: So at long last Hayavadana has become complete. (*To the Actors.*) You two go and tell the Revered Brahmin Vidyasagara that his grandson is returning home in triumph, riding a big, white charger.

ACTOR II: And the dolls?

BHAGAVATA: Throw them away. There's no further need for them.

(*The Actors go out with the dolls.*)

Unfathomable indeed is the mercy of the elephant-headed Ganesha. He fulfils the desires of all—a grandson to a grandfather, a smile to a child, a neigh to a horse. How indeed can one describe His glory in our poor, disabled words?

Come, Hayavadana, come. Enough of this dancing. Our play is over and it's time we all prayed and thanked the Lord for having ensured the completion and success of our play.

(*Hayavadana comes and stands by the Bhagavata. The Bhagavata helps the child down. At this point the curtain, with the fire painted on it—which has been there all the time—is dropped and Padmini, Kapila and Devadatta step forward and join the Bhagavata in prayer.*)

Grant us, O Lord, good rains, good crop,
Prosperity in poetry, science, industry and other affairs.
Give the rulers of our country success in all endeavours,
and along with it, a little bit of sense.

BALI: The Sacrifice

Bali: The Sacrifice was first presented at the Haymarket Theatre, Leicester, on 31 May 2002. The cast was as follows:

NASEERUDDIN SHAH	The Mahout
NEVE TAYLOR	The Queen
GARY TURNER	The King
RATNA PATHAK SHAH	The Queen Mother

Directed by	NONA SHEPPHARD
Designed by	MARSHA RODDY
Music by	ANDREW DODGE
Commissioning Producer	VAYU NAIDU

QUEEN: As the world is divided
           into two orbs:
           one lit up by the sun
           the other hid in the shade,
           so also the human soul,
           the habitation of gods,
           is split into two realms—
           one of the spirits that adore
           the blood and gore
           of the bright, shining blade
           slicing smoothly
           through the lamb
           and the other
           ruled by the spirits that bid
           you pause
           before you use
           the knife on a sapling
           or clap in the air—
           lest you harm a life.

Lights brighten to reveal the whole stage:
The inner sanctum of a ruined temple.
The pedestal on which the deity once stood is still intact. But as for
the image, only the feet survive, suggesting a standing figure.
In front of the pedestal is a low stone platform, meant for flowers,
incense, myrrh and other ingredients of worship.

When the play begins, the stage is dark.
We see two indistinct figures inside the sanctum: the Mahout and
the Queen. They are sitting apart from each other.
Pause.
The King enters the courtyard of the outer temple. He has a torch
in his hand.
He enters and sits on the outer steps of the temple. The two in the
inner sanctum are unaware of his presence.
Long pause.

KING: So we begin our tale—
             and in any tale
             the King and the Queen
             sitting on the throne
             should merge into one
             —she on his lap
             become half his royal frame
             or entwined in bed, tangled together
             they must turn
             into a four-armed deity
             thrashing and moaning
             for the good of the land.
             But
             woe betide the times
             where the King sits alone
             outside on the steps
             racked by sighs
             while the Queen is trapped
             in her lover's thighs.

MAHOUT: Who are you?
(*No reply.*)
     Tell me.

QUEEN: Let me go.
(*Pause.*)
   Please—

MAHOUT: Go.
(*She moves.*)
   But before you go, tell me your name.
(*Pause.*)
   Come on. What are you being so cussed about?

QUEEN: Why do you want my name?

MAHOUT: Ts! I told you—
(*Pause.*)

QUEEN: Please, it's getting late. I'm getting worried. Let me go.

MAHOUT: A name. Any name would have done. In fact, most
   women would have had a name coined and ready before
   stepping in here like this. But you!
(*Pause.*)
   I'll tell you something, you haven't seen me properly yet. I
   am ugly. Ugly as a bandicoot. I know. But I've had women.
   Plenty. When I've wanted a woman—needed a woman—my
   voice has never failed me. Can't remember any names though.

QUEEN: Then why do you want mine?

MAHOUT: After all, it's a matter of courtesy, isn't it? A mere
   formality. You can't just sleep with a woman and let her go—
   just like that. So you say 'What's your name?' She gives some
   name and that's the end of that. But you—the way you
   reacted to the question—recoil as though I had slapped you.
   Even in the dark I could feel that. After everything we'd done?
   God! I'm suffocating in here. I am going to open the
   window—

QUEEN: Look, I could also do with some fresh air. And it is getting
   late. I can't stay here any longer. Please let me go. We'll go
   our separate ways and not see each other again.

MAHOUT: That's why I want your name.

QUEEN: And I won't tell you.

(*Pause.*)

I hope you realize we are both repeating ourselves.

(*He goes and opens the window. She sinks into the darkest corner of the room. The moonlight streams into the sanctum and lights it up.*)

MAHOUT: Nice. The mist's cleared. Nice breeze. It's a beautiful night. Full moon. You can see every leaf in the tree. It's such a bright night, you won't know when it dawns. It'll flow from one into the other, seamlessly.

(*The Queen makes a sudden move to the door and tries to open it, but he is faster than her and grabs her. There is a scuffle. He drags her back and literally throws her into a corner. She moans in pain.*)

Don't. Don't make me angry. You don't know my temper. I have beaten women black and blue. You won't like it. Don't try any tricks. I don't like it.

(*She sits up, rubbing her wrists.*)

QUEEN: It's been lovely meeting you. Every minute of it. And you're ruining it.

MAHOUT: Listen, I could easily drag you to the window and see your face. You know that.

(*Pause.*)

But that won't be nice. Not after the time we've had together. So I say: you want to keep your face hidden? Fine! But tell me your name. I'm letting you off easy.

QUEEN: Let's say, my name is ... Kāmalatāsurasundari.

(*Pause.*)

MAHOUT: Trying to be funny, aren't you? I would have accepted any name earlier. But not now. Now I am curious. Now I want to know. Not be lied to. That's another thing I hate. Being taken for a moron.

QUEEN: I am not taking you for a moron.

MAHOUT: I don't like being taken for a moron just because I am ugly.

QUEEN: Why do you keep saying that?

MAHOUT: Because I am ugly. I know that. And I say it before others do.

QUEEN: I won't say it.

MAHOUT: Surely you have said it to yourself? When you came in here, the lamp was burning, you saw my face.

QUEEN: Yes.

MAHOUT: And what did you think?

QUEEN: I wasn't thinking. I was...just...
(*He waits. She doesn't complete the sentence.*)

MAHOUT: But you saw my face.

QUEEN: I suppose so.

MAHOUT: How did it strike you?

QUEEN: I don't know.
(*Pause.*)

MAHOUT: That's not nice.

QUEEN: But it's true.

MAHOUT: You came in here barely two hours ago. And you don't know what you thought of my face? That's not nice. Not nice at all.
(*He moves so that the moonlight falls directly on his face.*)
Well, you can see me now. What do you say?

QUEEN: If you mean you are not tall and fair with an aquiline nose and ruby lips—I live surrounded by such men and I am sick and tired of them.

MAHOUT: You are avoiding my question.

QUEEN: No, I'm not. Your looks don't matter to me. I came here because I heard you sing. You have a heavenly voice.
(*Pause.*)

I wanted the company of your voice.

MAHOUT: Then why did you put the light out as soon as you came in? You couldn't bear to see my mug while making love to me?

QUEEN: I didn't want you to see my face.

MAHOUT (*laughs*): Why? Are you ugly?

QUEEN: No, I don't think so. People usually describe me in flattering terms. Of course, they don't always mean what they say.

MAHOUT: I wish you would let me see your face. Just a glimpse.

QUEEN: No.

MAHOUT: Look, I am a low-caste mahout, the King's elephant keeper.
(*Looks at his arms.*)

And you? I am probably bleeding all over. There. You've almost scratched my skin off. Such long nails. You are no bazaar woman, I can see that. You are from the upper floors. And you haven't done a day's work. That's for sure. Those nails are for a dainty life.

QUEEN (*laughs*): You're right. They're not used to scrubbing the floor.

MAHOUT: I don't see many rich women. I'm not allowed near them. So it's not likely that I would have seen you. Or recognize you. So why are you hiding your face?
(*She changes the subject.*)

QUEEN: I'm sorry I hurt you.

MAHOUT: That's all right. I liked it. I like everything about bed. Everything. That's why I am good. I am good. Aren't I?
(*No reply.*)

Better than your husband?

QUEEN (*reacts*): How dare you!
(*The authority in her voice surprises him.*)
   He is the best of men.

MAHOUT: Maybe. But what about in bed?

QUEEN: There too.

MAHOUT: Then why are you here?

QUEEN: You won't understand that.

MAHOUT (*aggressive*): Are you saying I am stupid?

QUEEN: No, I'm not. So please don't keep saying that. My coming
   here has nothing to do with my husband. He is a marvellous
   person—affectionate, gentle, trusting.

MAHOUT: And if he's awake when you reach home now, what'll
   you tell him?

QUEEN: I'll say I'd gone out for a walk.

MAHOUT: In the streets? At midnight? And he'll accept that?

QUEEN: Will you please let me go? Please. I'm really getting scared.

MAHOUT: Any children?

QUEEN: Don't.

MAHOUT: Any children?

QUEEN: Don't let's talk about it.

MAHOUT: Why not?

QUEEN (*sharply*): I don't want to talk about it.

MAHOUT (*retreating*): All right. All right.

QUEEN: I want to go home.
(*The Mahout ignores her remark.*)

MAHOUT: I'll accept I am not very good at certain things. Like
   counting. I was lucky I was born in my caste. We only have
   to deal with elephants—and the elephants don't mind an
   ugly, misshapen man who can't count.
(*The Queen hums a tune to herself. It is not 'real' humming as much*

*as an expression of her mood. It's evident that the Mahout does not
hear her sing. He goes on talking.)*

You know why I am so ugly? I was born on a full moon. There
was an eclipse. As you know, the worst thing you can do to
yourself is to be born during an eclipse. The sun or the
moon—the god whose eclipse it is—is already in the grips of
the demons. The beneficial powers of that god are weak at
that moment, often ineffective. So it's free for all as far as the
forces of evil are concerned. A baby about to be born is fair
game. It'll be maimed. Or blind. Or even if it looks normal,
something will be wrong inside. The brain may be damaged.
You won't know till the baby grows up. My mother knew all
this and was scared. She was lying there on a torn piece of
mat and she heard sparrows chirping. In the middle of the
night? She looks up and what does she see? Up in the eaves,
a snake had crept into a sparrow's nest and was gobbling up
the eggs. She screamed in terror. And I was born. Like this.

*(The Queen Mother enters the courtyard. She has a large silver tray
in her hands and on it an object, about two foot high, covered by
a saffron cloth. There are flowers, incense sticks etc. in the tray, and
a sword.)*

People mock at mahouts. Call us 'low-born'. But where would
all your princes and kings be without us, I want to know.
What would happen to their elephants? No elephants. No
army. No pomp and splendour. No processions. No kings!
Ha!

QUEEN: Let me warn you—if we get caught together here, it won't
be pleasant for either of us.

MAHOUT: Several times I have asked God—Oh! Do you ever talk
to God?

QUEEN: No.

MAHOUT: Believe in one?

QUEEN: No. Though I have often wished He was there.

MAHOUT: But He is there. If you don't believe in Him, who do
you believe in?

QUEEN: The Saviour.

MAHOUT: Ah! you are a Jain, then. No God, but twenty-four
Saviours! Never could understand that. Who do you talk to
when you are lonely—when you are in trouble?

QUEEN: They're all there.

MAHOUT: But no God, eh? Funny what people will come up with.
But believe me, there is God. I talk to him. In my village,
outside the village limits, there's this banyan tree—enormous—hundreds of years old. And there's our God. A stone.
But not on the ground. The hanging roots of the banyan have
taken hold of Him and actually lifted Him up. The roots look
like trunks of elephants cradling our God. The God of the
Mahouts. Sometimes when I am sad, I am lost, I am upset,
I ask God. Of course, you can't demand anything of Him. He
meant everything to be as it is, you see. But I'm human, so
I ask, 'Why have you made me so ugly? Why not handsome,
like the Commander-in-Chief? Or the King? Why so ugly?' So
God says: 'Are the people laughing at you?' I say: 'No, not any
more. Not after I knocked the teeth of a couple of fellows
out!' God says: 'Well, I gave you the strength to do it. Didn't
I?' So I argue: 'But a handsome face! If I had one, then I
wouldn't need these muscles to shut them up!' So God says:
'Would you exchange your voice for good looks?' That puts
me in a proper spot. But God knows my answer in advance.
'No, I wouldn't,' I reply, so God says, 'Why not leave it at
that?'

QUEEN: You're not ugly, you know. You are lonely.

MAHOUT (*defensive*): I live alone, if that's what you mean. That's
all right by me.

QUEEN: That's why you are holding me prisoner. You don't want
to know my name. You want someone to talk to.

MAHOUT: I have my God.

QUEEN: God is no substitute—for anything!

MAHOUT (*angry*): All right, people avoid me. So what? They gather to hear me sing. Then they run away. So what are you saying?

QUEEN: That *that* may be a blessing. You can be surrounded by people who are talking—fawning on you—and you can be lonely. So lonely you are terrified. I should know.

MAHOUT: Is that why you came here?

QUEEN: No. I came here because I heard you sing. I had to come. But let me tell you something. Nobody has ever talked to me like you have. Nobody.

(*Pause.*)

I have to go back, but I like you.

(*Long pause.*)

MAHOUT: I think I'll let you go.

(*Pause.*)

Go.

(*She stands up with alacrity.*)

QUEEN: Thank you. I'll never forget you.

(*He strides to the window, almost angry at himself for letting her go. She covers her face with her sari and prepares to leave. He sees the Queen Mother outside. He can't see her full figure, so twists to get a better glimpse of her*).

There's someone there...in the courtyard.

(*The Queen freezes.*)

There's someone...there...outside the main door.

QUEEN: Who's there?

MAHOUT: A woman, I think.

QUEEN: Are you lying?

MAHOUT: If you think I'm lying, go out. See for yourself.

QUEEN: What's she doing?

MAHOUT: Must have just come in. Didn't see her earlier.

QUEEN: What's she doing?

MAHOUT: Just standing there. Still. Like a statue.
(*Pause.*)
   She is holding something in her hands, a bundle of some sort.

QUEEN: Is she alone?

MAHOUT: Yes. That's odd. Very odd. I mean—a woman, alone? At
   this time of the night?

QUEEN: What's she doing?

MAHOUT: That's what I want to know. I mean why here? A ruined
   temple. Most people would think it's haunted, evil. A
   wayfarer? At night? And then the traveller's shelter is just
   round the corner. Anyone would go there!

QUEEN: Anyone else with her?

MAHOUT: I don't know, I can't see.

QUEEN (*scared*): Are you trying to be funny?

MAHOUT: Stop repeating yourself like a parrot. Come and see.
   Quick. She is about to move...
(*The Queen moves to the window and looks out. Just at that
moment, the Queen Mother outside moves out of sight.*)

QUEEN: Where?

MAHOUT: She's come in. Inside the temple.
(*He sees the Queen's face.*)
   I have seen your face somewhere before.
(*The Queen turns her face away.*)

MAHOUT: Don't be absurd. After all that we've done together...I
   mean, this coyness, this fuss...

QUEEN: Look, no one must know I'm here. Please. I must go home.
   Immediately. Oh God! Is there any other way out of here?

MAHOUT (*laughs*): There's that hole there. If you could fly out, try.
   Listen, numbskull. This is the inner sanctum. It has a single
   door.

QUEEN: Please, please, help me. Here—
(*Reaches for her necklace, an almost automatic gesture.*)

MAHOUT (*irritated*): Keep it. If I'd wanted that bauble, I wouldn't have waited so long. That's your estimate of every lower-caste man, isn't it? He's a good lay and all he wants is a piece of gold. I am an elephant keeper, madam, not a fence, selling stolen jewellery. And if someone decides to investigate, I'll get my hands chopped off.

QUEEN: Please, please, keep your voice down. They mustn't know we're here—

MAHOUT: You aren't very bright, are you? I'm sure she is not alone. There must be others. We know there's no God's image here. But they may not. If they are travellers, before leaving in the morning, they may decide to bow down to the deity in here—

QUEEN: I can't stay here till the morning—

MAHOUT: And I don't want to get caught with you, whoever you are. God alone knows whose wife you are. I don't want to— Now listen. Listen! Let's see what they do. Let's see! If they try to come in, there's only one way to stop them. Let them know there's a couple in here…a man and a woman. So if anything like that happens, we have to raise our voices…make noise…

QUEEN: Oh God!…I must get away. Please, please help me!

MAHOUT: For goodness sake, don't start crying now. If they hear you, they'll decide you're in trouble and come to the rescue. People are so bloody nosey these days. Be quiet now and listen!

(*They listen, crouching next to the door, tense with fear.*
Outside, the Queen Mother, carrying the silver tray, comes to where the King is sitting. He gets up and, as though in a trance, removes the saffron cloth to see the object it is covering. He holds out the cloth in such a way that the audience cannot see the object.
He stares at the object and his stance changes as though the object

has communicated some message to him. He covers it again. Does namaskara to it.
The Queen Mother, with a nod of her head, signals to him to go ahead.
He takes the sword from the tray, ties it round his belt, picks up the torch and walks up the steps.
He knocks on the door. The knock startles the two inside. The Queen jumps to her feet and tries to run behind the pedestal. The Mahout grabs her.)

MAHOUT (*in a whisper*): Don't panic. Do as I say. Do as I tell you... Just laugh. Be merry. Come on.

(*The Queen tries to laugh but the attempt ends in a moan. The Mahout laughs loudly, theatrically. But he is scared. It's not easy. Knock.)*

MAHOUT: We must pant.

QUEEN: Pant?

MAHOUT: Yes, yes, pant. Heavy breathing. You and me—
(*He pants heavily.*)
Let them think something's going on...that we're making love here. You see what I mean? Sin in the inner sanctum. They'll slap themselves on their cheeks, say what's the world coming to, curse us and go away. Come on... Pant... heavy...
(*He demonstrates panting.*)
Hunnh... Hunnh... Yes. Like that. Come on.
(*The Queen moans in anguish.*)
That's it. Oh God! You're good, good, this is heaven. Yes. This is...aaaah... Come on. Come. Come. Aah.
(*The King knocks again. The Queen curls up in fear. The Mahout increases his labours.*)
Good. Oh God, you are good! uh...uh...uh... You're like no one I know... Oh! you are good—good...
(*Knocking again. The Mahout yells.*)

Hey, who's that? Are you deaf? Can't you hear I am with my woman? Go away. (*To the Queen.*) Come now...yes... Turn this way. That's it... Oh you're divine...

(*Urging her*)

Come on. Moan. Groan. Laugh.

(*The King knocks.*)

You bastard, get the hell out of here. Or else...I'll bash your brains out... Stamp you into mud...

QUEEN: Oh God!

MAHOUT (*to her*): Yes, that's right...

(*Knock again.*)

Bloody hell! Are you deaf? Or are you deliberately asking for trouble? I'll...I'll...

(*Knock again.*)

I said I'll kill you.

(*Knock again.*)

All right.

(*Jumps up. Picks up his stick.*)

QUEEN: No!

MAHOUT: So what do you want to do? Sit here all night while they knock? I'll give the rascals a taste of my stick...

(*Rushes to the door. The Queen, frightened, goes and crouches in a corner. The Mahout opens the door and raises the stick to hit out. He sees the King and freezes.*)

Oh my God! The King!

(*Reels back.*)

Your...Majesty...

(*The King steps in with the torch in his hand. The torch further lights up the interior. The King looks around for the Queen, while the Mahout quickly ties his dhoti in a knot.*)

I touch your feet, Your Majesty, there's no one here. It's just me! I fall to your feet, sir. Last night a bat entered the elephant stables, so we had to clear up the place. So I came here to sleep. But I am alone, sir, there's no one here. Only me...

KING (*calls*): Amritamati...

(*The Mahout recoils in horror. The King calls again.*)

   Amritamati...

(*The Queen gets up from behind the pedestal and comes out.*)

MAHOUT: Oh...God...the Queen! Forgive me, sir. I...didn't know. We didn't do anything, sir. I swear to you. I sang...she listened... Her Majesty was about to go back soon...

(*The King goes to her. Pushes back the veil covering her face. Takes the torch to her face. She recoils. He stares at her. Silence. Dazed, he looks at her as though he can't recognize her. Pinches her cheek as though to make sure she is there.*)

QUEEN (*gently*): Please...don't...

(*The King wakes up with a start. He is obviously embarrassed by what he's been doing.*)

KING (*dazed and without malice*): Is it you? I don't want to hurt you.

(*He turns, goes to a ring in the wall and sticks the torch into it. Then, in sheer exhaustion, leans his head against the wall.*
A long pause.
The Queen moves up to him. Almost in a whisper)

QUEEN: Let's go.

KING: Go?

(*She takes him by his hand and tries to lead him away. He does not move. They look at each other.*)

QUEEN (*gently*): Why did you come here?

(*Pause.*)

   Why did you? Until he saw you—

KING: I'm concerned about you. You about him.

QUEEN: I am talking about us both.

(*Pause.*)

   Until he saw you, he didn't know who I was. I was just a woman, any woman. Now he can gloat.

KING (*spits out contemptuously*): Him!

QUEEN: No, me. For one night, I was nameless.

MAHOUT (*scared*): Madam... Your Majesty... I swear to you I won't breathe a word of this to anyone. Who'll believe me anyway? They'll laugh at me... If I speak to any soul, may my tongue get worms in it. Rot and fall away. Please, madam. Please, sir—

KING: Shut up!

MAHOUT: If I shut up, Your Majesty, how will you know? I mean... you must hear me out. You could have me beheaded. Cut to pieces. Trampled under an elephant's foot. But that would be wrong, sir. Very wrong. I didn't do anything. A bat flew into the elephant stables last night, so I came here to sleep for a night. And I was singing by myself. Alone. I do that often. And she came. I didn't know who she was. It was dark. I was sitting here, singing, and she came in and she came to me and—

KING: I said shut up!

(*The King draws his sword and is about to slash at the Mahout when—*)

QUEEN: Your Majesty—

(*The Queen Mother on the steps too suddenly stands up as though she has sensed something. The King freezes, stares, uncomprehending, at the sword. Then almost with a sense of hopelessness, lets it slide back into the scabbard. The Mahout heaves a sigh of relief.*)

MAHOUT: Of course, how could I forget? You are a Jain. You can't indulge in violence. You aren't permitted to shed blood. Ooh! I forgot that—

(*He giggles in sheer relief. Giggling and talking to himself he retires to his corner.*)

Whew! That was close!... I mean... how could you draw the sword? You aren't allowed to kill. Huh!

(*The Mahout sits on his mattress. The King and the Queen stand, looking at each other, not knowing what move to make next. Lights slowly dim, plunging the pair into darkness. But we continue to see the Mahout as he begins to drink. Total darkness.*)

SINGER: Memories slide
                 meld and fuse.
                 Discrete moments
                 get flung together
                 strung in a single moment.

(*Lights come on the Queen and the King, acting young.*)

QUEEN: You there! What are you doing?

KING: Don't look. Look away—Don't come near—

QUEEN: You are peeing on our tree!

KING: I say...look away. Wait till I finish.

QUEEN: You are taking too long. You've got your leg wet.

KING: You startled me. I didn't know anyone was around.

QUEEN: I saw you. This garden is only for girls. Who are you?

KING: I am a prince.

QUEEN: Ohho! So you're the prince who's come to be my husband.
    But you are so—small. Don't husbands have moustaches?

KING: I'll grow my moustaches in good time, don't let that worry
    you. You aren't all that big yourself. You are like a doll—a rag
    doll.

QUEEN: If you tease me, I'll go and tell Father.

KING: Then you talk to me with respect. Is that how one talks to
    one's husband? 'You there!' 'You here!'

QUEEN: My maid does.

KING: I'm not going to marry a house-maid. I am a prince.

QUEEN: Good. Then I'll ask you a riddle. See if you can solve it.

KING: Tcha! I have no time for riddles. Solve them yourself.

QUEEN: You don't like riddles? What kind of a prince are you? In
    my house, everybody loves riddles.

KING: Even your father?

QUEEN: Him too. He knows millions of them. Millions of billions.

KING: Why should a king solve riddles? He must rule. He must
fight wars. He must make proclamations. He has other things
to do.

QUEEN: He does that too. And he knows proverbs.

KING: Can he throw a stone? Can he hunt lions?

QUEEN (*impressed*): You can hunt lions?

KING: Aw! Easy.

QUEEN: Will you show me? I have never seen a hunt. Never!

KING: I know. You are Jains, aren't you? Your kings can't hunt.
Your Saviours are all stark naked.

QUEEN (*miffed*): And…and…and my maid says your goddess
eats meat.

KING: She does too. But she is dressed in such gorgeous saris.
Bright, shiny silk saris. Clothed from neck to toe.

QUEEN (*losing the argument*): Your goddess eats…chicken…and
goats…and…and…

KING: But she is decked in gold. What kind of a king is your
father? Can't he even afford a jockstrap for your Saviour? Not
even a piece of rag to cover his shame?

(*The Queen's eyes fill up.*)

QUEEN: You're making fun of me. You are making me cry. I don't
want to marry you. I'll go and tell Mother.

(*He quickly intercepts her exit.*)

KING: Hey, hey! Listen! I'll show you something, if you promise
not to cry.

(*Looks around for something.*)

I could show you how to knock a bird off a branch but I
haven't got my catapult with me.

QUEEN: I am going.

KING: Show me a bird and I'll try to get it down with a stone,
without a catapult.

(*They look around.*)

QUEEN: I can't see any.

KING: It's midday.

QUEEN: Their babies must be sleeping.

KING: All right then, I'll knock a bird down from the branch in the evening. Just for you. Don't tell anyone. Otherwise your parents will be furious. So will mine.

QUEEN: If you show me, I'll let you pee on my rose bush. We can make babies.

KING: What's that? Revolting!

QUEEN: Why were you peeing here then?

KING: Because I haven't had a pee since morning. The front yard is full of guests. So I came here. It's got nothing to do with making babies.

QUEEN: It does too. That's why no boy is allowed to come in here. How did you get in?

KING: I made a hole in the hedge and crept in.

QUEEN: You should have waited till you became my husband.

KING: Why?

QUEEN: My maid says that if a boy pees on a bush and then if a girl smells the flowers from that bush, that's how babies are made.

KING: Really? I didn't know that.

QUEEN: You don't know a lot of things.
(*Suddenly*)
　　There!

KING: What?

QUEEN: A bird. There!

KING: Ah, yes. Shush now. Be absolutely quiet.
(*Picks up a stone, tiptoes nearer to the bird, takes aim and flings the stone. He shouts in triumph.*)
　　Got it!

(*They run to the fallen bird. The Queen recoils in horror at the sight of the bird.*)

QUEEN: Oh God! Blood. Poor birdie! It's bleeding.

(*The Queen kneels down and gently picks up the bird. She keeps caressing the bird and whispering to it. The King watches, almost mesmerized.*)

　　Poor baby! Poor dear baby!... Oh poor thing. Please, fetch some water. Please.

KING: I'm sorry, but it's no use. It's dead.

QUEEN: Dead? No. No. It can't be. It can't be. Wake up. Wake up, poor birdie.

KING: Here!

(*He gently tries to take the bird from her hand but she doesn't let him.*)

　　We have to bury it now.

QUEEN (*refusing to relinquish the bird*): But why did you kill it?

KING (*not accusing*): You wanted to see it knocked down.

QUEEN: But I didn't want you to kill it.

KING: I didn't realize—I'm sorry.

QUEEN: I didn't mean you to hurt it.

KING: I know that now. Stupid of me—

QUEEN: Poor birdie!

KING (*trying to take the bird again*): Your hand is covered with blood. Go wash your fingers. I'll bury the bird.

QUEEN (*withdrawing*): That was not nice.

(*He accepts that rebuke in silence.*)

　　You are cruel. You'll hurt it more. I won't give it to you. Wake up, birdie!

(*Runs off with the bird. He stands staring after her. Long pause. Suddenly he calls out.*)

KING: I am sorry.

SINGER: Memories slide,
                   meld and fuse.
                   Discrete moments
                   get flung together
                   strung in a single moment.
                   Then the moment
                   distends, spreads
                   into years.

(*The King and the Queen are older.*)

QUEEN: And Your Majesty has been urinating on my rose bush
    again!

KING (*almost shouting with joy*): Really? You are sure?

(*The Queen nods. Holds up four fingers.*)

    Four months? Four! Why didn't you tell me all these days?

QUEEN: You know why. (*Whispers*) I waited till I was sure.

(*He laughs delightedly. Kisses her all over. Then suddenly lifts her
up and whirls her around.*)

    Please—Please—you'll drop me.

KING (*plonking her down on the pedestal*): Never! I love you.
    You're pregnant! Pregnant! Oh, you're beautiful. And won-
    derful and glorious and...

QUEEN (*laughing*): Stop being silly.

KING: I am so happy. The entire kingdom will burst into
    festivities. But first we must tell Mother. She will be ecstatic.
    This is what she's been praying for...

QUEEN: Yes, we must. She first of all.

KING: Come. (*Calls out*) Mother! Mother!

(*They rush to the Queen Mother's quarters, she blushing, he
laughing. The Queen Mother enters.*)

MOTHER: What's it? Why are you shouting?

KING: Mother! Bless us—

MOTHER: You have my blessings. Always. What's happened now?

KING: Happy news. The happiest possible. We're going to have a baby—

(*The Mother looks at him warily.*)

MOTHER: Are you sure?

KING: Of course we are sure.

(*The Mother shuts her eyes and clutches her hands in a quick prayer. The King and the Queen come forward and touch her feet. The Mother lifts her daughter-in-law by her shoulders and embraces her. Smoothens her hair.*)

MOTHER: God bless you! You have made our family tree bloom. May you beget a son whose glory blinds the eight directions.

(*Gently seats her down.*)

Now, the next couple of months are most precious. You need to take special care.

KING: Yes, Mother. She'll be your obedient daughter-in-law.

(*The Queen blushes, laughs.*)

MOTHER: Good. Now I must go to my shrine and celebrate. We must thank the gods for this most wonderful gift.

KING: Yes, Mother.

MOTHER: I'll send you the offering.

(*Goes away. The King and the Queen return to their original place.*)

QUEEN: Yes! Yes! Now I'll show them. I'll show those swine. All these years I have waited for this moment. Prayed for it. Cringing at their glances—

KING: They meant well. They were only anxious.

QUEEN: They were vicious.

KING: As subjects of this land, they were interested in an heir. Fair enough.

QUEEN: Your subjects. For me, they were my judges, my interrogators, torturers—all clubbed together against me.

KING: 'Against' you?

QUEEN: Can you men even imagine what it feels like? To pretend you are unaware of their gaze as they scrutinize the roundness of your belly, the stain on your thigh! Line after line of carrion crows, watching, waiting, ready to caw at the palmful of blood that spurted. And spurt it did—every month—every bloody month. How I hated myself when that happened.

KING: Surely you can forget all that in your moment of triumph.

QUEEN (*suddenly laughs, tousles his hair*): Yes, I can. For you. You could have taken another wife. You didn't.

KING: Of course I didn't.

QUEEN: Sometimes I wished you had.

KING: You did?

QUEEN: Yes, purely for bearing children. Then I could make love to you—for its own sake—to make love. You don't know how I have pined for that. And now I can look forward to it.

KING: You mean it will get even better?

(*They laugh and embrace.*)

QUEEN: You are sure your mother isn't unhappy?

KING: Unhappy! Are you mad? She's wanted a grandson as badly as we've wanted a son.

QUEEN: All these years, she had some hope of getting you another queen. Now...

KING: She'll have a grandchild instead. Look, we can't change her. I can't bring myself another mother. She can't get herself another son. And (*laughing*) I won't look for another wife. So that seems to be a fairly unalterable situation.

(*Kisses her.*)

I wish you would stop being so full of doubts. About yourself. People don't dislike you—

QUEEN: She does. And I can't blame her. Because of me, you deserted her faith—her Mother Goddess.

(*The Queen moves to the window. Looks out.*)

I'm afraid.

KING: Of what?

QUEEN (*points out*): That bit of the thatched roof there. You have considerately built a wall round it to hide the shed. But the roof shows. As though it refuses to be dismissed.

KING: The earth there couldn't take a higher wall.

QUEEN: It's the shed in which your mother keeps her animals. (*Pause.*)
All these years I've been pretending that it doesn't exist. That I couldn't hear the bleat of sheep being taken out at night. (*Pause.*)
For slaughter.
(*Pause.*)
You sleep through it. You've grown up with those sounds. I haven't. They often wake me up—keep me awake. But I've pretended I didn't mind.

KING: I know. I'm sorry.

QUEEN: Because I didn't want to hurt your mother.

KING: Why are you bringing it up now?

QUEEN: When your mother says she'll celebrate, what does she mean?

KING (*gently*): Darling, how does it concern us? She doesn't make any demands on us.

QUEEN: The animals are graded according to the occasion. Poultry is offered at daily rites. Sheep, goats for the more important rituals. Then buffalo.

KING: You know that's been the family tradition.

QUEEN: Weren't human beings also offered in sacrifice to the goddess once?

KING: Yes. But that was generations ago.

QUEEN: So you see, a tradition can be given up. Or at least changed.

KING: Mother will not agree to give up her practices. You know

that. She feels she owes it to our ancestors. We've been
through all this before.

QUEEN: But now it concerns our child. What offerings will be
considered worthy of a royal birth, do you think?

(*No reply.*)

They say when you were born, every inch of the earth for
miles around was soaked in blood.

KING: People exaggerate.

QUEEN: Yes, you're right. I shouldn't be complaining about the
scale. Just the thought. Of bloodshed. Even a single drop of
blood.

(*Pause.*)

I don't want it. Not in the name of our child.

KING (*calmly*): I know how you feel. But look at it this way. She
has accepted the fact that we will not be party to her violent
rites. And she carries them out in her own separate shrine.
In her shell. Let's leave it at that.

QUEEN: I don't want to hurt her. She can live by her beliefs. But
we are Jains. Our son will be a Jain. He will have to uphold
the principle of compassion for all living beings, of non-
violence. Should we allow a blood rite to mark his arrival?
It would be wrong. Terribly wrong!

(*Suddenly she is overtaken by nausea. The King supports her. She
retches. When she recovers, he takes her back to the pedestal. She
sits on it. He moves to the Queen Mother's quarters.*)

KING: Mother—

MOTHER: Yes—

KING (*gently*): Mother, please don't get upset. But—

MOTHER: You don't have to beat around the bush. Come out with
it.

KING: I want you to promise me that there will be no blood
sacrifices in honour of our child.

(*Pause.*)

MOTHER: I was expecting this.

KING: Please, Mother.

MOTHER: You are denying me the right to my worship!

KING (*firmly*): No, Mother, I'm not.

MOTHER: You're treating my goddess as though she were a cheap, tribal spirit. And you are cutting off my path to her.

KING: Try and be sensible, Mother. No one is stopping you from worshipping your goddess or from your own form of worship. But I am a Jain. My son will be a Jain—a Jain King. I cannot have his birth greeted with the infliction of death.

MOTHER: You were not born a Jain. You were born my son. But you betrayed me and my faith. Instead of choosing the woman and bringing her to your faith, you chose hers.

KING: I accepted the faith because I found truth in it and compassion for the world in pain. I don't want to add to the pain. I will not let anyone do it. Certainly not in the name of my son.

MOTHER: He is my grandson too. I too have prayed for him. For me, he is the gift of my goddess.

KING: A king can follow only one path and I have chosen mine.

MOTHER: My feelings don't matter to you. It's mother, ranting and raving as usual. All right. Let her have her way. I'll move out of the palace.

(*The King tries to remonstrate.*)

I shall live in a separate cottage outside the palace.

KING: Mother, this is your home. This is where you gave birth to me, brought me up. We don't want you to go. Please, don't. I am only talking of this one occasion.

MOTHER: My gods have already been expelled from this house and live, shunned and starved, like outcastes. I should have followed them out. But I was blinded by my love for you.

(*Pause.*)

But I want you to promise me something.

KING: Yes?

MOTHER: I shall live away from the palace, in a corner of my own. And there, I shall live as I please. With my gods. My sacrificial animals. No further interference from you two.

KING: All right, Mother.

MOTHER: Promise.

KING: I promise.

MOTHER: All right. Will you arrange to have a cottage built next to the shrine for me? And a shed for my animals? Or should I look to it myself?

KING: I'll attend to it.

(*He turns to go.*)

MOTHER: Before you go, son—

(*He stops. He's been expecting this too.*)

I don't want to be nasty. But I am your mother and it worries me. Are you sure she's pregnant?

KING: Yes, I am.

MOTHER: Have you checked with the palace nurse?

KING: No, but she has.

MOTHER: I wanted to, but decided against it. If she heard that I was making enquiries, she would immediately decide I was doubting her word.

KING (*laughs*): But you are. However, there's no cause for it.

MOTHER: You should check personally.

KING: I'll accept my wife's word for it.

MOTHER: You know what happened last time.

KING: I do. But—

MOTHER: I hope it's not a repetition.

KING: She was still a child then. She knew very little. She was under such pressure to produce an heir. Her period was delayed by a few weeks and everyone went to town about her being pregnant. She too got carried away.

MOTHER: She claimed to be pregnant.

KING: She wanted to be pregnant. She was desperate.

MOTHER: She showed all the signs. Not just the stopping of periods. Her belly began to show. She had morning sickness—

KING: She couldn't have feigned all that.

MOTHER: Her problem is that she has too much imagination.

KING: She is sensitive.

MOTHER: She lives wrapped up in herself. She should listen to the world around her. Open her eyes to it: ears to it.

KING: She's been a good wife. A good queen.

MOTHER: You became the laughing stock of the world. You had to swallow public humiliation.

KING: Not swallow. Face. A king sometimes has to do that.

MOTHER: Soon after it came to light that it was a false pregnancy, I overheard two palace maids, giggling. 'A hen doesn't need a cock to lay eggs,' one of them was saying. 'She can do it on her own!' I could have died of shame.

KING: I hope you didn't dismiss them from service for saying so.

MOTHER: I did.

KING: Tongues won't wag any less outside the palace.

MOTHER: It was your palace. Yours and hers. That's why I couldn't chop that tongue off!

(*The King shrugs. The Mother walks out. As the lights brighten, we see the Mahout, still drinking. He casts surreptitious glances at the King and the Queen. Long pause. The Queen moves to the King.*)

QUEEN (*softly*): Let's go. Please.

(*The King does not respond.*)

MAHOUT: Why are you hanging on here? Why don't you go back to the palace—

KING (*in agony*): Oh God! God! God!

MAHOUT: I thought I was gone, finished, no more life. Now that I have been granted a few more years, I'd like to be left in peace. Go back to the palace.

QUEEN: I swear to you. It won't happen again. Ever. Please.
(*The King does not respond. Pause.*)
All right...
(*She moves to the door.*)

KING: No. Please. Stay!
(*She stops.*)
It won't take long.

QUEEN (*surprised, in a whisper*): What won't take long?

KING: I'll tell you. Let me recover. I'll tell you what's to be done.
(*Pause.*)
Let me get my breath. After all I've been through. Hours...

QUEEN (*taken aback*): How long have you been here?
(*He shrugs.*)
Have you been standing out there...all this while? Listening to everything going on inside?
(*Unbelieving*)
Oh God!

KING: What else could I do?
(*As the King speaks, lights change. The Mahout's song begins in the background, not sung by the Mahout but represented by a melody played on a wind instrument by a musician who appears on stage, while the Mahout mimes singing. A beam lights up the King as he relives his agony, moment by moment.*)
At midnight, he started singing in the distance. I felt you wake up. I felt you slide out of my bed. You got up. Left. I opened my eyes, saw you press yourself against the window and listen. And then, slip away. I followed. Through the biting chill and

you didn't even have a shawl on... You went out of the royal
garden... into the street. You entered this ruined temple. The
singing stopped. Those noises began. Those horrible, animal
noises of copulation. I couldn't... breathe.

(*The Queen covers her face in horror.*)

I was numb. Couldn't breathe. I needed fresh air. I ran. I ran
back into the garden.

(*The King runs into the garden. Almost breaks out into a scream
but gags himself with his fists. Sits clutching his head. Controls
himself.*

The Queen Mother enters. Sees him from a distance.)

MOTHER: Son—

(*The Queen takes a sudden intake of breath.*)

Son—

KING: Mother! What are you doing here?

MOTHER: You know my prayers finish only at midnight. Tonight
they went on a little longer. The lights. The songs. It was
beautiful. I was on my way back when I saw you. What are
you doing here at this hour?

KING: I felt suffocated in the palace, hot. Needed a breath of fresh
air. So I came here.

MOTHER: You felt hot? In the depth of winter? I'm freezing. And
you should be wearing something warmer.

KING: Thank you. I'm fine.

MOTHER: Don't be silly. Look, even the swans are frozen in the
lake. (*Laughs.*) They could be images carved in ice. Hot!

(*Pause. She notices something is wrong. She goes nearer. He half
turns away lest she notice his state.*)

But you are sweating. And your eyes are bloodshot. Are you
all right?

(*Long pause.*)

Son—

KING: Yes?

MOTHER: What is it? What's wrong?

KING: Me? Nothing.

MOTHER: Don't try to fool me. I know you. The moment I saw you from there, I knew. Even in the dark. There's something wrong, isn't there? Very wrong.

KING: What do you want me to say? I told you there's nothing wrong. I felt like a walk in the open—

MOTHER: Give me your hand.
(*She takes his hand and places it on her own head.*)
If you don't tell me what's on your mind, let my skull splinter into a thousand shards.
(*The King withdraws his hand, as though stung.*)

KING: Mother, why are you hounding me? Why don't you leave me alone?

MOTHER: You are telling lies. You are trying to hide something from your own mother. Must be something really serious.
(*Pause. Fiercely*)
Tell me. Tell me. I can't help you unless you tell me.

KING: Around midnight, I had a dream. It woke me up.

MOTHER: Yes? What was it?

KING: In the dream... (*Pause.*) I saw that the royal swan in our garden had got caught in mud and was flapping its wings.

MOTHER: It was asking for help.

KING: I don't know. I suppose so...

MOTHER: It was caught in mud. Trapped. And crying out for help?

KING: Yes.

MOTHER: Then?

KING: Nothing. I woke up. Felt wide awake. So I came out for a walk.

MOTHER: And you came to check if the swans were all right?

KING: No. Not really. I don't know. Perhaps yes. It was a vivid dream. It felt real.

(*Laughs.*)

Anyway the swans are there, safe, fast asleep. That's all. Are you happy now?

MOTHER: No, I'm not.

KING: I've told you the truth.

MOTHER: I know. And I'm glad you told me. It's a bad dream.

KING: Now, Mother...

MOTHER: It doesn't augur well.

KING: Don't start on that, Mother.

MOTHER: Dreams speak to us. They come to warn us.

KING: Now you know why I was reluctant to tell you about it.

MOTHER: Dreams have spoken to me. And whenever I ignored them, I suffered. Like when I lost your father. I was warned. You know that. I still blame myself. A dream like this is like an epidemic. The longer you ignore it, the more it spreads. Eats into more of the family and the populace. It's fortunate I came to know right now.

(*He makes a dismissive gesture.*)

You go back to your bed. Or wander around the garden. But then take this shawl. Leave the dream to me.

KING: And where are you going?

MOTHER: I'm going back to my goddess. She'll save us.

I know precisely what needs to be done.

KING: What are you going to do?

MOTHER: Don't ask.

(*Long pause. The King waits.*)

There's going to be a heavy mist soon. And you are dripping wet. Go back and change and go to bed.

KING: Why don't you tell me what you intend to do?

MOTHER: I shall offer the goddess a hundred fowl in sacrifice.
(*The King has anticipated something like this but cannot suppress a gasp. The Queen, too, concealed in the darkness, gasps.*)
    A hundred fowl. If we slake her parched throat, we may yet avert disaster.
(*Lights change: we see the King, the Queen and the Mahout.*)

MAHOUT: I knew it! I knew it would finally skewer me. No, no, that's not right, Your Majesty. A hundred fowl—I know what that slaughter means. It's witchcraft. Whip me, Sir, brand me. But don't don't take away my voice.

KING: Be quiet!

MAHOUT: What'll happen to me, if I lose my voice? I have nothing else...only my songs. Please, please, don't destroy me by taking them away.

QUEEN: Don't be alarmed. I'll see that nothing happens to you.

MAHOUT: Thank you, madam. You are like a mother to me. I'll never forget your kindness—
(*He literally touches her feet.*)

QUEEN (*no irony*): Trust me. I shall not deprive the world of your voice. I shall not desecrate it.
(*Caresses his hair.*)

KING (*turning his face away in disgust*): Bravo!

QUEEN: Spare me your disgust. You take your blood and gore. I'll choose his voice—

KING: Will you at least let me finish?

QUEEN: Yes?

KING: I refused. There was no question of any bloody rite.
(*The lights change. The King and the Mother.*)
    Mother, please. Don't do anything. Let things be. Please.

MOTHER: I am not asking you to join in.

KING: I know. It's just—I don't want you to do anything. No
rites. No sacrifices. (*Pause.*) Please, Mother, this once. No
bloodshed.

QUEEN (*from the dark*): Why didn't you tell her there was no
dream? No swan. That you'd made it up.

KING: Had I? I'm not so sure. I was talking about the swan. But
I was thinking of you.

MOTHER (*baffled*): Are you trying to stop me? When I moved out,
you promised that I would be allowed to live on my own
terms.

KING: Mother, you don't have to do anything, because…there was
no dream. That was a lie. I made it up.

(*The Mother stares at him, not comprehending.*)

MOTHER: No dream?

KING: No. The dream was a piece of fiction. So you don't have
to do anything about it.

(*He puts his palm on her head.*)

Here. I swear I made it up. Are you satisfied?

(*Withdraws his hand. The Mother is still trying to make sense.*)

MOTHER: No dream? Why did you say there was one then?

KING: I had to tell you something.

MOTHER: You're hiding something from me.

KING (*suddenly*): In God's name! Is there no way to escape this
hell?

(*The Queen Mother stares at him.*)

MOTHER (*quietly*): If you are going through hell, why isn't she
here by your side? She figures in it somewhere, doesn't she?
That's why you are tying yourself into such knots. At this time
of the night. Where is she?

(*Pause.*)

You are running away from her, aren't you?

(*Pause.*)

Why?

(*Pause.*)

I'll promise you something. On oath. Take me to her now. And I'll give up my faith and become a Jain.

(*Pause.*)

That's what you've always wanted. She has always wanted.

(*Pause.*)

You won't accept the offer. Why?

(*The truth dawns on her. She steps back in horror.*)

Oh my mother! Don't tell me! I knew it would happen ultimately... But don't tell me she's done it... She is with someone. A lover! Oh my God—

(*The King turns away.*)

When? Tonight?... It has to be. You were happy enough with her last evening... Is she in the palace?

(*No answer.*)

No. You mean she is lying between someone's thighs this moment?

KING: Mother—

MOTHER: Oh horrible! Horrible ! Where? Where is she? Tell me— In some hole? A god-forsaken garret? Where? Where did you see them?

KING: Control yourself—

MOTHER: Has she fallen so low? The whore—And you. How can you stand here like this? I should cut her to pieces...feed her to wolves and vultures. Do it, son, now!

KING: Don't be hysterical, Mother—

MOTHER: Throw her bones to the dogs. She has betrayed you. You are not bound by your vows now. All this nonsense about non-violence. It had to go. Let it go. Kill the harlot and her lover. If you won't do it, I'll do it. Let me fetch my sacrificial knife from the temple. I'll—

(*She turns to go to the temple. He holds her back.*)

KING: Calm down, Mother. Please—

MOTHER: What kind of a man are you? You have lost your manhood. You, you impotent...

(*Spits in his face. He reels back. But that action suddenly calms her. She suddenly realizes what she has done. Quickly moves forward and wipes his face.*)

Forgive me. Forgive me.

(*They look at each other. Their deep fondness for each other is clear in that look.*)

I am becoming decrepit—and still I haven't learnt to control my temper.

(*He smiles.*)

All right. You won't shed blood. Then throw her out. Get yourself another wife.

(*He does not respond. Incredulous*)

Surely you are not going to...forgive her? Continue as though nothing has happened?

KING: I don't know what to do.

MOTHER: You love her. But such love is meant for harlots. She has drowned our family in sin. She has called out to demonic forces.

KING: Mother, please. Please, help me.

MOTHER (*gentle*): Do you think I like tormenting you—my only child, the light of my life?

KING: Help me. Please.

(*Pause.*)

I am lost—

MOTHER: We have to do something.

(*She looks at him, deeply moved. Comes to him.*)

You won't offer a living animal in sacrifice.

KING: I can't.

MOTHER: So what if it isn't living? Will that do?

KING: What do you mean—

MOTHER: No, I don't mean a carcass. Silly ass! What you offer to the gods, you have to partake of. If it isn't living...
(*Laughs.*)
How dumb can you be! All right. There will be no bloodshed. We'll compromise.

KING: If anything has to be done, it'll be done by me. Promise. Not you. Nor anyone else. Mother, whatever's happened, concerns me, my wife. And I need her. (*Anguished*) I can't let her go.
(*The Mother stares.*)

MOTHER: All right. Go to her. I'll come there with the offering. There'll be no bloodshed.

KING: Thank you.

MOTHER: Go there and wait. I'll follow you.
(*As though answering an unasked question*)
I'll smell her out.
(*The Mother goes back to the silver tray on the steps of the temple. The King moves to the Queen.*)

QUEEN (*tense*): And so?

KING (*calls out*): Mother—Mother—

QUEEN (*aghast*): She's here? You brought her here with you?

KING: No. I didn't. She...smelt us out.

QUEEN: If only I knew you, as she does.

KING (*goes to the door*): Mother—
(*The Mother gets up, picks up the tray, and walks into the sanctum.*)
There. Put it down.
(*The Mother places the tray on the low platform in front of the altar.*)
Now, Mother. Leave us. Please.

(*The Mother doesn't move.*)
      I'll attend to everything.
(*The Mother goes out of the temple. The King goes to the tray and is about to take off the saffron cloth when they all freeze.*)

SINGER: The hunter,
                 dagger bright but sheathed,
                 back arching, the axe poised to strike
                 but frozen.
                 The dog
                 lunging behind, unmoving.
                 Patterns dotting welcome
                 on the winter's starry floor.
                 Why then suddenly
                 as the mists roll back
                 does my heart tremble
                 at the hound's burning eye?

(*The King takes off the saffron cloth covering the tray in which the offering is kept. The Mahout cannot resist stepping forward to take a look. Amidst ritual materials like flowers, saffron, myrrh and camphor stands a life-size replica of a cock with its head raised and beak open, as though it was crowing. The Queen gasps.*)

KING: This is the offering. A sacrifice of dough. A substitute for
      a live fowl.
(*The Queen stares at the cock of dough. The King, as though to reassure her*)
      It's dough. Inanimate.
(*The Mahout begins to giggle, more from relief than in derision.*)
      Don't you dare!
(*The Mahout retires to his corner trying to suppress his giggles.*)
      Don't you dare!

(*He turns and looks at the Queen. Trying to make it all sound normal, he holds the sword over the cock.*)

All you have to do is place your right hand on the back of my fist. Like this.

(*Demonstrates by placing his left hand on the back of his right.*)

And I'll push the blade into this lump of dough. We will, together. That's all. That'll be the end of it.

QUEEN: This is a temple! You want to violate it?

KING: But it's only dough. There's no violence in it.

QUEEN: But...but...this sword. This plunging in of the blade. The act...it's violence.

KING: There's no bloodshed.

QUEEN: Then why are you doing it? Why? Blood at least makes sense if you believe in bloodthirsty gods. But this... you can't knowingly fool yourself.

KING: It's a small thing. A symbolic gesture...

(*The Queen looks at the King, almost with compassion. He stares at her numbly.*)

QUEEN: You have taken this on to save me, haven't you? To ensure that your mother doesn't contaminate me with her violence?

(*Pause.*)

You are a good man. I have always known that.

(*Pause.*)

Perhaps, I don't deserve you.

KING (*softly*): I want you back. I can't live without you.

QUEEN: Nor can I.

KING: But we can't go back as though nothing has happened. Something has happened. Something terrible. We can't leave it to Mother to handle. It's my problem. Ours.

QUEEN: We'll face it together. But not here. At home.

KING: And take this cock home with us?

(*A new note has crept into the conversation which chills her.*)

QUEEN: Take it home? Why?

KING: How else do we tackle the problem?

QUEEN: I don't understand...

(*Pause.*)

KING: How do we face the problem...

(*He looks at the cock.*)

...without this?

QUEEN: How will it help?

KING: I don't know. But I have a feeling it will.

QUEEN: How?

KING: I don't know. But when I was waiting outside, lost, adrift, sunk in misery, Mother brought the offering. I looked at it and I felt better.

(*Pause.*)

I felt help was on its way.

(*Pause.*)

It sort of signalled to me.

(*Pause.*)

I could feel the reassurance. Don't keep questioning, it said, surrender.

(*Pause. The Queen stares.*)

Look at it. Just look. Please. And perhaps you'll see what I mean. I'm sure you will. It's there to help.

QUEEN: Perhaps. And you want to harm it?

KING: Not harm. Sacrifice. That's the whole point of its being there. That's its whole purpose.

QUEEN: Do you realize that those words would sum up my life as well?

(*Pause.*)

I won't take part in it.

KING (*desperate*): You don't have to believe! Merely carry out the rite. Along with me. That's enough.

(*She shakes her head firmly.*)

QUEEN: Why are you doing this to yourself? You are like a child. You want to hurt me. But you are hurting only yourself.

KING: But I have to do something. And I don't know what!

QUEEN: All right. Go ahead. Do as you wish. If it makes you feel better. I am going home.

KING: But you can't. I can't let you go.

QUEEN: Can't?

KING: Because we are husband and wife—coupled in the eyes of God, joined together with the sacred fire as the witness. We are bound by our vow—to do everything together.

QUEEN: You want me to play your wife so I can damn myself as an adulteress?

KING: Look, we don't know everything about this world. There may be...powers...forces we know nothing about.

(*Pause.*)

Who knows, if we had listened to Mother we may not have lost our child...

(*She looks at him horrified. Pause.*)

QUEEN: What did you say?

KING: I don't know—I mean—what do I—

QUEEN: So I lost my baby because I didn't follow your mother's orders? Because I didn't kill and maim?

KING: I am not saying that.

QUEEN: Yes, you are. Late in my life, I become pregnant and I have a miscarriage—and you are saying that it was a punishment meted out to me for my defiance.

KING: I didn't say punishment—

QUEEN: I lost my baby! I still haven't got over it. You know that

I still feel devastated by it. And you are now saying it was chastisement for my wickedness.

KING: Listen to me—

QUEEN: A curse I deserved? And all these years—when you were being loving and understanding, the ideal husband—you were only pretending. That's what you believed?

KING: I am not holding you responsible for your miscarriage. But you can't blame it on me or Mother either.

QUEEN: Sometimes I've felt—I had to abort to prove to you I was pregnant. To show you the proof.

KING: What are you talking about?

QUEEN: And I suppose that's why I haven't become pregnant since then. Your mother's goddess in her wrath has made me sterile! And all those years you have agreed with that—God! How I loathe you and your mother and your whole—

KING: No, I didn't. But can you blame me for believing that now? Now—after this betrayal—this treachery?

QUEEN: All right. Go ahead. Believe what you like. But I'll not agree to the sacrifice. I'll never.

(*Sudden laughter is heard from a distance. The Queen looks up surprised. The lights change. The Queen Mother enters from behind the pedestal, laughing. She is energetic, ebullient, a dancing, spectral figure, not the person we have seen earlier.*)

MOTHER (*laughing*): Bravo! Excellent! Excellent! More power to you!

QUEEN: What do you want?

MOTHER: We should strip ourselves bare and stand naked face to face. Let us. There's no one else. No one else can be here.

QUEEN: Why have you come here?

MOTHER: Don't agree to the sacrifice. Refuse. Let him plead. Don't yield. That's what I've come to tell you.

QUEEN: What are you up to now?

MOTHER: Me? Why?

QUEEN: This sudden, new tack? Is it some new game? A new opening?

MOTHER: Don't be so suspicious. I mean it. Don't agree to the sacrifice. Don't yield to his entreaties. The more you refuse, the more will my son suffer. Let him.

QUEEN: You've hated me from the day I stepped into this palace.

MOTHER: The only relationship in the world which does not wither and fade away is that of hate. That'll keep us together—at least so long as my son remains a Jain.

QUEEN: I refuse to discuss my religion with you.

MOTHER: I couldn't care less about your religion. It's my son's that concerns me.

QUEEN: You brought up your son drenched in bloody sacrifices, bile and gore. In violence. He was bound to turn away. He's a good man.

MOTHER: What do you know of violence? Or of pain? You seem so averse to blood that I wonder you didn't prefer to remain a virgin. For many years I was childless. Then—one day—I became pregnant.

(The Queen turns away.)

QUEEN: I don't want to know.

MOTHER: Of course you don't. You have a fickle womb. False pregnancy! Miscarriage! Mine is made of steel. We were ecstatic. But labour began and the child refused to come out. They said the foetus was set transverse in the womb. For four days and nights I screamed in pain. I prayed for death so my child could live. Ultimately they pinned me down to the floor, spreadeagled, and the nurse shoved her hand into my uterus, twisted him around and pulled him out. I was screaming through the gag they had thrust into my mouth. You couldn't

begin to imagine what I went through then. I knew I was
going to die. I cast one last glance at my darling son—a
farewell look, I thought—and saw him drenched in blood,
half-wrapped in my placenta, and I began to laugh. I lived.
I drowned him in blood. You, however, are drowning him in
guilt.

QUEEN: I'll never agree to the offering.

KING (*in the dark*): Please don't say that. Please.

MOTHER: Twist the knife in his wound. Let him flagellate himself,
revel in self-hatred. He is the offering, don't you see? Make
him bleed. It'll please the gods.

QUEEN: You disgust me.

(*The Queen Mother laughs. Disappears laughing. The lights change.*)

MAHOUT (*inebriated*): I may be speaking out of turn, sir, but I
think you are being hard on yourself. And there's no need for
it. I mean, a woman slips but it doesn't have to be for the
worse. I mean, take me. I am ugly, I know. People have called
me all sorts of names. But I tell you. I have known a few
women. They say there are six types of women...

KING (*gravely*): And what about the seventh?

MAHOUT (*stumped*): I only thought there were six.

KING: No one's written about her. While she sinks her teeth into
the man and drinks blood, plucks his entrails like strings, the
man's head only laughs and sings.

MAHOUT (*laughs*): You're joking, aren't you? You took me in there
for a minute, I tell you. I thought you were serious. No, no,
no, Your Majesty. You've got to take your life in your stride.
That's what I firmly believe. Do you believe in God? Of course
not. Stupid of me to ask. But if you did, then you would have
had someone to talk to now. To ask for guidance, if you see
what I mean. You can't dictate to Him, or demand things of
Him. But you can ask. And if I were you, I would ask: 'God,

why has this thing happened? What did you intend when you sent a bat into the elephant stables which brought this elephant-keeper into our lives? Surely you had a design?' And God might say to you—'Might', mind you, I am not saying He will—you never can say what God will answer, that's what makes Him what He is, doesn't it? But I reckon God might say: 'Look at the benefits!'

KING: Benefits. Quite right! We never gave any thought to the benefits.

MAHOUT: There! What did I tell you? Talk to God—ask Him— it makes you see things in a new light. The benefits. Now, there's a thing or two I've noticed about your queen.

KING: You have? What kind of thing?

MAHOUT: Touch her here on her shoulder. Rub gently. And you'll see for yourself what happens.

KING: The right shoulder!
(*Goes near the Queen and inspects her shoulders.*)
The right one. Here? I see. I must bear that in mind. I knew that sometimes caressing and pressing her down here—near the hips—that worked like magic. But this right shoulder thing, this is new to me.

QUEEN: Enough, sir. Please, you are making it worse for yourself.

KING (*ignoring her, to the Mahout*): Any other—shall I say, vulnerable—spots, would you say? Erogenous?

QUEEN: Don't you dare. I am not a piece of meat for you to pick and paw at.

MAHOUT: Sorry, lady. Didn't mean to upset you. I meant it all in good humour. Between the three of us, you know. Didn't mean to hurt.

QUEEN (*to the King*): How could you!

KING: What a pundit. A veritable sage. A guru. A man of divine wisdom...and beauty.

MAHOUT (*reacting*): Oh, don't worry about her sense of beauty. She put out the light as soon as she came in. I told you she knows what to do.

KING (*suddenly losing patience*): Enough of you. Go away!

MAHOUT: No. I won't. I am not going anywhere. I am staying. I came here first. I came here to have a drink and then sleep and that's what I'm going to do. Haven't had a moment to oneself and then one has to put up with rudeness. I was thinking of going. But now I won't. I'll stay.

(*Sits in his corner. Takes out a bottle and takes a long swig.*)

Yes, one more thing. Why do you carry that sword around if you aren't going to use it? Eh? I mean, it's like fangs in a sparrow's beak, isn't it? Pretty useless.

Oh, don't mind me. Go on. Cluck...clucking...

(*Burps.*)

I'm leaving in the morning. May have to walk for days before I get another job. So have to rest properly. Mind you, there is no shortage of kings in this land...nor of queens!

(*Laughs.*)

I'll tell you what. If you want to hang me by the tallest tree— make an example of me, you know—why don't you make an image of me with dough—

(*He giggles.*)

...with dough and string it up. After all, if you find it fit for gods, I don't see why dough shouldn't be good enough for you.

(*Pause.*)

Would a man of dough satisfy her though? Goodnight.

(*He covers himself and goes to sleep and is soon snoring.*)

QUEEN (*calmly*): Before we start again! I didn't say it earlier because I didn't want to hurt you. But it's the truth.

(*Pause.*)

I do not regret anything that has happened. I will not disown him or anything he gave me.

KING: How can you be so crass? So brazen? You—

QUEEN: Because it just happened. Without my willing it. It just happened. That's all.

KING: And you didn't pause to ask if I deserved it? I who have loved you all these years—above everything—
(*The Mahout's song, that is the music, begins.*)

QUEEN: I was sleeping by your side. His singing woke me up. The song was so—don't know how to describe it. But suddenly the notes caressed me, enveloped me. They carried me away. For a brief moment, nothing mattered. The palace. Me. You. Only the song. I felt like a flame burning bright. Pure. When I came to my senses, I was here. By his side. That's all there is to it. It just happened.
(*Pause.*)
And what happened was beautiful.

KING: No. I can't believe it's you. This isn't you! Why are you doing this to me? Because I blamed the miscarriage on you?

QUEEN (*gently*): No, of course not.
(*Pause.*)
I want to come back to you. I feel fuller. Richer. Warmer. But not ashamed. Because I didn't plan it. It happened. And it was beautiful.
(*A long pause. He stares at her.*)
I'm sorry. If this rite is going to blot the moment out, that would be the real betrayal. I'll do anything else.

KING: Anything else?

QUEEN: Yes. I promise.

KING: There's only one thing I want.
(*Pause.*)
You. I want you back. All this...this ritual...this...this here...all this is only so I can get you back.

QUEEN: I am yours. I'll never betray you again.

KING: Prove it.

QUEEN (*not quite sure*): I will. Let's go back—

KING: No. Here.

QUEEN: What do you mean?

KING: Prove that you'll be mine. Here. Now. In this place. After
all, this is where it all happened. Here in front of this...absent
God...

(*Startled, she looks at the Mahout who is fast asleep.*)
You promised. Before it dawns. I won't ask for anything else.
Come—

(*He extends his hand. She takes it. He leads her gently to where the
Mahout is sleeping. Then he unbuckles his sword and turns to her.
She stands petrified as he approaches her.*)

QUEEN (*in horror*): What's happened to you? What are you doing?

KING: You promised.

QUEEN: But...but you can't...not here.

KING: Yes, here.

(*He kneels in front of her and pulls her down, gently, almost
pleading, to her knees. Then as she kneels in front of him, he begins
to undress her. Takes off her pallu. The Mahout moans in his sleep.
Startled, she looks at him. The King, gently*)
Don't be afraid. Let him wake up. Let him see. What does it
matter? Let the whole world see. We are coupled in the eyes
of God. We need not be ashamed of anything. We must strip
ourselves of any sense of shame. Become naked like our
Saviours.

(*He loosens her hair. Kisses her shoulder. Caresses her bosom. Kisses
her gently in the cleft. She shudders. He tries to untie her blouse.
Suddenly the Mahout moans in his sleep and she reacts. Tries to
get away. But the King has anticipated that. They struggle. The
Mahout sits up with a start.*)

QUEEN (*viciously*): Get away from me...

(*She pushes the King aside and rolls away. He reaches out for her violently and then stops. He laughs.*)

KING: The fowl leave us no choice. Don't you see? There's no alternative!

QUEEN: Get away from me.

(*The Queen is trembling with humiliation, almost on the verge of tears. Suddenly she turns to the Mahout on his mat and then looks back at the King, defiantly.*)

KING: Yes, go back to that savage ape—that ugly beast—

(*The Mahout, has been, until now, sitting and watching in a kind of alcoholic stupor. He can barely understand what's going on. Now he reacts.*)

MAHOUT (*roars*): Enough!

(*Gets up.*)

> Enough, I say. I've had enough. I won't put up with any more. The insults. The abuses—no more. I've had enough. Now pick up that toy of yours and get out of here. Out! You may be the royalty. You may cut me to pieces tomorrow. But tomorrow's tomorrow. But now I tell you what to do. Pick that up and get out of here.

(*The King's hand automatically reaches out for his sword. But there's no sword round his waist.*)

> Stop reaching out for that sword...as though you are suffering from the itch. Pick that up now. Take it away. Now!

(*Pause.*)

> Now, are you going to do as I say or aren't you?

(*They watch each other tensely.*)

> You won't? Then I'll do it myself.

(*He reaches out for the cock. Then stops.*)

QUEEN: Go on. Go on. Don't hesitate now. Throw it out.

(*The Mahout looks at her. Then back to the cock.*)

> Don't be afraid, Mahout. Go ahead. Nothing'll happen to you. You've my word—

(*Pause.*)

    Go on.

(*The Mahout slowly steps back.*)

    You coward!

(*The Mahout goes back to his corner and starts rolling his mat, wrapping up his meagre belongings.*)

    You coward! Didn't you hear him call you an ape—an ugly beast? I'll stand by you. Fling it out—you—you—

MAHOUT (*quietly*): Madam, if you want to plunge your hand into a snake-pit, go ahead!

QUEEN (*imitating the Mahout*): And so the cock scared even our elephant man. Did it? I suppose now I have only this cock to make love to—

KING: Beware. Don't mock it.

QUEEN: Mock the cock? No, surely not. After all, not even that ape could lift that cock. All right then. I'll throw it out myself.

(*She reaches to the fowl, as though to pick it up.*)

KING: Amritamati, please—

(*In the distance she hears the laughter of the Queen Mother. Stops.*)

MOTHER: Twist the knife in his wound, let him suffer, make him bleed.

KING: Don't. Please, don't—I beg of you—

(*She stares, then looks around as though she is waking up.*)

MAHOUT: Listen, the two of you. Stop playing with these things, these forces. Look at those bats—hanging on the roof. Silent. Still. Watching us. Waiting for some signal. Go now. Fetch a witch-doctor. Let him deal with it. Take my advice. These things can eat into you. Go back to the palace. As for me, I am leaving town.

(*Pause. The Mahout stands looking at the Queen.*)

QUEEN (*gently*): I think I'll let you go.

MAHOUT: Thank you. I'll never forget you.
(*Goes out. Pause. The Queen turns to the King.*)

QUEEN: He's gone. The moment's gone. I am making you suffer. We are here. I love you. I don't want you to suffer. (*Pause.*)

I agree to the sacrifice.

KING: You do?

QUEEN: Yes.

KING: Then come.
(*He raises the sword. The Queen places her hand on the hilt of the sword.*)

SINGER:
Fowl, bird, cock of nine new moons,
bless us. Raise us from our darkness,
cleanse us of our sins.
Your curse covers not as words
but as the dying breath of an infant,
grows as the thorny cactus between bleached
rib-cages.
Remove the poison from the seed.
Remove the rust from the blade.
The worm from the flower.
Only you can save us now.
Only you.
Cock.
Divine Bird, help us—

(*The King tries to plunge the sword into the cock when the cock begins to crow.*)

COCK: Cock...a...doodle...doo—Cock...a...doodle...doo.
(*Total silence. The King drops the sword and stumbles back.*)

KING: What's that? What's that?

QUEEN: It's alive. The cock...is crowing. The cock's crowing!
(*Bursts into laughter.*)

The cock's crowing!
(*Kneels in front of the cock. Picks a palm full of grains from the tray and holds it up for the cock.*)
Here. Have some. Come on. Eat. Cluck...cluck...

KING: Stop it! Stop it!

QUEEN: Come on, please, eat. Have some.

KING (*screams*): Amritamati!

QUEEN: Cluck...cluck... Have some.

KING: Have you gone mad? It isn't alive! It's dough—

QUEEN (*ignoring him*): Come, Cockoo... Have shum...
(*Lallates as to a child.*)

KING: I said stop it—Look!
(*He picks up the dough and squashes it into a mass.*)
It's dough. Plain and simple! Dough.
(*The Queen looks up at him in sudden hatred, picks up the sword and lunges at him to stab him. She freezes. She stares at the sword in her hand, horrified.*
A cock crows outside. That takes the King by surprise. He turns to the door.
Suddenly, she presses the point of the blade on her womb and impales herself on the sword. Collapses into his arms.
The King holds her, uncomprehending, listening to the cock's crowing. It's dawn.
The Queen is lit by a beam. She stands up and they both sing.)

BOTH: In the World once divided into two orbs—
               one lit up by the sun,
               the other, hid in the shade,

               the orb in the shade
               opens itself to the light
               And warmth of the sun.

Night gives in to day.
Death yields to life.
Like monsoons piled on monsoons
So life follows life.

And through the days,
through endless rainy nights
through life after life
we hear the cock crow.

NĀGA-MANDALA
Play with a Cobra

NOTE

Nāga-Mandala is based on two tales from Karnataka which I first heard several years ago from Professor A. K. Ramanujan. But that is only the least of the reasons for dedicating this play to him.

I wrote *Nāga-Mandala* during the year I spent at the University of Chicago as Visiting Professor and Fulbright Scholar-in-Residence. I am most grateful to Professor Stuart M. Tave, Dean, Division of Humanities, and Professor C. M. Naim, Chairman, Department of South Asian Language and Civilizations as well as to the Council for International Exchange of Scholars for having made that visit possible. I am further indebted to Professor Naim for persuading me to write the play.

I am conscious that Naga's long speech on p. 276 owes much to Jean Anouilh, although I have been unable to identify the play.

GIRISH KARNAD

Nāga-Mandala was first presented in English by the Guthrie Theater, Minneapolis on 16 July 1993, as part of its thirtieth birthday celebrations. The principal cast was as follows:

RICHARD OOMS	The Man
MIRIAM LAUBE	The Story
NIRUPAMA NITYANANDAN	Rani
STAN EGI	Appanna/Naga
ISABELL MONK	Kurudavva
WILLIAM FRANCIS MCGUIRE	Kappanna
Directed by	GARLAND WRIGHT
Set Designed by	DOUGLAS STEIN
Music by	DAVID PHILIPSON

for
A. K. RAMANUJAN
friend, guru, hero

Prologue

The inner sanctum of a ruined temple. The idol is broken, so the presiding deity of the temple cannot be identified.
It is night. Moonlight seeps in through the cracks in the roof and the walls.
A man is sitting in the temple. Long silence. Suddenly, he opens his eyes wide. Closes them. Then uses his fingers to pry open his eyelids. Then he goes back to his original morose stance.
He yawns involuntarily. Then reacts to the yawn by shaking his head violently, and turns to the audience.

MAN: I may be dead within the next few hours.

(*Long pause.*)

 I am not talking of 'acting' dead. Actually dead. I might die right in front of your eyes.

(*Pause.*)

 A mendicant told me: 'You must keep awake at least one whole night this month. If you can do that, you'll live. If not, you will die on the last night of the month.' I laughed out loud when I heard him. I thought nothing would be easier than spending a night awake.

(*Pause.*)

 I was wrong. Perhaps death makes one sleepy. Every night this month I have been dozing off before even being aware of it. I am convinced I am seeing something with these eyes of mine, only to wake up and find I was dreaming. Tonight is my last chance.

(*Pause.*)

For tonight is the last night of the month. Even of my life, perhaps? For how do I know sleep won't creep in on me again as it has every night so far? I may doze off right in front of you. And that will be the end of me.

(*Pause.*)

I asked the mendicant what I had done to deserve this fate. And he said: 'You have written plays. You have staged them. You have caused so many good people, who came trusting you, to fall asleep twisted in miserable chairs, that all that abused mass of sleep has turned against you and become the Curse of Death.'

(*Pause.*)

I hadn't realized my plays had had that much impact.

(*Pause.*)

Tonight may be my last night. So I have fled from home and come to this temple, nameless and empty. For years I've been lording it over my family as a writer. I couldn't bring myself to die a writer's death in front of them.

(*Pause.*)

I swear by this absent God, if I survive this night I shall have nothing more to do with themes, plots or stories. I abjure all story-telling, all play-acting.

(*Female voices are heard outside the temple. He looks.*)

Voices! Here? At this time of night? Lights! Who could be coming here now?

(*He hides behind a pillar. Several Flames enter the temple, giggling, talking to each other in female voices.*)

I don't believe it! They are naked lamp flames! No wicks, no lamps. No one holding them. Just lamp flames on their own—floating in the air! Is that even possible?

(*Another three or four Flames enter, talking among themselves.*)

FLAME 3 (*addressing Flame I, which is already in the temple*):
Hello! What a pleasant surprise! You are here before us
tonight.

FLAME 1: That master of our house, you know what a skinflint
he is! He is convinced his wife has a hole in her palm, so he
buys all the groceries himself. This evening, before the dark
was even an hour old, they ran out of *kusbi* oil. The tin of
peanut oil didn't go far. The bowl of castor oil was empty
anyway. So they had to retire to bed early and I was permitted
to come here.
(*Laughter.*)

FLAME 2 (*sneering*): *Kusbi* oil! Peanut oil! How disgusting! My
family comes from the coast. We won't touch anything but
coconut oil.

FLAME 1: But at least I come here every night. What about your
friend, the kerosene flame? She hasn't been seen here for
months. She is one of the first tonight.

FLAME 4: Actually, from today on I don't think I'll have any
difficulty getting out...and early.

FLAME 1: Why? What's happened?
(*The other Flames giggle.*)

FLAMES: Tell her! Tell her!

FLAME 4: My master had an old, ailing mother. Her stomach was
bloated, her back covered with bed sores. The house stank
of cough and phlegm, pus and urine. No one got a wink of
sleep at night. Naturally, I stayed back too. The old lady died
this morning, leaving behind my master and his young
wife, young and juicy as a tender cucumber. I was chased out
fast.
(*Giggles.*)

FLAME 3: You are lucky. My master's eyes have to feast on his wife
limb by limb if the rest of him is to react. So we lamps have
to bear witness to what is better left to the dark.

(*They all talk animatedly. New Flames come and join them. They group and regroup, chattering.*)

MAN (*to the audience*): I had heard that when lamps are put out in the village, the flames gather in some remote place and spend the night together, gossiping. So this is where they gather!

(*A new Flame enters and is enthusiastically greeted.*)

FLAME 1: You are late. It is well past midnight.

NEW FLAME: Ah! There was such a to-do in our house tonight.

FLAMES: What happened? Tell us!

NEW FLAME: You know I have only an old couple in my house. Tonight the old woman finished eating, swept and cleaned the floor, put away the pots and pans, and went to the room in which her husband was sleeping. And what should she see, but a young woman dressed in a rich, new sari step out of the room! The moment the young woman saw my mistress, she ran out of the house and disappeared into the night. The old woman woke her husband up and questioned him. But he said he knew nothing. Which started the rumpus.

FLAMES: But who was the young woman? How did she get into your house?

NEW FLAME: Let me explain: My mistress, the old woman, knows a story and a song. But all these years she has kept them to herself, never told the story, nor sung the song. So the story and the song were being choked, imprisoned inside her. This afternoon the old woman took her usual nap after lunch and started snoring. The moment her mouth opened, the story and the song jumped out and hid in the attic. At night, when the old man had gone to sleep, the story took the form of a young woman and the song became a sari. The young woman wrapped herself in the sari and stepped out, just as the old lady was coming in. Thus, the story and the song created a feud in the family and were revenged on the old woman.

FLAME 1: So if you try to gag one story, another happens.

FLAMES (*all together*): But where are they now, the poor things? ...How long will they run around in the dark? What will happen to them?

NEW FLAME: I saw them on my way here and told them to follow me. They should be here any moment... There they are! The story with the song!

(*The Story, in the form of a woman dressed in a new, colourful sari, enters, acknowledges the enthusiastic welcome from the Flames with a languid wave of the hand and goes and sits in a corner, looking most despondent. The Flames gather around her.*)

NEW FLAME: Come on. Why are you so despondent? We are here and are free the whole night. We'll listen to you.

STORY: Thank you, my dears. It is kind of you. But what is the point of your listening to a story? You can't pass it on.

FLAMES: That's true...What can we do? Wish we could help.

(*While the Flames make sympathetic noises, the Man jumps out from behind the pillar and grabs the Story by her wrist.*)

MAN: I'll listen to you!

(*The Flames flee helter-skelter in terror. The Story struggles to free herself.*)

STORY: Who are you? Let me go!

MAN: What does it matter who I am, I'll listen to you. Isn't that enough? I promise you, I'll listen all night!

(*The Story stops struggling. There is a new interest in her voice.*)

STORY: You will?

MAN: Yes.

STORY: Good. Then let me go.

(*He does not.*) I need my hands to act out the parts.
(*He lets her go.*)

There is a condition, however—

MAN: What?

STORY: You can't just listen to the story and leave it at that. You must tell it again to someone else.

MAN: That I certainly shall, if I live. But first I must be alive to... That reminds me. I have a condition, too.

STORY: Yes?

MAN: I must not doze off during the tale. If I do, I die. All your telling will be wasted.

STORY: As a self-respecting story, that is the least I can promise.

MAN: All right then. Start. (*Suddenly.*) But no! No! It's not possible. I take back my word. I can't repeat the story.

STORY: And why not?

MAN: I have just now taken a vow not to have anything to do with themes, plots or acting. If I live, I don't want to risk any more curses from the audience.

STORY (*gets up*): Good-bye then. We must be going.

MAN: Wait! Don't go. Please.
(*Thinks.*)
    I suppose I have no choice.
(*To the audience.*)
    So now you know why this play is being done. I have no choice. Bear with me, please. As you can see, it is a matter of life and death for me.
(*Calls out.*)
    ` Musicians, please!
(*Musicians enter and occupy their mat.*)
    The Story and the Song!
(*Throughout the rest of the play, the Man and the Story remain on stage. The Flames too listen attentively though from a distance.*)
    (*To the Story.*) Go on.

Act One

The locked front door of a house with a yard in front of the house, and on the right, an enormous ant-hill. The interior of the house—the kitchen, the bathroom as well as Rani's room—is clearly seen.

STORY: A young girl. Her name... it doesn't matter. But she was an only daughter, so her parents called her Rani. Queen. Queen of the whole wide world. Queen of the long tresses. For when her hair was tied up in a knot, it was as though a black King Cobra lay curled on the nape of her neck, coil upon glistening coil. When it hung loose, the tresses flowed, a torrent of black, along her young limbs, and got entangled in her silver anklets. Her fond father found her a suitable husband. The young man was rich and his parents were both dead. Rani continued to live with her parents until she reached womanhood. Soon, her husband came and took her with him to his village. His name was—well, any common name will do—

MAN: Appanna?

STORY: Appanna.

(Appanna enters, followed by Rani. They carry bundles in their arms, indicating that they have been travelling. Appanna opens the lock on the front door of the house. They go in.)

APPANNA: Have we brought in all the bundles?

RANI: Yes.

APPANNA: Well, then, I'll be back tomorrow at noon. Keep my lunch ready. I shall eat and go.

(*Rani looks at him nonplussed. He pays no attention to her, goes out, shuts the door, locks it from the outside and goes away. She runs to the door, pushes it, finds it locked, peers out of the barred window. He is gone.*)

RANI: Listen—please—

(*She does not know what is happening, stands perplexed. She cannot even weep. She goes and sits in a corner of her room. Talks to herself indistinctly. Her words become distinct as the lights dim. It is night.*)

...So Rani asks him: 'Where are you taking me?' And the Eagle answers: 'Beyond the seven seas and the seven isles. On the seventh island is a magic garden. And in that garden stands the tree of emeralds. Under that tree, your parents wait for you.' So Rani says: 'Do they? Then please, please take me to them—immediately. Here I come.' So the Eagle carries her clear across the seven seas...

(*She falls asleep. Moans 'Oh, Mother!' 'Father' in her sleep. It gets light. She wakes up with a fright, looks around, then runs to the bathroom, mimes splashing water on her face, goes into the kitchen, starts cooking. Appanna comes. Opens the lock on the front door and comes in. Goes to the bathroom. Mimes bathing, then comes to the kitchen and sits down to eat. She serves him food.*)

RANI: Listen—(*fumbling for words*) Listen—I feel—frightened—alone at night—

APPANNA: What is there to be scared of? Just keep to yourself. No one will bother you. Rice!

(*Pause.*)

RANI: Please, you could—

APPANNA: Look, I don't like idle chatter. Do as you are told, you understand?

(*Finishes his meal, gets up.*)

  I'll be back tomorrow, for lunch.

(*Appanna washes his hands, locks her in and goes away. Rani watches him blankly through the window.*)

STORY: And so the days rolled by.

(*Mechanically, Rani goes into the kitchen, starts cooking. Talks to herself.*)

RANI: Then Rani's parents embrace her and cry. They kiss her and caress her. At night she sleeps between them. So she is not frightened any more. 'Don't worry,' they promise her. 'We won't let you go away again ever!' In the morning, the stag with the golden antlers comes to the door. He calls out to Rani. She refuses to go. 'I am not a stag,' he explains, 'I am a prince'...

(*Rani sits staring blankly into the oven. Then begins to sob. Outside, in the street, Kappanna enters, carrying Kurudavva on his shoulders. She is blind. He is in his early twenties.*)

KAPPANNA: Mother, you can't do this! You can't start meddling in other people's affairs the first thing in the morning. That Appanna should have been born a wild beast or a reptile. By some mistake, he got human birth. He can't stand other people. Why do you want to tangle with him?

KURUDAVVA: Whatever he is, he is the son of my best friend. His mother and I were like sisters. Poor thing, she died bringing him into this world. Now a new daughter-in-law comes to her house. How can I go on as though nothing has happened? Besides, I haven't slept a wink since you told me you saw Appanna in his concubine's courtyard. He has got himself a bride—and he still goes after that harlot?

KAPPANNA: I knew I shouldn't have told you. Now you have insomnia—and I have a backache.

KURUDAVVA: Who's asked you to carry me around like this? I haven't, have I? I was born and brought up here. I can find my way around.

KAPPANNA: Do you know what I ask for when I pray to Lord
    Hanuman of the Gymnasium every morning? For more
    strength. Not to wrestle. Not to fight. Only so I can carry you
    around.

KURUDAVVA (*pleased*): I know, I know.
(*Suddenly Kappanna freezes.*)
    What is it? Why have you stopped?
(*He doesn't answer. Merely stands immobile and stares. A touch of
panic in Kurudavva's voice.*)
    What is it, Kappanna? Kappanna!

KAPPANNA: Nothing, Mother. It's just that I can see Appanna's
    front door from here.

KURUDAVVA (*relieved*): Oh! For a moment I was worried it was
    that—who-is-that-again? That witch or fairy, whatever she
    is—who you say follows you around.

KAPPANNA: Mother, she is not a witch or a fairy. When I try to
    explain, you won't even listen. And then, when I'm not even
    thinking of her, you start suspecting all kinds of—

KURUDAVVA: Hush! Enough of her now. Tell me why we have
    stopped.

KAPPANNA: There doesn't seem to be anyone in Appanna's house.
    There is a lock on the front door.

KURUDAVVA: How is that possible? Even if he is lying in his
    concubine's house, his bride should be home.

KAPPANNA: Who can tell about Appanna? He's a lunatic.

KURUDAVVA: You don't think he could have sent his wife back to
    her parents already, do you? Come, let us look in through the
    window and check.

KAPPANNA: Of course not, Mother! If someone sees us—

KURUDAVVA: Listen to me. Go up to the house and peep in. Tell
    me what you see.

KAPPANNA: I refuse.

KURUDAVVA (*tearful*): I wouldn't have asked you if I had eyes. I don't know why God has been cruel to me, why he gave me no sight...

KAPPANNA (*yielding*): All right, Mother.

(*They go near the house. Kappanna peers through the window.*)

KAPPANNA: The house is empty.

KURUDAVVA: Of course it is, silly! How can anyone be inside when there is a lock outside on the door? Tell me, can you see clothes drying inside? What kind of clothes? Any saris? Skirts? Or is it only men's clothes?

KAPPANNA: I can't see a thing!

RANI: Who is it? Who is that outside?

KAPPANNA: Oh my God!

(*Lifts Kurudavva and starts running.*)

KURUDAVVA: Stop! Stop, I tell you! Why are you running as though you've seen a ghost?

KAPPANNA: There is someone inside the house—a woman!

KURUDAVVA: You don't have to tell me that! So what if there is a woman inside the house? We have come here precisely because a woman is supposed to be in the house.

KAPPANNA: Mother, what does it mean when a man locks his wife in?

KURUDAVVA: You tell me.

KAPPANNA: It means he does not want anyone to talk to his wife.

RANI (*comes to the window*): Who is it?

KAPPANNA: Let's go.

(*Starts running again. Kurudavva hits him on the back.*)

KURUDAVVA: Stop! Stop! (*To Rani*) I am coming, child! Right now! Don't go away! (*To Kappanna*) He keeps his wife locked up like a caged bird? I must talk to her. Let me down—instantly!

(*He lets her down.*)

You go home if you like.

KAPPANNA: I'll wait for you here under the tree. Come back soon. Don't just sit there gossiping.

KURUDAVVA (*approaching Rani*): Dear girl...

RANI: Who are you?

KURUDAVVA: Don't be afraid. I am called Kurudavva, because I am blind. Your mother-in-law and I were like sisters. I helped when your husband was born. Don't be frightened. Appanna is like a son to me. Is he not in?

RANI: No.

KURUDAVVA: What is your name?

RANI: They call me Rani.

KURUDAVVA: And where is Appanna?

RANI: I don't know.

KURUDAVVA: When did he go out?

RANI: After lunch yesterday.

KURUDAVVA: When will he come back?

RANI: He will be back for lunch later in the day.

KURUDAVVA: You don't mean, he is home only once a day, and that too...only for lunch?
(*No reply.*)
    And you are alone in the house all day?
(*Rani begins to sob.*)
    Don't cry child, don't cry. I haven't come here to make you cry. Does he lock you up every day like this?

RANI: Yes, since the day I came here.

KURUDAVVA: Does he beat you or ill-treat you?

RANI: No.

KURUDAVVA (*pause*): Does he...'talk' to you?

RANI: Oh, that he does. But not a syllable more than required. 'Do this', 'Do that', 'Serve the food'.

KURUDAVVA: You mean—? That means—you are—still—hmm! Has he...?

RANI: Apart from him, you are the first person I have seen since coming here. I'm bored to death. There is no one to talk to!

KURUDAVVA: That's not what I meant by 'talk'. Has your husband touched you? How can I put it? (*Exasperated.*) Didn't anyone explain to you before your wedding? Your mother? Or an aunt?

RANI: Mother started shedding tears the day I matured and was still crying when I left with my husband. Poor her! She is probably crying even now.
(*Starts sobbing.*)

KURUDAVVA: Dear girl, it's no use crying. Don't cry! Don't! Come here. Come, come to the window. Let me touch you. My eyes are all in my fingers.
(*She feels Rani's face, shoulder, neck through the bars of the window.*)
Ayyo! How beautiful you are. Ears like hibiscus. Skin like young mango leaves. Lips like rolls of silk. How can that Appanna gallivant around leaving such loveliness wasting away at home?

RANI: I am so frightened at night, I can't sleep a wink. At home, I sleep between Father and Mother. But here, alone— Kurudavva, can you help me, please? Will you please send word to my parents that I am, like this, here? Will you ask them to free me and take me home? I would jump into a well—if only I could—

KURUDAVVA: Chih! Chih! You shouldn't say such things. I'll take care of everything.
(*Calls out.*)
Son! Son!

KAPPANNA (*from behind the tree*): Yes?

KURUDAVVA: Come here.

KAPPANNA: No, I won't.

KURUDAVVA: Come here, you idiot.

KAPPANNA: I absolutely refuse, Mother. I told you right at the start that I won't.

KURUDAVVA: Honestly!
(*Comes to him.*)
   Listen, Son. Run home now. Go into the cattle shed—the left corner—

KAPPANNA: The left corner—

KURUDAVVA: Just above where you keep the plough, behind the pillar, on the shelf—

KAPPANNA: Behind the pillar—on the shelf—

KURUDAVVA: There is an old tin trunk. Take it down. It's full of odds and ends, but take out the bundle of cloth. Untie it. Inside there is a wooden box.

KAPPANNA: A wooden box. All right—

KURUDAVVA: In the right hand side of the wooden box is a coconut shell wrapped in a piece of paper. Inside are two pieces of a root. Bring them.

KAPPANNA: Now?

KURUDAVVA: Now. At once. Before Appanna returns home.

KAPPANNA: Mother, listen to me. If he finds you here—

KURUDAVVA: Don't waste time now. Do as I say. Run.
(*Gets up and comes back to the house. Kappanna leaves.*)
   Are you still there?

RANI: Yes. Who is that?

KURUDAVVA: My son, Kappanna. Oh, don't let his name mislead you. He isn't really dark. In fact, when he was born, my husband said: 'Such a fair child! Let's call him the Fair One!'

I said: 'I don't know what Fair means. My blind eyes know only the dark. So let's call this little parrot of my eyes the Dark One!' And he became Kappanna.

RANI: And where have you sent him?

KURUDAVVA: I'll tell you. I was born blind. No one would marry me. My father wore himself out trudging from village to village, looking for a husband. But to no avail. One day a mendicant came to our house. No one was home. I was alone. I looked after him in every way. Cooked hot food specially for him and served him to his heart's content. He was pleased with me and gave me three pieces of a root. 'Any man who eats one of these will marry you', he said.

RANI: And then?

KURUDAVVA: 'Feed him the smallest piece first', he said. 'If that gives no results, then try the middle-sized one. Only if both fail, feed him the largest piece.'

RANI (entranced): And then?

KURUDAVVA: One day a boy distantly related to me came to our village and stayed with us. That day I ground one of the pieces into paste, mixed it in with the food, and served him. Can you guess which piece I chose?

RANI (working it out): Which one now? The smallest one, as the mendicant said? No, no, surely the biggest piece.

KURUDAVVA: No, I was in such a hurry I barely noticed the small one. The biggest scared me. So I used the middle-sized root.

RANI: And then?

KURUDAVVA: He finished his meal, gave me one look and fell in love. Married me within the next two days. Never went back to his village. It took the plague to detach him from me.

(Rani laughs.)

KAPPANNA (entering): Mother—

KURUDAVVA: Ha! There he is! Wait!
(*Goes to him.*)
Have you brought them?
(*Kappanna gives her the two pieces of root. Kurudavva hurries back to Rani.*)
Are you still there?

RANI: Yes, I am.

KURUDAVVA: Here.

RANI: What is that?

KURUDAVVA: The root I was telling you about.

(*Rani Starts.*) Here. Take this smaller piece. That should do for a pretty jasmine like you. Take it! Grind it into a nice paste and feed it to your husband. And watch the results. Once he smells you he won't go sniffing after that bitch. He will make you a wife instantly.

RANI: But I am his wife already.

KURUDAVVA: Just do as I say.
(*Rani takes the piece. Kurudavva tucks the other one in the knot of her sari. Kappanna whistles. She turns.*)
That must be Appanna coming.

RANI (*running in*): Go now, Kurudavva. But come again.

KURUDAVVA: I shall too. But don't forget what I told you.
(*Kurudavva starts to go. Appanna crosses her.*)

APPANNA (*suspicious*): Who is that? Kurudavva?

KURUDAVVA: How are you, Appanna? It's been a long time—

APPANNA: What are you doing here?

KURUDAVVA: I heard you had brought a new bride. Thought I would talk to her. But she refuses to come out.

APPANNA: She won't talk to anyone. And no one need talk to her.

KURUDAVVA: If you say so.
(*Exits.*)

APPANNA (*so she can hear*): I put a lock on the door so those with
sight could see. Now what does one do about blind meddlers?
I think I'll keep a watch dog.

(*Opens the door and goes in. To Rani.*)

I am lunching out today. I'll have my bath and go. Just heat
up a glass of milk for me.

(*Goes into the bathroom. Mimes bathing. Rani boils the milk. Pours
it in a glass and starts to take it out. Notices the piece of root.
Stops. Thinks. Runs out. Sees that he is still bathing. Runs back into
the kitchen, makes a paste of the root.*)

APPANNA (*dressing*): Milk!

(*Rani jumps with fright. Hurriedly mixes the paste into the milk.
Comes out and gives Appanna the glass of milk. He drinks it in a
single gulp. Hands the glass back to her. Goes to the door, ready to
put the lock on. She watches him intently. He tries to shut the door.
Suddenly clutches his head. Slides down to the floor. Stretches out
and goes to sleep on the door-step, half inside and half outside the
house. Rani is distraught. Runs to him. Shakes him. He doesn't wake
up. He is in deep sleep. She tries to drag him into the house, but
he is too heavy for her. She sits down and starts crying.*)

APPANNA (*groggily*): Water! Water!

(*She brings a pot of water. Splashes it on his face. He wakes up
slowly, staggers up. Washes his face. Pushes her in. Looks the door
from outside. Goes away. Rani watches, stunned. Slowly goes back
to her bedroom. Starts talking to herself. It becomes night.*)

RANI: ...So the demon locks her up in his castle. Then it rains
for seven days and seven nights. It pours. The sea floods the
city. The waters break down the door of the castle. Then a
big whale comes to Rani and says: 'Come, Rani, let us go...'

(*She falls asleep. Midnight. Kappanna enters carrying Kurudavva.
Stumbles on a stone. They fall.*)

KURUDAVVA: Thoo! That's the problem with having eyes: one can't
see in the dark. That's why I have been telling you to let me
go out on my own at least at night

KAPPANNA: Go! Go! From this point on you can certainly go on
  alone. I refuse to come any closer to that house. And what
  are you doing, Mother? Suppose he is in the house. And he
  hears you. What will you say? That you have come to gossip
  with his wife in the dead of night?

KURUDAVVA: Shut up! We are here only to find out if the lock is
  gone yet. If it's gone, he is inside now. That means success
  is ours. We'll leave right away.

(*Goes and touches the door. It is closed. Tip-toes to feel the latch.
The lock is still there. Recoils in surprise.*)

  I can't believe it. The lock is still there! (*Thinks.*)

  Perhaps he has taken her out to the fields or the garden!
(*Laughs.*)

RANI (*wakes up*): Who is that?

KURUDAVVA: Me.

RANI (*comes running*): Who? Kurudavva? This time of the night?

KURUDAVVA: What happened, child? Why is the lock still there?
(*No reply.*)

  Did you feed him the root?

RANI: Yes.

KURUDAVVA: And what happened?

RANI: Nothing. He felt giddy. Fainted. Then got up and left.

KURUDAVVA: That's bad. This is no ordinary infatuation then.
  That concubine of his is obviously—

RANI: Who?

KURUDAVVA: Didn't want to tell you. There is a woman, a bazaar
  woman. She has your husband in her clutches. Squeezes him
  dry. Maybe she's cast a spell. There is only one solution to
  this—

RANI: What?

KURUDAVVA (*giving her the bigger piece*): Feed him this largest
  piece.

RANI: No!

KURUDAVVA: Yes!

RANI: That little piece made him sick. This one—

KURUDAVVA: It will do good, believe me. This is not hearsay. I am
    telling you from my own experience. Go in. Start grinding
    it. Make a tasty curry. Mix the paste in it. Let him taste a
    spoonful and he will be your slave. And then? Just say the
    word and he will carry you to my house himself.

(*Rani blushes.*)

    Son! Son!

    (*To Rani*) Remember. Don't let anything frighten you.

(*Rani goes into the kitchen. Kurudavva wakes up Kappanna. They
exit. It gets brighter. Appanna comes. He has a vicious-looking dog
on a chain with him. He brings it to the front yard and ties it to
a tree stump there. Then comes to the front door and unlocks it.
The dog begins to bark. Surprised at the bark, Rani peers out of
the window.*)

RANI: Oh! A dog—

APPANNA: That blind woman and her son! Let them step in here
    again and they'll know! I'll bathe and come to eat. Serve my
    food.

(*Goes to the bathroom and starts bathing. Rani takes down her pot
of curry. Removes the lid. Takes out the paste of the root.*)

RANI (*to the Story*): Shall I pour it in?

STORY: Yes.

(*Rani prays silently to the gods and pours the paste into the curry.
There is a sudden explosion. She runs and hides in a corner of the
room. The curry boils over, red as blood. Steam, pink and
dangerous, coils out of the pot. Rani shuts her eyes in fear. Appanna
calmly continues his bath. It is evident he has heard nothing.*)

RANI: Oh my god! What horrible mess is this? Blood. Perhaps
    poison. Shall I serve him this? That woman is blind, but he
    isn't. How could he possibly not see this boiling blood, this

poisonous red? And then—even if he doesn't see it—how do
I know it is not dangerous? Suppose something happens to
my husband? What will my fate be? That little piece made him
ill. Who knows...?

(*Slaps herself on her cheeks.*)

No, no. Forgive me, God. This is evil. I was about to commit
a crime. Father, Mother, how could I, your daughter, agree
to such a heinous act? No, I must get rid of this before he
notices anything.

(*She brings the pot out. Avoids the husband in the bathroom. Steps
out of the house. Starts pouring out the curry. Stops.*)

No! How awful! It's leaving a red stain. He is bound to notice
it, right here on the door-step! What shall I do? Where can
I pour it, so he won't see?

STORY: Rani, put it in that ant-hill.

RANI: Ah, the ant-hill!

(*Runs to the tall ant-hill. Starts pouring the liquid into it. The dog
starts howling in the front yard.*)

APPANNA: Rani! See what is bothering the dog!

(*Surprised at receiving no reply.*) Rani! Rani!

(*Goes to the kitchen, drying himself. She is not there. Comes to the
front door looking for her. By this time Rani has poured the curry
into the ant-hill and is running back to the house. The moment she
turns her back to the ant-hill, a King Cobra lifts its hood, hissing,
out of the ant-hill. Looks around. It sees Rani and follows her at
a distance. By the time she has reached the front door of her house,
it is behind a nearby tree, watching her.*

*Rani comes to the front door and freezes. Appanna is waiting for
her.*)

APPANNA: Rani, where have you been?

(*No answer.*)

I said, where have you been? Rani, answer me!

(*Moves aside so she can go in. But the moment she steps in,*

Appanna slaps her hard. Rani collapses to the floor. He does not look at her again. Just pulls the door shut, locks it from outside and goes away. There is not a trace of anger in anything he does. Just cold contempt. The dog barks loudly at the King Cobra which watches from behind the tree, hissing, excited, restless. Appanna goes away. Rani goes to her bedroom. Throws herself down in her usual corner, crying.

When it is dark, the Cobra moves toward the house.

The barking becomes louder, more continuous. Rani wakes up, goes to the window, curses and shouts. Goes back to bed. The Cobra enters the house through the drain in the bathroom.)

STORY: As you know, a cobra can assume any form it likes. That night, it entered the house through the bathroom drain and took the shape of—

(*The Cobra takes the shape of Appanna. To distinguish this Appanna from the real one, we shall call him Naga, meaning a 'Cobra'.*

Naga searches for Rani in the house. Finds her sleeping in the bedroom. He moves nearer her and then gently caresses her. She wakes up with a start.)

RANI: You—you—

NAGA: Don't get up.

RANI: But, when did you come? Shall I serve the food?

NAGA (*laughs*): Food? At midnight?

RANI: Then something else. Perhaps—
(*Doesn't know what to say. Stands dazed, leaning against the wall.*)

NAGA: Why don't you sit? Are you so afraid of me?
(*She shakes her head.*)
    Then sit down.

RANI: No.

NAGA: I will go and sit there. Away from you. Will you at least sit then?

(*Moves away, sits on the floor at a distance from her.*)
    Now?
(*Rani sits on the edge of the bed. Long silence. She is dozing but struggles to keep her eyes open.*)

NAGA: You are very beautiful.

RANI (*startled*): Hm? What? Do you—want something?

NAGA: No. I said you are very beautiful. Poor thing!

RANI: Poor thing—?

NAGA: That a tender bud like you should get such a rotten husband.

RANI: I didn't say anything!

NAGA: You didn't. I am saying it. Did it hurt—the beating this morning?

RANI: No.

NAGA: Locked up in the house all day... You must be missing your parents.

RANI (*struggles to hold back a sob*): No.

NAGA: They doted on you, didn't they?
(*She suddenly bursts out into a fit of weeping.*)

NAGA (*startled*): What is it?
(*Rani continues to howl.*)
    I know, you want to see your parents, don't you? All right. I'll arrange that.
(*She looks at him dumbfounded.*)
    Truly. Now, smile. Just a bit. Look, I'll send you to them only if you smile now.
(*Rani tries to smile. A new outburst of barking from the dog.*)
    Oh! Does this dog carry on like that all night? How long is it since you have had a good night's sleep?

RANI: But—

NAGA (*happy to see her react*): But what?

RANI: Nothing.

NAGA (*in order to provoke her*): Listen to that racket! Have you
   had even one good night's sleep since coming here?

RANI: But—

NAGA: What are you 'but'ting about? But what?

RANI: But you brought the dog here only this morning! There was
   no problem all these days.

NAGA (*trying to cover up*): Yes, of course.

RANI: Till this morning, once the housework was over, what was
   there to do? I used to sleep through the day and lie awake
   at night. Today this wretched dog has been barking away since
   it was brought here. That's why I was dozing when you came
   in. I'm sorry—

NAGA (*teasing*): Quite right! That won't do any more. From
   tomorrow I want you to be fresh and bright when I come
   home at night—

RANI (*uncertain*): At night?

NAGA: Yes. I shall come home every night from now on. May I?
(*Rani laughs shyly. Pause. She is sleepy.*)
   May I sit by you now? Or will that make you jump out of your
   skin again?
(*Rani shakes her head. Naga comes and sits very close to her. When
she tries to move away, he suddenly grabs her, with frightening
speed.*)

NAGA: Don't be afraid. Put your head against my shoulder.
(*She slowly puts her head on his shoulder. He gently puts his arm
around her.*)

NAGA: Now, don't be silly. I am not a mongoose or a hawk that
   you should be so afraid of me. Good. Relax. Tell me about
   your parents. What did all of you talk about? Did they pamper
   you? Tell me everything—
(*She has fallen asleep against his chest. He slowly unties her hair.*

*It is long and thick and covers them both. He picks up her hair in
his hand, smells it.*)

NAGA: What beautiful, long hair! Like dark, black, snake princesses!

(*He lays her down gently. Gets up. Goes to the bathroom, turns into
his original self and slithers away. Morning. Rani wakes up, and
looks around. No husband. Comes to the front door. Pushes it. It
is still locked. Baffled, she washes her face, goes to the kitchen and
starts cooking.*
The dog starts barking. Appanna comes. Pats the dog.)

APPANNA: Hello, friend! No intruders tonight, eh?

(*He unlocks the door and steps in. At the noise of the door, Rani
comes out running. She is laughing.*)

RANI: But when did you go away? I'm...

(*Freezes when she sees the expression of distaste on his face.*)

APPANNA: Yes?

RANI: Oh! Nothing.

APPANNA: Good.

(*Goes to the bathroom. Rani stares after him, then returns to the
kitchen.*)

RANI: I must have been dreaming again—

(*Appanna bathes, then eats silently as usual and leaves. It grows
dark. Night. Rani lies in bed, wide awake. A long silence. The Cobra
comes out of the ant-hill and enters the darkened front yard of her
house. The dog suddenly begins to bark. Then, sounds of the dog
growling and fighting, mixed with the hiss of a snake. The racket
ends when the dog gives a long, painful howl and goes silent. Rani
rushes to the window to see what is happening. It is dark. She cannot
see anything. When silence is restored, she returns to her bed.*
*The Cobra enters the house through the drain and becomes Naga.
In the bathroom, he washes blood off his cheeks and shoulder and
goes to Rani's room. When she hears his step on the stairs, she covers
her head with the sheet. Naga comes, sees her, smiles, sits on the*

edge of her bed. Waits. She peeps out, sees him, closes her eyes tight.)

NAGA: What nonsense is this?

(*Without opening her eyes, Rani bites her forefinger. Gives a cry of pain.*)

    What is going on, Rani?

RANI (*rubbing her finger*): I must be going mad.

NAGA: Why?

RANI (*to herself*): His visit last night—I assumed I must have dreamt that. I am certainly not dreaming now. Which means I am going mad. Spending the whole day by myself is rotting my brain.

NAGA: It is not a dream. I am not a figment of your imagination either. I am here. I am sitting in front of you. Touch me. Come on! You won't? Well, then. Talk to me. No? All right. Then I had better go.

RANI: Don't. Please.

NAGA: What is the point of sitting silent like a stone image?

RANI: What do you—want me to say?

NAGA: Anything. Tell me about yourself. About your parents. Whatever comes into your head. If you want me to stay, tell me why. If you want me to go, say why.

RANI (*pouting*): What can I say if you behave like this?

NAGA: Like what?

RANI: You talk so nicely at night. But during the day I only have to open my mouth and you hiss like a...stupid snake.

(*Naga laughs.*)

    It's all very well for you to laugh. I feel like crying.

NAGA: What should I do then? Stop coming at night? Or during the day?

RANI: Who am I to tell you that? It's your house. Your pleasure.

NAGA: No, let's say, the husband decides on the day visits. And the wife decides on the night visits. So I won't come at night if you don't want me to.

RANI (*eyes filling up*): Why do you tease me like this? I am sick of being alone. And then tonight, I was terrified you might not come—that what I remembered from last night may have been just a dream. I was desperate that you should come again tonight. But, what am I to say if you spin riddles like this?

NAGA (*seriously*): I am afraid that is how it is going to be. Like *that* during the day. Like *this* at night. Don't ask me why.

RANI: I won't.

NAGA: Come. You slept like a child in my arms last night. You must be sleepy now. Come. Go to sleep.

RANI (*moves into his arms, suddenly stops*): But, what is this? (*Touches his cheek.*)
Blood on your cheeks! And your shoulders! That looks like tooth-marks. Did you run into a thorn bush or a barbed-wire fence on your way here?

NAGA: Don't worry about it.

RANI: Wait. Let me apply that ointment Mother gave me. Where is it? I took it out the other day when I cut my thumb slicing onions. Where did I put it? Oh, yes! The mirror-box!
(*She rushes to the mirror-box and opens it. Before Naga can move away so Rani won't see his reflection, she looks at him in the mirror. Screams in fright. He moves with lightening speed, pulls her away from the mirror and holds her in his arms. She is trembling.*)

NAGA: What is it? What is it, Rani?
(*He gently shuts the mirror-box and pushes it away. Rani turns and looks at where he had been sitting.*)

RANI: When I looked in the mirror, I saw there—where you were sitting—instead of you, I saw a—

(*Mimes a cobra hood with her fingers.*)
  —sitting there.

NAGA: What? A cobra?

RANI (*silencing him*): Shh! Don't mention it. They say that if you
  mention it by name at night, it comes into the house.

NAGA: All right. Suppose a cobra does come into this house...

RANI: Don't! Why are you tempting fate by calling that unmen-
  tionable thing by its name?

NAGA: ...why shouldn't it come with love?

RANI: May God bless our house and spare us that calamity. The
  very thought makes me shudder.

NAGA: I am here now. Nothing more to fear.
(*They sit on the bed together.*)

RANI: Oh no! What am I to do with myself? In all this, I forgot
  to put the ointment on your wounds.
(*She tries to get up. He forces her down. She gently touches his
wounds. Shivers.*)
  Your blood is so cold. It's the way you wander about day and
  night, heedless of wind and rain—

(*Stares into his eyes. Suddenly shuts her eyes and clasps him.*)

NAGA: What is it now?

RANI (*looking up*): Since I looked into the mirror, I seem to be
  incapable of thinking of anything else. Father says: 'If a bird
  so much as looks at a cobra—'

NAGA: There! Now you said 'cobra'. Now he is bound to come—
(*He mimes a cobra's hood with his hand.*)

RANI: Let it. I don't feel afraid any more, with you beside me.
  Father says: 'The cobra simply hooks the bird's eyes with its
  own sight. The bird stares—and stares—unable to move
  its eyes. It doesn't feel any fear either. It stands fascinated,
  watching the changing colours in the eyes of the cobra. It

just stares, its wings half-opened as though it was sculpted in
the sunlight.'

NAGA: Then the snake strikes and swallows the bird.

(*He kisses her. The Flames surround them and dance, and sing.
Naga and Rani join them*).

> FLAMES: *Come let us dance*
> *through the weaver-bird's nest*
> *and light the hanging lamps*
> *of glow-worms*
> *through the caverns in the ant-hill*
> *and set the diamond*
> *in the cobra's crown ablaze*
> *through the blind woman's dream*
> *through the deaf-mute's song*
> *Come let us flow*
> *down the tresses of time*
> *all light and song.*

Act Two

Rani is sitting in a corner, hiding her face behind her knees, her arms wrapped around her legs. Naga is watching her with a smile, from the bed. The Flames are watching them humming the last lines of the song.

FLAMES (*sing*):   *Come let us flow*
                          down the tresses of time
                          all light and song.

(*As the song fades away*)

NAGA: What is it now?

RANI: Go away! Don't talk to me.

NAGA: But why are you crying?

RANI: I said be quiet.

(*Pause.*)

I didn't know you were such a bad man. I should have known the moment you started using honeyed words.

(*Pause.*)

Had I known, I would never have agreed to marry you. What will Father and Mother say if they come to know?

NAGA: They will say: 'Good! Our daughter is following nicely in our footsteps—'

RANI (*exploding*): Quiet! I warn you, I am your wife and you don't
have to answer anyone about me. But I will not have you say
such things about my parents. They are not like—like—like
dogs!

NAGA (*laughs*): What have dogs done to deserve sole credit for it,
you silly goose? Frogs croaking in pelting rain, tortoises
singing soundlessly in the dark, foxes, crabs, ants, rattlers,
sharks, swallows—even the geese! The female begins to smell
like the wet earth. And stung by her smell, the King Cobra
starts searching for his Queen. The tiger bellows for his mate.
When the flame of the forest blossoms into a fountain of red
and the earth cracks open at the touch of the aerial roots of
the banyan, it moves in the hollow of the cottonwood, in the
flow of the estuary, the dark limestone caves from the womb
of the heavens to the dark netherworlds, within everything
that sprouts, grows, stretches, creaks and blooms—everywhere, those who come together, cling, fall apart lazily! It is
there and there and there, everywhere.

RANI: Goodness! Goats have to be sacrificed and buffaloes
slaughtered to get a word out of you in the mornings. But
at night—how you talk! Snakes and lizards may do what they
like, but human beings should have some sense of shame.

NAGA (*suddenly looks out*): It is almost dawn. I must go.

RANI: No! No!

NAGA: Listen! The drongo. And the *koel*.

RANI: Why don't those birds choke on their own songs? Who has
given them the right to mess about with other creatures'
nights?

NAGA: I'll be back again at night.

RANI: Only at night? Not for lunch?

NAGA: Of course. There's always that. (*Pause.*) Listen, Rani. I shall
come home every day twice. At night and of course again at
mid-day. At night, wait for me here in this room. When I come

and go at night, don't go out of this room, don't look out of the window—whatever the reason. And don't ask me why.

RANI: No, I won't. The pig, the whale, the eagle—none of them asks why. So I won't either. But they ask for it again. So I can too, can't I?

(*Runs to him and embraces him.*
While the above scene is in progress, Kurudavva and Kappanna have arrived outside. As usual, he lowers her to the ground and sits under the tree. She goes to the door. Stumbles over the dog. Surprised, she feels it, makes sure it is dead. Feels the lock on the door. Calls out in a whisper.)

KURUDAVVA: Kappanna!

KAPPANNA: Yes.

KURUDAVVA: Come here.

KAPPANNA: No, I won't.

KURUDAVVA: I said come here. This fool doesn't understand a thing. Quick. Something funny is happening here.

(*Reluctantly, Kappanna comes to the door.*)
Look here.

KAPPANNA: A dog. And it is dead!

KURUDAVVA: It wasn't here the night before. And the lock is still there. I wonder what the silly girl has gone and done. Look inside the house. Can you see anything?

KAPPANNA (*looking*): No!

KURUDAVVA: Listen.

(*They listen. Naga walks toward the bathroom.*)

KAPPANNA: Footsteps.

KURUDAVVA: It's a man.

KAPPANNA: Appanna! He is inside. He will be out any minute!

KURUDAVVA: He can't! What about the lock? (*Thinks.*) And if Appanna locked the door from the outside, who is in there now? Look, look. See who it is.

KAPPANNA: I can't see anything from here.

KURUDAVVA: Try the window at the back.

(*Reluctantly he goes to the backyard. Naga goes to the bathroom, turns into a King Cobra and goes out of the drain, just as Kappanna arrives at the spot and sees the Cobra emerge.*)

KAPPANNA (*screams*): Snake! Snake! A cobra!

(*Rushes to the front door, picks up Kurudavva and starts to run.*)

KURUDAVVA: Where?

KAPPANNA: In the backyard! Out of the bathroom drain!

KURUDAVVA: Then why are you running? It isn't following us, is it? It should be gone by now. Let me down! Let me down!

(*Rani hears the commotion, comes running to the front door.*)

RANI: Who is it? Kurudavva?

KURUDAVVA: Let me down! Yes, it's me, child.

(*Comes back to the door.*)

KAPPANNA: Don't go too near, Mother. It may still be there—

RANI: What is it. Kurudavva? Who was that shouting?

KURUDAVVA: I won't come any closer. I'll speak from here. Kappanna says he saw a cobra there.

RANI: Where?

KURUDAVVA: Coming out of your bathroom drain.

RANI: Oh my God! I hope he didn't go to the bathroom—

(*Rushes to the bathroom, calling out to Appanna.*)

Listen—listen—

(*She is relieved to find it empty. Comes back to the front door.*)

KURUDAVVA: Who are you calling? Appanna?

RANI: Yes, he left just a few minutes ago. I think he's gone—thank God!

KURUDAVVA: He must be inside the house. We have been here the last half hour. No one has come out.

RANI: He certainly isn't in the house!
(*Pushes the door.*)
> There! The door is locked from the outside. It wouldn't be if he was in here, would it? Perhaps you didn't see him come out?

KURUDAVVA: May be so. Well, my child, have you started your married life?

RANI (*blushing*): Yes, Kurudavva.
(*Yawns.*)

KURUDAVVA (*laughs*): Tired? Poor thing! So you see the power of my root? Didn't I tell you your husband will cling to you once he tastes it?
(*Rani, embarrassed, tries to laugh.*)

KURUDAVVA: Well, my work is done. I'll be off now. Bless you. Burn incense in a ladle and stick it into the drain. Keeps the reptiles out.

RANI: Please come again.
(*Kappanna lifts up Kurudavva. They talk in whispers.*)

KAPPANNA: If the steps we heard were Appanna's, well, he certainly hasn't come out of the house.

KURUDAVVA: Of course, he is in there. Once couples start playing games, they begin to invent some pretty strange ones. Come on. Let's go.
(*They move. Rani thinks for a while, goes into the bedroom. Kappanna, carrying Kurudavva, suddenly stiffens. Stands frozen, staring at something in the distance.*)

KURUDAVVA: Kappanna—Kappanna—
(*He does not respond. She hits him on his back in an effort to wake him up. But he is immobile.*)

KURUDAVVA (*panicky*): Kappanna! What is it? Why do you act like this? Kappanna—
(*He suddenly wakes up.*)

KAPPANNA: Eh? Nothing.

KURUDAVVA: What do you mean nothing? Giving me a scare like that—

KAPPANNA: You won't believe me if I tell you. It was her again—

KURUDAVVA: Why shouldn't I believe you if you talked sense? Just admit it's one of the girls from a nearby village, instead of making up fancy stories about some—

KAPPANNA: She is not a village girl. Which village girl will dare step out at this hour? And I am not making up stories. That day she floated out from the haunted well. Just now she stepped out of the cemetery. Looked at me. Smiled and waved.

KURUDAVVA: Perhaps she is an ogress. Of demon birth. Or someone from the netherworld, perhaps. A spirit. Why don't you just say who it is—

KAPPANNA: You won't let me—

KURUDAVVA: When you talk like this I feel we are falling apart. It's a fear I have never felt before.

KAPPANNA: Mother, just listen—

KURUDAVVA: Shut up now!

(*They exit, arguing. It gets brighter. It is mid-day. Appanna enters. Sees the dead dog.*)

APPANNA: What's wrong with this dog? Why is it asleep in the hot sun?

(*Whistles. Then comes nearer and inspects.*)

It is dead! Dead! I paid fifty rupees for it!

(*Rani comes to the front window and looks out.*)

APPANNA: Something has bitten it. Perhaps that cobra—from that ant-hill...

(*To Rani.*) This was no ordinary hound. It cornered a cheetah once. It must have sensed the cobra. It must have given a fight. Didn't you hear anything at night?

(*She shakes her head. He gets up.*)

APPANNA: I'd better go and find an Untouchable to bury the carcass.

(*Appanna exits. Rani stares after him nonplussed. Touches herself on her cheek.*)

RANI: But last night... he had blood on his cheeks... and shoulders. Now...

(*Goes to the kitchen. Starts cooking. Appanna comes, bathes, sits down to eat. She serves him food. He gets up. Locks the door and goes away.*

While all this is going on, the Story narrates the following.)

STORY: The death of the dog infuriated Appanna. He next brought a mongoose. The mongoose lasted only one day. But it had evidently given a tougher fight: its mouth was full of blood. There were bits of flesh under its claws. Bits of snakeskin were found in its teeth.

Rani fainted when she saw the dead mongoose. That night he did not visit her. There was no sign of him the next fifteen days. Rani spent her nights crying, wailing, pining for him. When he started visiting again, his body was covered with wounds which had only partly healed. She applied her ointment to the wounds, tended him. But she never questioned him about them. It was enough that he had returned. Needless to say, when her husband came during the day, there were no scars on him.

(*It gets dark on stage. Rani hurriedly lights the lamps in the house.*)

RANI: Wait now. Don't be impatient. It won't be long... It will open out. Reach out with its fragrance.

(*Rushes into her bedroom. Waits tensely. Suddenly jumps up, breathes in deeply.*)

There it is... The smell of the blossoming nightqueen! How it fills the house before he comes! How it welcomes him! God, how it takes me, sets each fibre in me on fire!

(*Naga comes, they embrace. They make love. Naga plays with her loose hair. She suddenly laughs.*)

NAGA: What is it?

RANI: Thank God.

NAGA: Why?

RANI: All these days I was never sure I didn't just dream up these nightly visits of yours. You don't know how I have suffered. When I saw your scowling face in the morning, I would be certain everything was a fantasy and almost want to cry. But my real anxiety began as the evening approached. I would merely lie here, my eyes shut tight. What is there to see after all? The same walls. The same roof. As the afternoon passed, my whole being got focused in my ears. The bells of cattle returning home—that means it is late afternoon. The cacophony of birds in a far-away tree—it is sunset. The chorus of crickets spreading from one grove to another—it is night. Now he will come. Suppose he doesn't tonight? Suppose the nightqueen does not blossom? Suppose it's all a dream? Every night the same anxiety. The same cold feeling deep within me! Thank God. That's all past now.

NAGA: Why?

RANI: I have definite evidence to prove I was not fantasizing.

NAGA: What evidence?

RANI: I am pregnant.

(*He stares at her, dumbfounded.*)

Why are you looking at me like that? There is a baby in my womb.

(*He stares blankly.*)

We are going to have a baby.

(*Pause.*)

It doesn't make you happy?

(*Anguished.*) What am I going to do with you? Laugh? Cry? Bang my head against the wall? I can never guess how you'll react. I thought you would dance with joy on hearing the news. That you would whirl me around and fondle me. Feel my stomach gently and kiss me. All that—

(*Pause.*)

Actually, I was also afraid you might not do anything of the sort. That's why I hid the news from you all these months. I can't make any sense of you even when it is just the two of us. Now a third life joins us! I didn't know if that would be too much for you. So I was silent.

(*Her eyes fill up.*)

What I feared has come true. What kept me silent has happened. You are not happy about the baby. You are not proud that I am going to be a mother. Sometimes you are so cold-blooded—you cannot be human.

(*Forcibly puts his hand on her belly.*)

Just feel! Feel! Our baby is crouching in there, in the darkness, listening to the sounds from the world outside—as I do all day long.

NAGA (*dully*): I am glad you hid the news from me all this time. Even now, try to keep from speaking about it as long as possible. Keep it a secret.

RANI: From whom?

NAGA: From me.

RANI: What are you talking about? I have already told you. How can it be a secret again? And how long can it remain a secret? Another fifteen days? Three weeks?

NAGA (*sadly*): I realize it cannot remain a secret for long. That is why I said, as long as possible. Please, do as I tell you.

RANI (*blankly*): Yes, I shall. Don't ask questions. Do as I tell you. Don't ask questions. Do as I tell you. No. I won't ask questions. I shall do what you tell me. Scowls in the day. Embraces at night. The snarl in the morning unrelated to the caress at night. But day or night, one motto does not change: Don't ask questions. Do as I tell you.

(*He is silent.*)

I was a stupid, ignorant girl when you brought me here. But

now I am a woman, a wife, and I am going to be a mother. I am not a parrot. Not a cat or a sparrow. Why don't you take it on trust that I have a mind and explain this charade to me? Why do you play these games? Why do you change like a chameleon from day to night? Even if I understood a little, a tiny bit—I could bear it. But now—sometimes I feel my head is going to burst!

(*Naga opens his mouth to say something.*)

RANI: I know. Don't ask questions. Do as I say.

NAGA (*laughs*): That is not what I was going to say.

RANI: You don't want the child, do you? If I had remained barren, I could have spent my whole life happily trying to work out whether all of this was real or a dream. But this is no dream now. Dreams remain in heads. This one has sent roots deep down into my womb.

(*Suddenly.*)

What shall I do? Shall I have an abortion?

(*Naga stares, blankly.*)

I may find a sharp instrument in the kitchen—a ladle, a knife. Or I can ask Kurudavva's help. No, it's too late. It's five months old. Too big to be kept a secret. Forgive me. I know it's my fault. But the secret will be out whatever I do.

NAGA: It's almost morning. I must go.

RANI (*waking up*): What?

NAGA: I have to go.

RANI (*gently*): Go.

(*She turns away. Naga takes a step to go. They both freeze. The lights change sharply from night to mid-day. In a flash, Naga becomes Appanna: Pushes her to the floor and kicks her.*)

APPANNA: Aren't you ashamed to admit it, you harlot? I locked you in, and yet you managed to find a lover! Tell me who it is. Who did you go to with your sari off?

RANI: I swear to you I haven't done anything wrong!

APPANNA: You haven't? And yet you have a bloated tummy. Just pumped air into it, did you? And you think I'll let you get away with that? You shame me in front of the whole village, you darken my face, you slut—!
(*He beats her. The Cobra watches this through a window and moves about, frantic. Neither notices it.*)

APPANNA: I swear to you I am not my father's son, if I don't abort that bastard! Smash it into dust! Right now—
(*Drags her into the street. Picks up a huge stone to throw on her. The Cobra moves forward, hissing loudly, drawing attention to itself. Rani screams.*)

RANI: Oh my God! A snake! A cobra!
(*Appanna throws the stone at the Cobra which instantly withdraws. Rani uses this moment to run into the house and lock herself in. Appanna runs behind her and bangs on the door.*)

APPANNA: Open the door! Open the door, you whore! All right then, I'll show you. I'll go to the Village Elders. If they don't throw that child into boiling oil and you along with it, my name is not Appanna.
(*He exits. She rushes to her bedroom. Lights change to night. She is crying on the floor. Naga comes and sits glumly nearby.*)

RANI: Why are you humiliating me like this? Why are you stripping me naked in front of the whole village? Why don't you kill me instead? I would have killed myself. But there's not even a rope in this house for me to use.

NAGA: Rani, the Village Elders will sit in judgement. You will be summoned. That cannot be avoided.

RANI: Look at the way you talk—as if you were referring to someone else. After all, you complained to the Elders about me. Now you can go and withdraw the complaint. Say my wife isn't a whore.

NAGA: I'm sorry, but it can't be done. Rani, listen. You do trust
   me, don't you?

RANI: You ask me that? Isn't all this a result of trusting you?
   (*Suddenly helpless.*) Who else is there for me?

NAGA: Then listen to me carefully. When you face the Elders, tell
   them you will prove your innocence. Say you will undertake
   the snake ordeal.

RANI: Snake ordeal? What is that?

NAGA: You know the ant-hill under the banyan tree. Almost like
   a mountain. A King Cobra lives in it. Say you will put your
   hand into the ant-hill—

RANI (*screams*): What?

NAGA: Yes. And pull out the King Cobra. And take your oath by
   that Cobra.

RANI: I can't! I can't!

NAGA: There is no other way.

RANI: Yes, there is. Give me poison instead. Kill me right here.
   At least I'll be spared the humiliation. Won't the cobra bite
   me the moment I touch it? I'll die like your dog and your
   mongoose.

NAGA: No, it won't bite. Only, you must tell the truth.

RANI: What truth?

NAGA: The truth. Tell the truth while you are holding the cobra.

RANI: What truth? Shall I say my husband forgets his nights by
   next morning? Shall I say my husband brought a dog and a
   mongoose to kill this cobra, and yet suddenly he seems to
   know all about what the cobra will do or not do?

NAGA: Say anything. But you must speak the truth.

RANI: And if I lie?

NAGA: It will bite you.

RANI: God!

(*And then gently, almost menacingly.*)

And suppose what I think is the truth turns out to be false?

NAGA: I'm afraid it will have to bite you. What you think is not of any consequence. It must be the truth.

(*Anguished.*)

I can't help it, Rani. That's how it has always been. That's how it will always be.

RANI: Oh, God!

NAGA (*gets up*): All will be well, Rani. Don't worry. Your husband will become your slave tomorrow. You will get all you have ever wanted.

(*He turns to go.*)

RANI: Wait!

(*She suddenly runs to him and embraces him.*)

Please hold me tight. I'm afraid. Not of the cobra. Nor of death! Of you. For you. You say you'll become my slave tomorrow. That we will be together again. Why then does your heart hammer so frantically? I had not even noticed it until now. And now, why is it fluttering like a bird ambushed in a net? Why this welcome to my child?

(*He slowly moves her away. Unable to look at him, unable to keep quiet, she leans her forehead against the wall.*)

The night is almost over. You must go. But I know this is not a morning like any before. Tomorrow won't be a day like any other day. I don't want any tomorrows. Or days after. I want this night to last forever. Remain unchanged. I mustn't let you go. I must listen to my heart and hold you back. Take you like a baby in my arms and keep you safe.

(*As she talks, Naga moves down the steps, turns into a snake and goes away. She suddenly turns to him. He is not there.*)

Listen. Please. Wait.

(*She rushes out. Runs to the front door. Lifts her hand to open the latch. And freezes.*)

But the door...I had locked it from inside. And it is still
locked.

(*A new thought occurs to her. Almost unconsciously, she runs to the*
bathroom. Looks inside, it is empty.)

Where are you? Where are you?

(*Sudden commotion. Crowds of villagers fill the stage from all sides.*
The three Elders come and take their positions near the ant-hill.
The stage becomes the village square.)

ELDER I: Dear child, we have done our best. But you refuse to
listen to us. We have no alternative now but to give in to your
demands.

ELDER II: It brings no credit to the village to have a husband
publicly question his wife's chastity. But Appanna here says:
since the day of our wedding, I have not once touched my
wife or slept by her side. And yet she is pregnant. He has
registered the complaint, so we must judge its merits.

ELDER III: The traditional test in our Village Court has been to
take the oath while holding a red-hot iron in the hand.
Occasionally, the accused has chosen to plunge the hand in
boiling oil. But you insist on swearing by the King Cobra. The
news has spread and, as you can see, attracted large crowds.

ELDER I: This Village Court has turned into a Country Fair. Such
curiosity is not healthy for the village, nor conducive to
justice.

ELDER III: Listen to us even now. If something goes wrong and
the Cobra bites you, not just your life but the life of the child
you carry will be in jeopardy. We risk the sin of killing your
unborn child.

ELDER II: To risk visiting such a sin on the whole village and on
the Village Elders purely for a personal whim of yours is not
right. Think again. Listen to us. Desist from this stupidity.

ELDER I: We shall be content if you go through the ordeal of the
red-hot iron.

RANI: I am young and immature. I know nothing. But I ask pardon of the Elders. I must swear by the King Cobra.

(*The Elders discuss animatedly among themselves.*)

ELDER I: All right. If you insist. Come now child. Truth shall prevail. Come.

(*Rani steps up to the ant-hill. The crowds surge forward. The Cobra rears its head out of the ant-hill. The crowd steps back in terror. Even Rani is scared and runs back. The Cobra waits, swaying its hood. Rani steps farther and farther back. The Cobra goes back into the ant-hill.*)

ELDER II: Go on, child. Don't delay now.

RANI: I am scared. Please, if the Cobra bites me, what shall I do? I am afraid—

(*Runs to Appanna.*)

Please, please, help me—

APPANNA: You whore!

ELDER III: Appanna, there is no need to be vituperative. She may have erred. But she is a child yet. Even we feel shaken by the sight of the King Cobra. So her fright is quite understandable.

ELDER I: If you are afraid, there is no need to go through with the ordeal. Accept your guilt. We shall then go on to consider the punishment.

RANI: But I have not done anything wrong. I am not guilty of anything. What shall I plead guilty to?

ELDER II (*angry*): Listen to me. We have been patient until now because of your youth. We have given in to your whims. But you have tested us enough. Either confess or accept the ordeal.

ELDER III: Remember, child, you have a choice of ordeals even now.

RANI (*looking at the ant-hill*): All right. I shall take my oath, holding the red-hot iron.

(*A roar of disappointment from the crowds. But the Elders are delighted.*)

APPANNA: This is ridiculous! You can't allow this harlot...

ELDER I: Heaven be praised. It's a load off our conscience.

ELDER II: We have been saved.

ELDER III: Hurry up now. Heat the iron rod. Quick!
(*In all this confusion, Kurudavva enters calling her son.*)

KURUDAVVA: Kappanna, my son! Where are you? Can you hear me?

RANI: Kurudavva—

KURUDAVVA: Has my son come here? Why is he teasing me like this? Kappanna—

RANI: Kurudavva—
(*Tries to rush after her but is stopped by Appanna.*)

APPANNA: Where do you think you are going?

ELDER I: Do you know that old woman? Don't you know she has gone mad?

ELDER II: Her son disappeared a week ago.

ELDER III: We have all told her he is not in the village. But she won't listen. Wanders around day and night calling him.

KURUDAVVA: Kappanna, son—

RANI (*snarling at Appanna*): If you don't let go, I'll—
(*Taken aback by her fury, Appanna lets her go.*)

ELDER III: Let her. The rod isn't hot yet.

RANI (*runs to Kurudavva*): Help me, Kurudavva. Help me, please!

KURUDAVVA: Do you know where he is? He—

RANI: It's me. Rani. What shall I do? I don't know...

KURUDAVVA: My Kappanna is gone. Melted away.

RANI: I am innocent, Kurudavva. I haven't done anything, what shall I do?

KURUDAVVA: I woke up. It was midnight. I heard him panting. He was not in his bed. He was standing up...stiff...like a wooden pillar. Suddenly I knew. There was someone else in the house. A third person.

RANI (*mesmerized*): Who was it?

KURUDAVVA: If only I had eyes! I would have seen her. I would have recognized. But what can one do with these pebbles? When he tried to tell me I didn't listen. I was deaf. A temptress from beyond? A *yaksha* woman? Perhaps a snake woman? But not a human being. No. What woman would come inside our house at that hour? And how? She wasn't even breathing. I shouted: 'Who are you? What do you want from us? Go away!' Suddenly the door burst open. The rushing wind shook the rafters. He slipped from my hands and was gone. Never came back.

ELDER I: Rani—

KURUDAVVA: Now I wander about calling him. They tell me he is not in the village. They think I am mad. I know he is not here. I know he won't come back. But what can I do? How can I sit in the house doing nothing? I must do something for him.

ELDER II: Rani—

KURUDAVVA: I must go. Look for my son. Can't waste time like this. Kappanna. Son, it's your Mother. Don't torment me now, child...

(*Goes out. Rani stands staring in her direction. Then turns to the Story.*)

RANI: Why should she suffer like this? Would sight have helped? Do desires really reach out from some world beyond right into our beds?

(*The crowd has become restive. So Rani's remaining questions get lost in the increasing hubub. We only see her addressing the Story, who does not answer.*)

ELDER I: Silence! Silence!

(*The crowd falls silent. Only the last part of Rani's dialogue is heard.*)

RANI (*to the Story*): Why should I let you push me around? Isn't it better to accept the kiss of the Cobra and the dark silence of the ant-hill?

ELDER II: Come, child. The iron rod is hot and ready.

RANI: No. I'll opt for the ordeal by the Cobra.
(*Goes to the ant-hill, plunges her hand into it and pulls the Cobra out.*)

ELDER III: Be quick now.

RANI: Since coming to this village, I have held by this hand, only two...

APPANNA (*triumphant*): There. She admits it. Two, she says. Two! Who are they?

RANI: My husband and...

APPANNA: And—say it, who else?

RANI: And this Cobra.
(*Suddenly words pour out.*)
   Yes, my husband and this King Cobra. Except for these two, I have not touched any one of the male sex. Nor have I allowed any other male to touch me. If I lie, let the Cobra bite me.
(*The Cobra slides up her shoulder and spreads its hood like on umbrella over her head. The crowd gasps. The Cobra sways its hood gently for a while, then becomes docile and moves over her shoulder like a garland. Music fills the skies. The light changes into a soft, luminous glow. Rani stares uncomprehending as the Cobra slips back into the ant-hill. There are hosannas and cheers from the crowd.*)

ELDER I: A miracle! A miracle!

ELDER II: She is not a woman. She is a Divine Being!

ELDER III: Indeed, a Goddess—!
(*They fall at her feet. The crowd surges forward to prostrate itself*

before her. Appanna stands, uncomprehending. The Elders shout,
'Palanquin! Music!' They lift her into the palanquin. Then, as an
afterthought, Appanna is seated next to her. The couple is taken in
procession to their house.)

ELDER I: Appanna, your wife is not an ordinary woman. She is a
     goddess incarnate. Don't grieve that you judged her wrongly
     and treated her badly. That is how goddesses reveal them-
     selves to the world. You were the chosen instrument for the
     revelation of her divinity.

ELDER II: Spend the rest of your life in her service. You need merit
     in ten past lives to be chosen for such holy duty.

ELDER III: Bless us, Mother. Bless our children.

(*All disperse, except Rani and Appanna. Appanna opens the lock
on the door, throws it away. He goes in and sits, mortified, baffled.
She comes and stands next to him. Long pause. Suddenly he falls
at her feet.*)

APPANNA: Forgive me. I am a sinner. I was blind.

RANI: Hush, now!

(*She gently takes him in her arms. Music starts in the background
and the words they speak to each other cannot be heard.*)

STORY: So Rani got everything she wished for, a devoted husband,
     a happy life. For Appanna's concubine was present at the trial.
     When she saw Rani's glory, she felt ashamed of her sinful life
     and volunteered to do menial work in Rani's house. Thus
     Rani even got a life-long servant to draw water for her house.
     In due course, Rani gave birth to a beautiful child. A son.
     Rani lived happily ever after with her husband, child and
     servant.

(*Her last sentence is drowned in the hubub created by the Flames
as they prepare to leave. 'That was a nice story!', 'Has it dawned
yet?', 'I don't want to be late', 'Poor girl!'*)

MAN (*exasperated*): These Flames are worse than my audience.
     Can't they wait till the story is over?

FLAMES: But isn't it?... It will be dawn soon.

MAN: It can't be. No one will accept this ending.

STORY: But why not?

MAN: Too many loose ends. Take Kappanna's disappearance, for instance.

STORY: Oh, that is Kurudavva's story. If you are interested in that one, you may find her yet, meet her unexpectedly as you met me here, in some remote place. Even in the market place perhaps. Or someone in the audience may know. Or you can invent the missing details. That would be quite in order. I am only Rani's story.

MAN: Even then, the present ending just doesn't work.

STORY: And why not?

MAN: It's all right to say Rani lived happily ever after. But what about Appanna, her husband? As I see him, he will spend the rest of his days in misery.

(*Appanna suddenly moves out of Rani's embrace. Speaks to himself.*)

APPANNA: What am I to do? Is the whole world against me? Have I sinned so much that even Nature should laugh at me? I know I haven't slept with my wife. Let the world say what it likes. Let any miracle declare her a goddess. But *I* know! What sense am I to make of my life if that's worth nothing?

STORY: Well then, what about her?

(*Rani does not speak but responds restlessly to the Story's following dialogue.*)

STORY: No two men make love alike. And that night of the Village Court, when her true husband climbed into bed with her, how could she fail to realize it was someone new? Even if she hadn't known earlier? When did the split take place? Every night this conundrum must have spread its hood out at her. Don't you think she must have cried out in anguish to know the answer?

MAN: So? The story is not over then?

STORY: When one says, 'And they lived happily ever after', all that
is taken for granted. You sweep such headaches under the
pillow and then press your head firmly down on them. It is
something one has to live with, like a husband who snores,
or a wife who is going bald.

(*As the Story speaks, Rani and Appanna come together, smile,
embrace and are plunged into darkness.*)

MAN: But that ending lacks something. (*Remembering.*) Of
course, the Cobra!

STORY: Yes, the Cobra. One day the Cobra was sitting in its ant-
hill and it thought of Rani and said: 'Why should I not go
and take a look?'

(*During the above dialogue, the Cobra enters the house, takes on
his human form.*)

NAGA: Why should I not take a look? I have given her everything.
Her husband. Her child. Her home. Even her maid. She must
be happy. But I haven't seen her. It is night. She will be asleep.
This is the time to visit her. The familiar road. At the familiar
hour. (*Laughs.*) Hard to believe now I was so besotted with
her.

(*Goes into Rani's bedroom. Rani is sleeping next to her husband,
her head on his shoulders, her long loose tresses hanging down from
the edge of the cot. Her child is by her side. There is a quiet smile
of contentment on her face. Naga looks at the group and recoils in
sudden anguish. Covers his face as though he cannot bear to see the
scene.*)

NAGA: Rani! My queen! The fragrance of my nights! The blossom
of my dreams! In another man's arms? In another man's
bed? Does she curl around him as passionately every night
now? And dig her nails into his back? Bite his lips? And
here I am—a sloughed-off skin on the tip of a thorn. An
empty sac of snake-skin. No. I can't bear this. Someone must

die. Someone has to die. Why shouldn't I kill her? If I bury
my teeth into her breast now, she will be mine. Mine forever!

(*Moves to her swiftly. But stops.*)

No, I can't. My love has stitched up my lips. Pulled out my
fangs. Torn out my sac of poison. Withdraw your veils of
light, Flames. Let my shame float away in the darkness. Don't
mock, gecko. Yes, this King Cobra is now no better than a
grass snake. Yes, that is it. A grass snake. A common reptile.
That's what I am and I had forgotten that. I thought I could
become human. Turn into my own creation. No! Her thighs,
her bosom, her lips are for one who is forever a man. I shed
my own skin every season. How could I even hope to retain
the human form? For me—yes, only her long locks. Dark, jet-
black snake princesses.

(*Smells them.*)

They are like me. Reptilian. Cold. Long. They are right for
me. I shall summon my magical powers for the last time—
to become the size of her tresses. To become so thin, so small,
that I can hide in them, play with them, swim away in their
dark flow.

(*Presses her hair to his body.*)

Become their size now! Enter her tresses! Make love to them.
They have no sensation. They will not disturb her dreams.
But for you, that will suffice.

(*A beam of light on him. The rest is plunged into darkness. Long
dark hair appear to descend and cover him. He covers himself with
the hair and dances.*

*Finally, Naga ties a tress into a noose and places it around his neck.
The stage slowly becomes dark.*

Long silence.

Then Kurudavva's voice is heard in the distance.)

KURUDAVVA'S VOICE: Son! Where are you?

(*Lights comes on. Rani, Appanna and child are sleeping.*)

KURUDAVVA'S VOICE: Kappanna—
(*Appanna sits up.*)

APPANNA: Yes?

RANI (*waking up*): What is it?

APPANNA: I thought I heard someone calling me.

KURUDAVVA'S VOICE: Kappanna! Where are you?

RANI: The poor soul! Kurudavva.

APPANNA: In my sleep, it sounded like my mother calling me—

RANI: Poor you!
(*Tries to sit up. Groans and clutches her hair.*)

APPANNA: What is it?

RANI: My head. It feels so heavy. Ahh! Please. Can you give me
a comb? My head weighs a ton. I must comb my hair.
(*He gives her a comb. She tries to comb her hair, but cannot. There
is something caught up in her tresses.*)
    (*To Appanna.*) Could you please help?

APPANNA: Certainly.
(*He combs her hair. He has to struggle to get the comb through. A
dead cobra falls to the ground.*)
    A cobra! Stay away!
(*They look at it from afar*)

RANI: Oh! Poor thing, it is dead!

APPANNA (*examining the dead snake*): You know, it seems to have
got caught in your hair and strangled itself. Your long hair
saved us, Rani. The Elders were right. You are no common
person. You are a goddess.

RANI: We are not important. But our son is the blossom of our
family. He has been saved. He has been given the gift of life
by the Cobra, as by a father.

APPANNA: So?

RANI (*almost to herself*): A cobra. It has to be ritually cremated.
Can you grant me a favour?

APPANNA: Certainly.

RANI: When we cremate this snake, the fire should be lit by our son.

APPANNA: As you say.

RANI: And every year on this day, our son should perform the rituals to commemorate its death.

APPANNA: But aren't you going too far? I mean—that's done only for one's own father. And I am still alive.

RANI: Please don't say no.

APPANNA: Of course, there is no question of saying no. You are the goddess herself incarnate. Any wish of yours will be carried out.

(*He exits. She sits staring at the snake. Her eyes fill with tears. Music. She bows down to the dead snake, then picks it up and presses it to her cheeks. Freezes. The Story of course is gone.*)

FLAMES: Is it really over?...Oh! What a lovely tale! etc.

MAN (*looks out*): No sign of any light yet!

FLAME 3: Pity it has to end like that.

FLAME 2: These unhappy endings...

FLAME 4: Why can't things end happily for a change?

MAN: But death! It's the only inescapable truth, you know.

FLAME 5: Don't be so pompous!

FLAME 1 (*sharply*): Then why are you running away from it?

FLAME 2: If darkness were the only option, we might as well have embraced it at home!

MAN: But—that's how the story is. That's how it ends. I'm not to blame.

FLAMES: Stop making excuses! You are a playwright, aren't you? The story may be over. But you are still here and still alive!... Listen, we don't have much time left... Get on with it, for goodness' sake, etc.

MAN: All right! All right! Let me try.
(*The Flames rush back to their corners and wait expectantly.
Rani and Appanna are sleeping, with the child next to them.
Rani suddenly moans and sits up, holding her hair. Appanna wakes
up.*)

APPANNA: What is it?

RANI: My head! It hurts—as though someone were pulling out my
    hair! Ahh! Please. Can you give me a comb? I can't bear the
    pain.
(*He gives her a comb. She tries to comb her hair, but cannot. She
gives the comb to Appanna.*)

    Would you please help?

(*He takes the comb. Combs her hair. A live snake falls out of her
hair and lies writhing on the floor.*)

APPANNA: A snake! Stay away! It's tiny, but it's a cobra, all right.
    And alive. How did it get into your hair? Thank god for your
    thick tresses. They saved you. Wait. We must kill it.
(*Backs away from the snake, then runs out, shutting the bedroom
door behind him. Searches for a stick in the kitchen.
Rani watches the snake transfixed.*)

APPANNA: Isn't there a stick anywhere here?

RANI (*softly, to the Cobra*): You? What are you doing here? He'll
    kill you. Go. Go away. No! Not that way. He's there. What
    shall we do? What shall we do? Why did you ever come back
    here, stupid? (*Suddenly*) My hair! Of course, Come, quick.
    Climb into it.
(*She lets her hair down to the floor.*)
    Quick now. Get in. Are you safely in there? Good. Now stay
    there. And lie still. You don't know how heavy you are. Let
    me get used to you, will you?
(*Appanna comes in with a stick.*)
    It went that way—toward the bathroom.

(*Appanna rushes out of the bedroom, toward the bathroom, looking for the snake. Rani pats her hair.*)

> This hair is the symbol of my wedded bliss. Live in there happily, for ever.

(*Picks the baby up. Turns to the Man, gives him a thumbs-up sign. Walks out triumphant.*

It gets brighter. The Flames disappear, one by one.

We are back in the inner sanctum of the temple. The Man is sitting alone. He looks up. Sunlight pours in through the cracks in the temple roof. It is morning. The man vigorously stretches himself, bows to the audience and goes out.)

APPENDIX 1*

Note on *Tughlaq, Hayavadana,*
and *Nāga-Mandala*[1]

My generation was the first to come of age after India became independent of British rule. It therefore had to face a situation in which tensions implicit until then had come out in the open and demanded to be resolved without apologia or self-justification: tensions between the cultural past of the country and its colonial past, between the attractions of Western modes of thought and our own traditions, and finally between the various visions of the future that opened up once the common cause of political freedom was achieved. This is the historical context that gave rise to my plays and those of my contemporaries.

In my childhood, in a small town in Karnataka, I was exposed to two theatre forms that seemed to represent irreconcilably different worlds. Father took the entire family to see plays staged by troupes of professional actors called *natak companies* which toured the countryside throughout the year. The plays were staged in semipermanent structures on proscenium stages, with wings and drop curtains, and were illuminated by petromax lamps.

---

* Condensed from Introduction, *Three Plays: Nāga-Mandala, Hayavadana, Tughlaq,* Girish Karnad, Delhi: Oxford University Press, 1994.

[1] This is a considerably revised and expanded version of my paper, 'In Search of a New Theatre', in *Contemporary India,* Carla M. Borden, ed., Delhi: Oxford University Press, 1989.

Once the harvest was over, I went with the servants to sit up nights watching the more traditional *Yakshagana* performances. The stage, a platform with a back curtain, was erected in the open air and lit by torches.

By the time I was in my early teens, the *natak companies* had ceased to function and *Yakshagana* had begun to seem quaint, even silly, to me. Soon we moved to a big city. This city had a college and electricity, but no professional theatre.

I saw theatre again only when I went to Bombay for my postgraduate studies. One of the first things I did in Bombay was to go and see a play, which happened to be Strindberg's *Miss Julie*, directed by the brilliant young Ebrahim Alkazi.

I have been told since then that it was one of Alkazi's less successful productions. The papers tore it to shreds the next day. But when I walked out of the theatre that evening, I felt as though I had been put through an emotionally or even a physically painful rite of passage. I had read some Western playwrights in college, but nothing had prepared me for the power and violence I experienced that day. By the norms I had been brought up on, the very notion of laying bare the inner recesses of the human psyche like this for public consumption seemed obscene. What impressed me as much as the psychological cannibalism of the play was the way lights faded in and out on stage. Until we moved to the city, we had lived in houses lit by hurricane lamps. Even in the city, electricity was something we switched on and off. The realization that there were instruments called dimmers that could gently fade the lights in or out opened up a whole new world of magical possibilities.

Most of my contemporaries went through some similar experience at some point in their lives. We stepped out of mythological plays lit by torches or petromax lamps straight into Strindberg and dimmers. The new technology could not be divorced from the new psychology. The two together defined a stage that was like nothing we had known or suspected. I have often wondered whether it wasn't that evening that, without being actually aware of it, I decided I wanted to be a playwright.

At the end of my stay in Bombay, I received a scholarship to go abroad for further studies. It is difficult to describe to a modern Indian audience the traumas created by this event. Going abroad was a much rarer

occurrence in those days; besides, I came from a large, close-knit family
and was the first member of the family ever to go abroad. My parents
were worried lest I decide to settle down outside India, and even for me,
though there was no need for an immediate decision, the terrible choice
was implicit in the very act of going away. Should I, at the end of my
studies, return home for the sake of my family, my people and my country,
even at the risk of my abilities and training not being fully utilized in
what seemed a stifling, claustrophobic atmosphere, or should I rise above
such parochial considerations and go where the world drew me?

While still preparing for the trip, amidst the intense emotional
turmoil, I found myself writing a play. This took me by surprise, for I
had fancied myself a poet, had written poetry through my teens, and had
trained myself to write in English, in preparation for the conquest of the
West. But here I was writing a play and in Kannada, too, the language
spoken by a few million people in south India, the language of my
childhood. A greater surprise was the theme of the play, for it was taken
from ancient Indian mythology from which I had believed myself
alienated.

The story of King Yayati that I used occurs in the Mahabharata. The
king, for a moral transgression he has committed, is cursed to old age
in the prime of life. Distraught at losing his youth, he approaches his
son, pleading with him to lend him his youth in exchange for old age.
The son agrees to the exchange and accepts the curse, and thus becomes
old, older than his father.[2] But the old age brings no knowledge, no self-
realization, only the senselessness of a punishment meted out for an act
in which he had not even participated. The father is left to face the
consequences of shirking responsibility for his own actions.

While I was writing the play, I saw it only as an escape from my
stressful situation. But looking back, I am amazed at how precisely the
myth reflected my anxieties at that moment, my resentment with all
those who seemed to demand that I sacrifice my future. By the time I
had finished working on *Yayati*—during the three weeks it took the ship
to reach England and in the lonely cloisters of the college—the myth had
enabled me to articulate to myself a set of values that I had been unable

[2] In the Mahabharata, King Yayati has five sons; after the elder four refuse
their father, the youngest yields to his entreaties.

to arrive at rationally. Whether to return home finally seemed the most
minor of issues; the myth had nailed me to my past.

Oddly enough the play owed its form not to the innumerable
mythological plays I had been brought up on, and which had partly kept
these myths alive for me, but to Western playwrights whom until then
I had only read in print or seen on stage only in Bombay: Anouilh (his
Antigone particularly) and also Sartre, O'Neill, and the Greeks. That is,
at the most intense moment of self-expression, while my past had come
to my aid with a ready-made narrative within which I could contain and
explore my insecurities, there had been no dramatic structure in my own
tradition to which I could relate myself.

Indeed this contradiction haunts most contemporary playwriting and
theatre in India. Even to arrive at the heart of one's own mythology, the
writer has to follow signposts planted by the West, a paradoxical
situation for a culture in which the earliest *extant* play was written in
AD 200! The explanation lies in the fact that what is called 'modern
Indian theatre' was started by a group of people who adopted 'cultural
amnesia' as a deliberate strategy. It originated in the second half of the
nineteenth century in three cities, Bombay, Calcutta and Madras. None
of these seaports built by the British for their maritime trade had an
Indian past of its own, a history independent of the British. These places
had developed an Indian middle class that in all outward respects aspired
to 'look' like its British counterpart. The social values of this class were
shaped by the English education it had received and by the need to work
with the British in trade and administration.

Inevitably the theatre it created imitated the British theatre of the
times, as presented by visiting troupes from England. Several new
concepts were introduced, two of which altered the nature of Indian
theatre. One was the separation of the audience from the stage by
the proscenium, underscoring the fact that what was being presented
was a spectacle, free of any ritualistic associations and which therefore
expected no direct participation by the audience in it; and the other
was the idea of pure entertainment, whose success would be measured
entirely in terms of immediate financial returns and the run of the
play: the practice of selling tickets to cover costs.

Until the nineteenth century, the audience had never been expected
to pay to see a show. Theatre had depended upon patronage—of kings,

ministers, local feudatories, or temples. With the myth-based story line already familiar to the audience, the shape and success of a performance depended on how the actors improvised with the given narrative material each time they came on stage. Actors did not rehearse a play so much as train for particular kinds of roles, a system still followed in folk and traditional theatre forms. The principle here is the same as in north Indian classical music, where the musician aims to reveal unexpected delights even within the strictly regulated contours of a raga, by continual improvisation. It is the variability, the unpredictable potential of each performance that is its attraction. The audience accepts the risk.

With the new theatre, in conformity with the prevailing laissezfaire philosophy, risk became the producer's responsibility, the factor determining the company's investment policy. The audience paid in cash to see a show guaranteed as a 'success' and in return received as much entertainment as could be competitively fitted within the price of a ticket. A performance became a carefully packaged commodity, to be sold in endless identical replications.[3]

The proscenium and the box office proclaimed a new philosophy of the theatre: secularism—but a commercially viable secularism.

The secularism was partly necessitated by the ethnic heterogeneity of the new entrepreneurial class. In Bombay, for instance, the enterprises were financed by the Parsis, who spoke Gujarati. But the commonly understood language was Urdu, popularized by the Muslim chieftains who had ruled over most of India since the sixteenth century. Naturally many of the writers employed by the Parsi theatre were Muslim. And the audience was largely Hindu!

The consequences of this secularism were that every character on stage, whether a Hindu deity or a Muslim legendary hero, was alienated from his true religious or cultural moorings; and myths and legends, emptied of meaning, were reshaped into tightly constructed melodramas with thundering curtain lines and a searing climax. Unlike traditional

---

[3] Interestingly, although in Bombay ticketing of shows was the logical result of bringing theatre within the free market economy, in Bengal, where the Anglophile landed gentry had immediately made theatre their exclusive privilege, ticketing was the means by which this privilege was attacked and the form made accessible to the middle class.

performances, which spread out in a slow, leisurely fashion, these plays demanded total attention, but only at the level of plot. Incident was all. Even in *natak companies* run entirely by Hindus, the basic attitude was dictated by this Parsi model.

There was, however, a far more important reason for the superficiality of the fare. The audience that patronized the Parsi theatre professed values it made no effort to realize in ordinary life. Whereas in public it accepted the Western bourgeois notions of secularism, egalitarianism, and individual merit, at home it remained committed to the traditional loyalties of caste, family, and religion. Only a society honest enough to face squarely the implications of this division within itself could have produced meaningful drama out of it. But as the new bourgeoisie claimed to be ashamed of the domestic lifestyle to which it nevertheless adhered tenaciously, the theatre certainly would never be allowed to acknowledge and project these contradictions.

It is possible to argue, as Ashis Nandy has done, that this inner division was not psychologically harmful at all but was a deliberate strategy adopted by this class to ensure that its personality was not totally absorbed and thereby destroyed by the colonial culture. Whatever the case, the effect on drama was to render it sterile. Despite its enormous success as spectacle over nearly seventy years, the Parsi theatre produced no drama of any consequence.

With the advent of 'talking' films in the 1930s, the Parsi theatre collapsed without a fight. In the West, movies diminished the importance of theatre but did not destroy it. In India, professional theatre was virtually decimated by the film industry, which had learned most of its tricks from the theatre and could dish out the made-to-order entertainment on a scale much larger than the theatre could afford and at cheaper rates. India has not seen a professional theatre of the same proportions since.

In the process of settling down, the Parsi theatre had absorbed several features of traditional or folk performing arts, such as music, mime, and comic interludes. In Maharashtra, for instance, where this theatre flourished and continues to survive, its greatest contribution was in the field of music, in the form of a rich and varied body of theatre songs. However, to my generation of playwrights, reacting against memories of the Parsi stage in its decadence, music and dance seemed irrelevant to genuine drama. The only legacy left to us then was a lumbering, antiquated style of staging.

Yet there was no other urban tradition to look to, and in my second play, having concluded that Anouilh and Co. were not enough, I tried to make use of the Parsi stagecraft. This time the play was historical and therefore, perhaps inevitably, had a Muslim subject. (I say inevitably, for the Hindus have almost no tradition of history: the Hindu mind, with its belief in the cycle of births and deaths, has found little reason to chronicle or glamourize any particular historical period. Still, independence had made history suddenly important to us; we were acutely conscious of living in a historically important era. Indian history as written by the British was automatically suspect. The Marxist approach offered a more attractive alternative but in fact seemed unable to come to terms with Indian realties. Even today Marxist ideologues are lost when confronted with native categories like caste. It was the Muslims who first introduced history as a positive concept in Indian thought, and the only genuinely Indian methodology available to us for analysing history was that developed by the Muslim historians in India.)

My subject was the life of Muhammad Tughlaq, fourteenth-century sultan of Delhi, certainly the most brilliant individual ever to ascend the throne of Delhi and also one of the biggest failures. After a reign distinguished for policies that today seem far-sighted to the point of genius, but which in their day earned him the title 'Muhammed the Mad', the sultan ended his career in bloodshed and political chaos. In a sense, the play reflected the slow disillusionment my generation felt with the new politics of independent India: the gradual erosion of the ethical norms that had guided the movement for independence, and the coming to terms with cynicism and realpolitik.

The stagecraft of the Parsi model demanded a mechanical succession of alternating *shallow* and *deep* scenes. The shallow scenes were played in the foreground of the stage with a painted curtain—normally depicting a street—as the backdrop. These scenes were reserved for the 'lower class' characters with prominence given to comedy. They served as *link* scenes in the development of the plot, but the main purpose was to keep the audience engaged while the deep scenes, which showed interiors of palaces, royal parks, and other such visually opulent sets, were being changed or decorated. The important characters rarely appeared in the street scenes, and in the deep scenes the lower classes strictly kept their place.

The spatial division was ideal to show the gulf between the rulers and the ruled, between the mysterious inner chambers of power politics and the open, public areas of those affected by it. But as I wrote *Tughlaq*, I found it increasingly difficult to maintain the accepted balance between these two regions. Writing in an unprecedented situation where the mass populace was exercising political franchise, in however clumsy a fashion, for the first time in its history, I found the shallow scenes bulging with an energy hard to control. The regions ultimately developed their own logic. The deep scenes became emptier as the play progressed, and in the last scene, the 'comic lead' did the unconventional—he appeared in the deep scene, on a par with the protagonist himself. This violation of traditionally sacred spatial hierarchy, I decided—since there was little I could do about it—was the result of the anarchy which climaxed Tughlaq's times and seemed poised to engulf my own.

(An aside: whatever the fond theories of their creators, plays often develop their own independent existence. In his brilliant production of *Tughlaq*, E. Alkazi ignored my half-hearted tribute to the Parsi theatre and placed the action on the ramparts of the Old Fort at Delhi; and it worked very well.)

Another school of drama had arisen in the 1930s, at the height of the struggle for national independence. When social reform was acknowledged as a goal next only to independence in importance, a group of 'realistic' playwrights had challenged the emptiness and vapidity of Parsi drama. The contemporary concerns of these playwrights gave their work an immediacy and a sharp edge lacking in the earlier theatre, and a few plays of great power were written. While trying to awaken their audience to the humiliation of political enslavement, many of these new playwrights made a coruscating analysis of the ills that had eaten into Indian society. This was essentially the playwright's theatre; the plays were presented by amateur or semiprofessional groups and were mostly directed by the playwrights themselves. Unlike in the Parsi theatre, where a hardheaded financial logic was the guide, here the writers, the actors, and the audience were all united by a genuine idealism. They created a movement, if not a theatre, for the times.

Although its form aimed at being realistic, it must be pointed out at once that this drama concentrated on only a small corner of the vast canvas explored by Western realistic theatre.

The door banged by Nora in *The Doll's House* did not merely announce feminist rebellion against social slavery. It summed up what was to be the main theme of Western realistic drama over the next hundred years: a person's need to be seen as an individual, as an entity valuable in itself, independent of family and social circumstance. Indian realism, however, could not progress beyond analyses of social problems, for in India, despite the large urban population, there really has never been a bourgeoisie with its faith in individualism as the ultimate value. 'Westernization' notwithstanding, Indians define themselves in terms of their relationship to the other members of their family, caste, or class. They are defined by the role they have to play. In Sudhir Kakar's words, they see themselves in 'relational' terms in their social context, and they naturally extend the same references to theatre as well.

Let me give an example. A few years ago Arthur Miller's *A View from the Bridge* was presented in Madras. Eddie Carbone, the play's protagonist, is an Italian dock worker. He is a good man, but tragedy is brought about by his incestuous passion for his orphaned niece. He harbours two young, illegal Italian immigrants in his house, one of whom falls in love with the niece. Consumed by jealousy, Eddie breaks his code of honour, betrays the immigrants to the authorities, and is killed by one of them.

The audience watching the play in Madras was English-educated, familiar with Western literature. Many of them frequently travelled abroad and had a living contact with the Western way of life. The production was a success. But most of the audience entirely missed the element of incest in the play; rather, they chose to ignore it as an unnecessary adjunct to an otherwise perfectly rational tale. After all, Eddie was his niece's guardian, a surrogate father. It was only right that he should be interested in her welfare. You certainly could not blame him for trying to safeguard her future. On the contrary, the illegal immigrants emerged as unsympathetic, for they had betrayed their host's confidence by seducing the niece's affections.

Even apart from considerations of social duties that led the Madras audience to write its own *A View from the Bridge*, Eddie Carbone perfectly fits an Indian archetype: the father figure aggressing toward its offspring. Our mythology is replete with parental figures demanding sacrifices from their children—as in my own *Yayati*; Eddie's position was not one in which the Indian audience was likely to find any tragic flaw.

To get back to realistic theatre, its great improvement over the Parsi theatre was that it took itself seriously both as art and as an instrument of social change. Yet it remained saddled with the European model. Bernard Shaw was its presiding deity. The proscenium continued, only now the grand spectacles gave way to the interior set with the invisible fourth wall. And that three-walled living room succinctly defined the basic limitation of this school of writing.

From Ibsen to Albee, the living room has symbolized all that is valuable to the Western bourgeoisie. It is one's refuge from the sociopolitical forces raging in the world outside, as well as the battleground where values essential to one's individuality are fought out and defended. But nothing of consequence ever happens or is supposed to happen in an Indian living room! It is the no-man's-land, the empty, almost defensive front the family presents to the world outside.

Space in a traditional home is ordered according to the caste hierarchy as well as the hierarchies within the family. Whether a person is permitted inside the compound, allowed as far as the outer verandah, or admitted into the living room depends on his or her caste and social status. And it is in the interior of the house, in the kitchen, in the room where the gods are kept, or in the backyard, where family problems are tackled, or allowed to fester, and where the women can have a say. Thus the living room as the location of dramatic action made nonsense of the very social problems the playwright set out to analyse, by distorting the caste dimensions as well as the position of women in the family.

How could these playwrights have so misunderstood the geography of their own homes? The three-walled living room was a symptom of a much more serious malaise: the conceptual tools they were using to analyse India's problems were as secondhand and unrealistic as the European parlour. The writers were young, angry, and in a hurry. The concepts defined for them by their English educators were new and refreshing and seemed rational. If the tools didn't quite fit the shifting ambiguities of social life, reality could be adjusted to fit these attractive imports. It could be argued that the refusal to go beyond the living room exactly mirrored the reluctance of these Westernized, upper-caste writers to go to the heart of the issues they were presenting.

To my generation, a hundred crowded years of urban theatre seemed to have left almost nothing to hang on to, to take off from. And where was one to begin again? Perhaps by looking at our audience again by trying to understand what experience this audience expected to receive from theatre? This at least partly meant looking again at the traditional forms that had been sidelined by the Parsi theatre. The attempt, let me hasten to add, was not to find and reuse forms that had worked successfully in some other cultural context. The hope, rather, was to discover whether there was a structure of expectations—and conventions—about entertainment underlying these forms from which one could learn.

The most obvious starting point should have been the Sanskrit theatre. *Sakuntala* and *Mrcchakatika*, two Sanskrit masterpieces, had been presented successfully on the Marathi stage in the early part of this century. Recently, Ratan Thiyam, K. N. Panicker, and Vijaya Mehta have brought Sanskrit plays alive again for today's audience. But no modern playwright has claimed, or shown in his work, any allegiance to Sanskrit sensibility. Sanskrit drama assumed a specific social setting, a steady, well-ordered universe in which everyone from the gods to the meanest mortals was in his or her allotted slot. Even in its heyday it was an elitist phenomenon confined to a restricted group of wealthy and educated courtiers, remote from the general populace.

Along with this court theatre there had existed other, more popular forms—more flexible, varying in their emphasis on formal purity. The exact relationship between Sanskrit theatre and these popular forms is of course difficult to determine. Sanskrit was not a language spoken in the homes; it was the language of courtly, literary, and philosophical discourse. The popular forms, on the other hand, used the natural languages of the people. Further, most of these languages came into their own as vehicles for literary expression only about AD 1000, by which time Sanskrit literature—particularly drama—was already moribund. Even the aesthetics of these two theatre traditions differed. Sanskrit drama underplayed action and emphasized mood. It avoided scenes that unduly excited the audience. The popular forms wallowed in battles and hard-

won marriages, blood and thunder. The biggest hurdle from our
perspective is that unlike in Sanskrit, in which plays were written down,
this class of performing arts used no written texts and depended on
improvisatioh within limits prescribed by their separate conventions,
making it difficult to trace their historical growth. But in India as has
often been pointed out the past is never totally lost; it coexists with the
present as a parallel flow. A rich variety of regional theatre forms still
exists, with a continuous history stretching over centuries, though
through these centuries they have undoubtedly undergone changes and
even mutilations.

For the first two decades after independence, how traditional forms
could be utilized to revitalize our own work in the urban context was
a ceaseless topic of argument among theatre people. The poet Vallathol
had given a new identity to *Kathakali*, Shivaram Karanth a new lease
on life to *Yakshagana*. Habib Tanvir has gone to areas in which the
traditional troupes operate, taking with him his urban discipline. He has
taught, lived, worked, and toured with the local troupes and evolved
through them a work that is rich, vital, and meaningful.

But what were we, basically city-dwellers, to do with this stream?
What did the entire paraphernalia of theatrical devices, half-curtains,
masks, improvisation, music, and mime mean?

I remember that the idea of my play *Hayavadana* started crystallizing
in my head right in the middle of an argument with B. V. Karanth (who
ultimately produced the play) about the meaning of masks in Indian
theatre and theatre's relationship to music. The play is based on a story
from a collection of tales called the *Kathasaritsagara* and the further
development of this story by Thomas Mann in 'The Transposed Heads'.
Two young men behead themselves and, when brought back to life, find
that their heads have got mixed up.

The story initially interested me for the scope it gave for the use of
masks and music. Western theatre has developed a contrast between the
face and the *mask*—the real inner person and the exterior one presents,
or wishes to present, to the world outside. But in traditional Indian
theatre, the mask is only the face 'writ large'; since a character represents
not a complex psychological entity but an ethical archetype, the mask
merely presents in enlarged detail its essential moral nature. (This is why
characters in *Hayavadana* have no real names. The heroine is called

Padmini after one of the six types into which Vatsyayana classified all women. Her husband is Devadatta, a formal mode of addressing a stranger. His friend is Kapila, simply 'the dark one.') Music—usually percussion—then further distances the action, placing it in the realm of the mythical and the elemental.

The decision to use masks led me to question the theme itself in greater depth. All theatrical performances in India begin with the worship of Ganesha, the god who ensures successful completion of any endeavour. According to mythology, Ganesha was beheaded by Shiva, his father, who had failed to recognize his own son (another aggressive father!). The damage was repaired by substituting an elephant's head, since the original head could not be found. Ganesha is often represented onstage by a young boy wearing the elephant mask, who then is worshipped as the incarnation of the god himself.

Ganesha's mask then says nothing about his nature. It is a mask, pure and simple. Right at the start of the play, my theory about masks was getting subverted. But the elephant head also questioned the basic assumption behind the original riddle: that the head represents the thinking part of the person, the intellect.

It seemed unfair, however, to challenge the thesis of the riddle by using a god. God, after all, is beyond human logic, indeed beyond human comprehension itself. The dialectic had to grow out of grosser ground, and I sensed a third being hovering in the spaces between the divine and the human, a horse-headed man. The play *Hayavadana*, meaning 'the one with a horse's head', is named after this character. The story of this horse-headed man, who wants to shed the horse's head and become human, provides the outer panel—as in a mural—within which the tale of the two friends is framed. Hayavadana, too, goes to the same Goddess Kali and wins a boon from her that he should become complete. Logic takes over. The head is the person: Hayavadana becomes a complete horse. The central logic of the tale remains intact, while its basic premise is denied.

The energy of folk theatre comes from the fact that although it seems to uphold traditional values, it also has the means of questioning these values, of making them literally stand on their head. The various conventions—the chorus, the masks, the seemingly unrelated comic episodes, the mixing of human and nonhuman worlds—permit the simultaneous presentation of alternative points of view, of alternative attitudes to the central problem. To use a phrase from Bertolt Brecht, these conventions then allow for 'complex seeing'. And it must be admitted that Brecht's influence, received mainly through his writings and without the benefit of his theatrical productions, went some way in making us realize what could be done with the design of traditional theatre. The theatrical conventions Brecht was reacting against—character as a psychological construct providing a focus for emotional identification, the willing-suspension-of-disbelief syndrome, the notion of a unified spectacle—were never a part of the traditional Indian theatre. There was therefore no question of arriving at an 'alienation' effect by using Brechtian artifice. What he did was to sensitize us to the potentialities of nonnaturalistic techniques available in our own theatre.

Nāga-Mandala is based on two oral tales I heard from A. K. Ramanujan. These tales are narrated by women—normally the older women in the family—while children are being fed in the evenings in the kitchen or being put to bed. The other adults present on these occasions are also women. Therefore these tales, though directed at the children, often serve as a parallel system of communication among the women in the family.

They thus express a distinctly woman's understanding of the reality around her, a lived counterpoint to the patriarchal structures of classical texts and institutions. The position of Rani in the story of *Nāga-Mandala*, for instance, can be seen as a metaphor for the situation of a young girl in the bosom of a joint family where she sees her husband only in two unconnected roles—as a stranger during the day and as a lover at night. Inevitably, the pattern of relationships she is forced to weave from these disjointed encounters must be something of a fiction. The empty house Rani is locked in could be the family she is married into.

Many of these tales also talk about the nature of tales. The story of the flames comments on the paradoxical nature of oral tales in general: they have an existence of their own, independent of the teller and yet live only when they are passed on from the possessor of the tale to the listener. Seen thus, the status of a tale becomes akin to that of a daughter, for traditionally a daughter too is not meant to be kept at home too long

but has to be passed on. This identity adds poignant and ironic
undertones to the relationship of the teller to the tales.

It needs to be stressed here that these tales are not left-overs from the
past. In the words of Ramanujan, 'Even in a large modern city like
Madras, Bombay or Calcutta, even in western-style nuclear families with
their well-planned 2.2 children, folklore…is only a suburb away, a
cousin or a grandmother away'.[4]

The basic concern of the Indian theatre in the post-independence
period has been to try to define its 'Indianness'. The distressing fact is
that most of these experiments have been carried out by enthusiastic
amateurs or part-timers, who have been unable to devote themselves
entirely to theatre. I see myself as a playwright but make a living in film
and television. There is a high elasticity of substitution between the
different performing media in India; the participants—as well as the
audiences—get tossed about.

The question therefore of what lies in store for the Indian theatre
should be rephrased to include other media as well—radio, cinema,
audio cassettes, television, and video. Their futures are inextricably
intertwined and in this shifting landscape, the next electronic gadget
could easily turn a mass medium into a traditional art form.

Perhaps quite unrealistically, I dream of the day when a similar ripple
will reestablish theatre—flesh-and-blood actors enacting a well-written
text to a gathering of people who have come to witness the performance—where it belongs, at the centre of the daily life of the people.

[4] A. K. Ramanujan, 'Introduction', *Folktales from India* (New Delhi: Viking,
1993), p. xiii.

A. K. Ramanujan, 'Two Realms of Kannada Folklore', in *Another Harmony*,
Stuart H. Blackburn and A. K. Ramanujan, eds, Berkeley: University of California
Press, 1987.

A. K. Ramanujan, 'Telling Tales', *Daedalus*, Fall, 1989.

APPENDIX 2*

Note on *Bali: The Sacrifice*

It is a tribute to the astuteness and sensitivity of Mahatma Gandhi that he saw so clearly the importance of non-violence to the cultural and political survival of India. Violence has been the central topic of debate in the history of Indian civilization. Vedic fire sacrifices, conducted by Brahmin priests, involved the slaughter of animals as offerings to the gods, which the Jains found repugnant. To the Jain, indulging in any kind of violence, however minor or accidental, meant forfeiting one's moral status as a human being. Later, the Buddhists too joined the debate, arguing for non-violence, but from their own philosophical standpoint.

The dialectic found some resolution when the Brahmins renounced blood sacrifice. Miniature figurines, made of dough, were substituted for live animals, a practice that continues to this day. Still, the Jains argued that this was no solution. Although no animals were slaughtered and no meat consumed, these figures of dough, mimicking the forms of real animals, clearly carried the original violent impulse within them. And why dough rather than, say, mud or chalk? Because an offering makes sense only if it is meant as food for gods and is, therefore, cooked and consumed by the devotees. Thus the priests had merely replaced actual violence with violence in intention, which, said the Jains, was no less

---

* Taken from Preface, *The Dreams of Tipu Sultan, Bali: The Sacrifice: Two Plays by Girish Karnad* (Delhi: Oxford University Press, 2004).

dehumanizing. This argument gave the debate a much more complex ethical twist. The Jain position raises the question: if intended violence condemns one as surely as actual violence, that is, if one is morally responsible for merely intending to commit an act one has not actually carried out in real life, is one not shutting oneself up in a solipsistic world, a bleak, guilt-ridden existence with no hope of absolution?

For *Bali: The Sacrifice*, I have drawn upon the thirteenth-century Kannada epic, *Yashodhara Charite*, by Janna, which in turn refers back through an eleventh-century Sanskrit epic by Vadiraja to the ninth-century Sanskrit epic, *Yashastilaka*, by Somadeva Suri. Some elements of the tale have been traced back to the first century.

Stories and legends play multiple roles in Indian culture. As the late Professor Bimal Krishna Matilal of All Souls, Oxford, has pointed out: 'Great epics, apart from being the source of everything else, constitute an important component of what we may term as moral philosophical thinking of the Indian tradition. ...Professional philosophers of India over the last two thousand years...have very seldom discussed what we call moral philosophy today.... The tradition itself was very self-conscious about moral values, moral conflicts and dilemmas, as well as difficulties of what we call practical reason or practical wisdom. This consciousness found its expression in the epic stories and narrative literature.'

I first came across the myth of the Cock of Dough when I was still in my teens. Since then, my career as playwright has been littered with discarded drafts of dramatized versions of it written in Kannada. But looking back, I am happy that closure eluded me, for the myth continued to reveal unexpected meanings with passing years. Though many of these versions were presented on stage, helping me to come to terms with the tale, I must remember with gratitude an early production, in Hindi, by Satyadev Dubey, featuring Naseeruddin Shah, Ratna Pathak Shah, Sunila Pradhan and Satyadev himself.

I rewrote the play from scratch, not for the first time but this time in English, when the Leicester Haymarket Theatre commissioned me to write for them. The decision to end the play with the Queen impaling herself on the sword was the outcome of the rehearsals at Leicester. However, it is equally conceivable that she kills the King: indeed, such a development would be more in accord with the original myth. The action could also end with the two staring at each other, frozen in horror, as she is poised to lunge at him.

I must also acknowledge the kindness of Neelum Singh, who has retyped innumerable drafts and put up cheerfully with my niggling alterations.

Plays by Girish Karnad
in English

Translation

Dates refer to the year of publication. All the plays have been published by Oxford University Press, except *Talé-Daṇḍa*, which was initially published by Ravi Dayal, Publisher.